Played at the Pub

The pub games of Britain

Played at the Pub
© English Heritage 2009

English Heritage
is the government's statutory
advisor on all aspects of the
historic environment

Kemble Drive
Swindon SN2 2GZ
www.english-heritage.org.uk

Design work by Jörn Kröger
Series designer Doug Cheeseman

Production and additional research
by Jackie Spreckley

Series editor Simon Inglis

For image credits see page 180

Malavan Media is a creative
consultancy responsible
for the Played in Britain series

www.playedinbritain.co.uk

Printed by Zrinski, Croatia
ISBN: 978 1 905624 973
Product code: 51373

Played at the Pub

The pub games of Britain

Arthur Taylor

Editor Simon Inglis

ENGLISH HERITAGE

The Murrell Arms, Barnham, West Sussex is a treasure trove of trinkets, trophies and games. Apart from the slate shove ha'penny board on the table, mounted on the wall (from left to right) can be seen quoits, cribbage boards, Ring the Bull and the ubiquitous London, or Trebles dartboard.

Previous page Bedford coal merchant Jack Fowler and his pals enjoy a lunchtime game of dominoes at the Balloon Inn, in October 1937, as his horse Sam (apparently a regular) studies his master's tiles.

Title page Ringing the Bull in one of the rock-hewn bars at Ye Olde Trip to Jerusalem in Nottingham – one of the oldest and most exasperating of pub games, in one of Britain's oldest and most enchanting pubs.

Contents

'The pub is the club, in which the real people consort for friendship. There are no kinder people, and no better tempered people, than the inhabitants of the Crown. They are never drunk, and they would not mind if they were. They go for love and comfort, and they get it. You can do anything in a pub, except be mean.

'One of the things about the public house recently has been the arty fashion for it. The mechanics and fund-holders stream out from the Wen, sometimes screaming and giggling, and condescending, always at heart uncomfortable. It takes six months in the same pub to evict condescension without condescending. It takes the same time to learn darts and to appreciate beer. The people in the Crown are there for direct reasons: they want a little love, three pints of hops.

'To pass the time away, and as an excuse for the beer (for there is a half a pint betted on every game), they play darts, or nap (if tired), or crib, or tipit, or shove-penny. They play these games with the same interest and attention as the Wen-man plays his billiards, but with warmer hearts.

'Darts is a good and difficult game, not a light-opera country pastime like dancing round the maypole.'

From *England Have My Bones*, by TH White, 1936. The Crown, if that was its real name, would have been somewhere near Stowe School, Buckinghamshire, where White taught English before he went on to write the Arthurian blockbuster, *The Sword in the Stone*. The Wen, for those who have not read their William Cobbett, is London.

Foreword

There is a pub in Middleton, Lancashire, called Who'd a Thowt It. That translates from the Lancastrian, my native language, as 'well bless my soul, that really is quite extraordinary'.

This is my third book on pub games. The first was published in 1976, the second in 1992, and now here you have number three, in 2009. That is, a span of over 30 years of going down to the pub; for the beer, the company, the chat... and of course the games.

It has been strenuous and demanding work, but I do not complain. I am taking the strain.

Who'd a thowt it?

The good news is that the glorious, chaotic variety and complexity of Britain's pub games repertoire, remains as inspiring, stimulating and enjoyable as ever.

It has been a joy to catch up with such old friends as hood skittles in Northamptonshire, long alley in Leicestershire, skittles in all their splendid confusion across the West Country, bat and trap in Kent, and Aunt Sally in Oxfordshire.

I have been able to experience events quite new to me: the world bar billiards championships in Jersey, for example; the log end darts championships at Moston, north Manchester; the world tippit championships in mid-Wales; a shooting match under the auspices of the Devizes & District Miniature Rifle League, and the first British quoits championships for a generation or more, featuring teams from Wales, Scotland and England.

Also to be celebrated is the meeting up of players from two surviving centres for the playing of rings; those of Essex, who have thirteen hooks on their boards and six rings per throw, and those from Ventnor on the Isle of Wight, with their fifteen hooks and four rings. (In the arcane world of pub games, such differences matter, even if no-one knows how and why they ever came about.)

Equally pleasurable was the discovery that toad in the hole, a game that had plunged deep into the doldrums when I researched my previous book, has since enjoyed such a spirited revival in and around Lewes in East Sussex.

And there was the exhilarating revelation that the Childwall Quoiting Club are still playing cheerfully and noisily at the Childwall Abbey Hotel, on the outskirts of Liverpool, as they have been doing since at least 1811.

Having now had the pleasure of joining them for one evening, I understand fully why they are loath to let this august association fade into oblivion, as so many of their counterparts have done at clubs and pubs all over Britain.

For the plain truth is that in revisiting the pub games of Britain, for every tale of cheer I have encountered, there have been many more of woe.

There used to be a Granada TV series called *Disappearing World*, in which a film crew would follow an anthropologist to some remote corner of the planet to record the last rites of a tribe whose traditional way of life was about to be obliterated by progress.

I genuinely believe that such an approach, perhaps prompted by *Played at the Pub*, is now necessary in order to record threatened pub games, and the social and cultural worlds that surround them. »

» I well remember as a student in London during the 1960s that I spent many a summer weekend energetically spectating the centuries old game of lawn billiards (or pall mall as it was also known), at the Freemasons Arms, in Hampstead.

The beer, as I recall, was Bass.

The Freemasons had the last lawn billiards pitch in the country.

Yet by the time I put nostalgic pen to paper for my first book, in 1976, the brewery had concreted over the pitch to enlarge the outdoor drinking area.

This time round it further transpires that the basement skittle alley at the Freemasons is now also the only Old English skittle alley left in any London pub.

When preparing the second book, in the 1990s, I was able to watch several demonstration games of knur and spell, an extraordinary long-hitting (and hard-betting) game in Yorkshire, known also as 'poor man's golf'.

This time round, the game has vanished.

The same can be said for nipsy, played by miners in a league around Barnsley, up until the 1990s. But today, no miners, and no nipsy.

I miss them both.

Even those games that one always imagined were immune from the ravages of time and fashion are now suffering.

As I began working on this third book, in 2007, the organiser of the British dominoes championships, finally threw in the towel.

Partly this was because he had lost his sponsorship. Partly it was because the hall at Bridlington, where the event had been held for two decades, had been declared smoke-free, and too many domino players refused to turn up if they could not light up.

But the main reason why the event petered out, and the main reason why so many of our pub games are now under threat, is that so few young people appear interested in playing, let alone taking over the reins of office from long serving organisers.

Time and time again I have heard league secretaries bemoan today's youth. Said one, 'The young lads won't play the game because they find it too difficult.'

Said another, 'They're not interested if it takes more than ten minutes or if no screens or buttons are involved.'

And this familar complaint. 'They give it a week or so, then drift away.'

You will notice the common denominator. Old folk putting down the young generation.

'Twas ever thus, for sure.

But somehow the generation gap today does seem wider than ever before. For centuries pub games have been handed on from fathers to sons, and then onto grandsons. Now it would appear that the grandchildren have a totally different agenda when it comes to personal entertainment.

But wait, let us not panic.

Pub games, it must be emphasised, have always been in

a state of flux. Some come and go. Some come and stay around. Some are ousted because something better takes its place.

Consider, for example, that organised pub quizzes in Britain started at a working men's club in York in 1946. And that pétanque, or boules, began to appear in pub gardens in the south east in the mid 1960s (one of several pub games to have crossed the Channel, as we shall discover throughout this book). By 1970 Britain had also imported its first pool tables (again from France, and also from Italy and Australia, though not, as often thought, from the USA).

Nowadays of course, pub quizzes, pétanque and pool are firmly rooted in pub life.

There have been revivals as well. Toad in the hole in Lewes, as mentioned earlier, is one. Regardless of the Save Our Skittles campaign launched in 2008 (as featured later), in parts of the West Country participation is actually holding up well, and in a few centres even growing, partly boosted by the setting up of British championships.

For centuries a characteristic of the pub game scene has been that a team in one village may know very little about how things are done only a few miles away. Now, courtesy of the internet, the ability of players in different locations to learn what others are doing, and make contact, is of huge benefit to pub games. In some instances the digital revolution has even made

up for the loss of local newspaper coverage – another trend that has made research in the last few years so very different from how it was only a decade ago.

Now, on the other hand, let us panic.

The real spectre of gloom that overshadows any study of pub games in the early 21st century is not so much the state of pub games as the state of pubs themselves.

As anyone who has picked up a newspaper on almost any day over the last year or so will know only too well, Britain's pubs are closing at a shocking and unnerving rate.

According to Peter Haydon's *The English Pub*, published in 1994 (*see* Links), there were an estimated 99,000 pubs in Britain in 1905 (itself a drop since the reforming zeal of the Victorians had led to thousands of closures in the late 19th century). By 1935, as licensing authorities clamped down further on smaller, less reputable drinking dens and the like, the total had dropped to 77,500.

In 1975, as I embarked upon my first book, the total had fallen still further to 60,000.

Over the next two decades that number appears to have fallen only marginally. According to figures kept by the British Beer and Pub Association (BBPA), the total in 2007 stood at 57,500.

Since then, however, the industry appears to have gone into freefall. In 2005, reported the BBPA, 102 pubs closed in this country (balanced, it has to be said, by those that also opened).

In 2007 the number of closures shot up to 1,409.

In 2008 it rose again to 2,028, or the equivalent of a frightening 39 pubs closing per week.

That is, six a day.

In virtually every area of the licensed drinks industry the figures make deeply depressing reading. The Campaign for Real Ale (CAMRA), whose own efforts to highlight the plight of our more treasured pubs are to be applauded, reckons that between 2003 and 2008, 37 breweries closed down, with the loss of 44,000 jobs overall.

This is not a book about the brewing industry, nor even about the history of licensed premises. Several fine histories already exist and are listed at the end of this book (*see Links*). But it is as well to summarise the main factors that most experts believe lie behind the grisly statistics. Readers will no doubt be familiar with them all.

The first concerns pubs' status as business enterprises, especially since a report to the Monopolies and Mergers Commission in 1989 led to large conglomerates, called 'pubcos', owning thousands of pubs between them. Critics claim that in order to satisfy their shareholders (rather than pub goers) these companies charge high rents, require landlords to buy high priced drinks from selected breweries, and prefer to sell off loss-making premises for more profitable residential or retail purposes rather than sell them to a prospective landlord.

Good news for those who read only the financial pages, but depressing in the extreme for the rest of us in the normal world.

Secondly, we drink, on average, much less in pubs than we used to. According to the BBPA, today's pubs sell 14 million fewer pints per day than in 1979. In 2009 sales were lower than at any time since the great depression of the 1930s.

It is true that many of us lead more abstemious lives, or have switched to wine as our daily preference. But it is also true that beer is now sold so cheaply in supermarkets – cheaper than bottled water in some instances – that pubs simply cannot compete.

The third factor most frequently cited in the decline of the pub trade is the ban on smoking in public places, introduced in July 2007. Whatever one's views on this ban – and I write as a non-smoker who would be happy for pubs to have retained smoking lounges, as of old – various statistics can be called up that support both sides of the argument.

As for the BBPA, it estimated in 2007 that 3,000 pubs would close because of the smoking ban. A year after the ban was set in place it upped this estimate to 5–6,000.

Of course the fewer pubs there are, the more likely it is that pub games will suffer.

But it goes deeper than that, because as survival gets ever harder, breweries and landlords are increasingly and actively stopping pub games from taking place on their premises.

They mainly do this in order to devote more space to bar and dining areas. But it is also partly because they do not see pub games as fitting in with the image and ambience they are seeking to create. Beer and skittles are being replaced by wine and fine dining.

But, as we are so often told, a glass half empty is also half full.

We who believe that the provision of pub games could well be part of the solution, rather than part of the problem, must remind ourselves that there remain thousands of wonderful pubs in Britain, run by dedicated landlords who support pub games to the hilt (and even play a bit themselves).

Similarly, there exist a number of family-run, regional breweries whose support for pub games is absolutely vital; the likes of Hook Norton (sponsors of Aunt Sally), Blackthorn (supporters of skittles), Joseph Holt (friends of Manchester's log end darts community), and Theakston (sponsors of quoits).

These and other sponsors too many to mention deserve thanks for helping to maintain games that form such an important part of our nation's heritage.

To which I must add in conclusion that the correlation between 'good' beer, that is to say traditional cask conditioned beer, and traditional pub games, is a very real one.

Just as cask beer needs care and attention, so too do pub games.

The pub where perhaps darts, dominoes and cribbage are played, or maybe some other regional game in season; the pub where there is a flutter of notices pinned to a wall, publicising league fixtures, away matches or excursions; where there is a well filled charity box; where there is a buzz of conversation, perhaps just a touch of eccentricity and a range of good beer on offer, is the sort of pub that I, for one, home in on.

Games form only part of that cocktail of bonhomie and belonging, but without them, the mix is so much less enduring.

If this books helps in any way to keep those games going, and to lead you, the reader, to maybe try your hand at an unfamiliar game or two as you venture forth, then there is a fighting chance that *Played at the Pub* will not prove to be the valedictory report many will fear, but merely yet another progress report along the way.

Whichever, I do not expect to be around for the next 30 years to see how things pan out.

But to have enjoyed the games, the beer, and the company of the regulars for the last 30 years, well, what a joy.

Who'd a thowt it?

Arthur Taylor
Shaw, Lancashire. January 2009

Postcript: Sod's Law. Since I wrote this foreword, Who'd a Thowt It, the pub in Middleton, has closed.

So reader beware. If planning to visit any of the pubs mentioned on these pages, check first, and best not leave it too long.

Chapter One

Played at the pub

This is the Essex-born antiquarian and engraver, Joseph Strutt, whose monumental work, *The Sports and Pastimes of the People of England*, published in 1801 (shortly before he died at the age of 53), is cited frequently throughout this book. Strutt did most of his research not in the field but at the British Museum (he was a chronic asthmatic). He was condescending towards 'rustics' and ale houses. But without his researches the modern study of sports and games would be very much the poorer.

Games have been played in and around pubs for as long as there have been pubs, and there have been pubs, or at least houses selling ale, for well over a thousand years.

The problem for those of us who seek to study their history is that so many of these games constitute what the sports historian Richard Holt has called 'the submerged tradition... at the other end of the social scale'.

In other words, we know little about them until the modern era because for centuries they were played by people who did not write or occupy positions of power, and therefore did not leave their imprint upon history.

As a result, and as in virtually every other area of sporting history, what little we do know of the games played by ordinary people before the 17th century derives mainly from the steady flow of prohibitions issued by the Crown, local assizes and so on.

One of the earliest, in the 13th century, was issued by Henry III to prohibit the clergy from playing either dice or chess. A century later Edward III imposed a ban on a number of named activities (including handball and football), not because of gambling but because they diverted boys and men of military age from their archery practice.

Many of the games that feature in this book are named in further statutes issued during the reigns of Henry VII and Henry VIII, from 1485 to 1547. Their wording – familiar to many students of sporting history – carry an authoritarian menace, intent on imposing one law for the rich and another for virtually everyone else.

For example, in 1496 it was enacted that 'no prentice should play at tenys, clash, dice, cards, bowles, or such like unlawful games' except during the Christmas holidays, and then only within their masters' houses.

Any householder caught flouting this would be fined 6s 8d for every offence.

The keepers of 'hostelries, inns or ale-houses' were further ordered in 1529 not to permit the use on their premises of 'tables, dyce, cardes, bowles, closshes, pynnes, balles, and all other thynges pertayning unto the said unlawfull games'.

Had this been an era of piety and abstention in high places such bans might have carried some moral weight. But the Tudor elite was itself passionately devoted to sport and gaming.

So while Henry VIII installed bowling alleys in his palaces and gambled heavily, in 1541 he ordered that anyone found guilty of running 'an alley or place of bowling' be fined 20s for every day on which the law had been broken, and anyone caught bowling in such a place, 6s 8d.

Should anyone then think of playing on open ground, or in gardens or orchards, the 1541 Act went on to order that 'no manner of Artificer or Craftsman of any handicraft or occupation, Husbandmen, Apprentice, Labourer, Servant at Husbandry, Journeyman or Servant of Artificer, Mariners, Fishermen, Watermen or any Serving men' should play bowls or other banned games other than at Christmas, subject to a swingeing fine of 20s.

Joseph Strutt sums up the Played in Britain ethos in his seminal study of 1801, *The Sports and Pastimes of the People of England*

IN order to form a just estimation of the character of any particular people, it is absolutely necessary to investigate the Sports and Pastimes most generally prevalent among them.

Naturally this prohibition did not extend to the rich, who, as long as they were worth £100 or more per annum were permitted to play at any time, without penalty, provided only that it was within 'the Precinct of his or their Houses, Gardens or Orchards'.

Policing these orders cannot have been easy, particularly as the instinct to play, then as now, permeated every level of society, the yeomanry and clergy included. But there are sufficient examples from Court Leet records to suggest that, if nothing else, catching and fining perpetrators brought in a steady flow of income.

In Southwark, for example, that cauldron of bear baiting, theatre and carousing on what we now call London's South Bank, reports from the 1630s show not only a sliding scale of fines, from 13s 4d for a first offence up to £2 13s 4d for repeat offenders, but also that certain alehouse and inn keepers were hauled up before the bench year after year for permitting shovel boards or nine pins on their premises, offences for which the penalties could go as high as £5.

Clearly these publicans saw such fines as routine expenditure, rather as some today might regard parking tickets; an inconvenient if unavoidable part of business life.

Not all prohibited games were linked directly with drinking. But as shown by Peter Clark's social history of ale houses during the period 1200–1830 (see Links), a fair number can be considered what we would today call pub games.

Listed in various prohibitions between 1500 and 1650, their names are a mix of the familiar and the quaintly obscure.

Bowls, dice, card games, shovelhalfpenny or slide thrust, nine and ten holes, alleys (or »

▲ Customers at a 17th century ale house enjoy games of tric trac (an early variant of backgammon) and cards, while others prefer to warm their feet by the fire.

Along with his contemporaries Jan Steen and David Teniers, the Haarlem artist **Adriaen van Ostade**, who painted this scene in 1674 or 1675, was one of the earliest European painters to document ordinary working people, thereby bequeathing us a precious glimpse of how pubs and games formed a natural part of everyday life.

No British artist would tackle such scenes until the late 18th century, and even then, the likes of James Gilray, Thomas Rowlandson and George Cruikshank seemed far more interested in caricature than in social realism.

But just as importantly, it is to the bars and cafés, the pubs and *estaminets* of the Netherlands, Flanders and northern France that we will return throughout this book to discover the roots of so many of the pub games that we play today, not least billiards, bar billiards, bagatelle, table football and pétanque. Even our earliest mass produced darts came from France.

MONSTER
DERBY SWEEP
At the "Tidley Wink"
2000 Subscribers
at one Shilling each
First horse £50
Second do   25
Third do   10
Starters   10
Non-Starters

▲ While Dutch artists portrayed the benign characteristics of an ale house, until the 20th century their English counterparts invariably focused on negative traits.

Typical is this 1848 illustration, highlighting the links between alcohol and gambling, as the bookmaker – a copy of the populist *Lloyd's Weekly* at his feet – draws in punters to pay a shilling per head to enter the **Monster Derby Sweep**, one of many sweeps that were then illegal under legislation governing lotteries, yet were openly advertised by publicans.

Note that the pub is named on the notice as **The Tidley Wink**. Cockney rhyming slang for drink, tiddlywink was a 19th century nickname for drinking dens of the lowest sort. Also that in the corner there is a 'cheese' and a pile of Old English, or London skittles (of which more in Chapter Three).

That pubs and pub culture were not more sympathetically depicted in England is all the more surprising given their ubiquity, and that all kinds of artists and writers – the likes of Samuel Pepys and John Evelyn – frequented them for all kinds of reasons, games included.

A Swiss traveller to London in the 1590s, Thomas Platter, for example, remarked favourably on the 'great many inns, taverns, and beer-gardens scattered about the city, where much amusement may be had with eating, drinking, fiddling, and the rest, as for instance in our hostelry, which was visited by players almost daily.'

By players he meant of course actors and musicians. Indeed coaching inns, with their courtyards surrounded by galleries, were especially suited to theatre. Shakespeare's work was regularly staged at the Cross Keys Inn on

Gracious Street, the Boar's Head at Aldgate, and the Bel Savage Inn on Ludgate Hill, while in provincial centres without theatres, inns served a similar and vital role.

Platter also noted how many women enjoyed taverns and ale-houses, taking it as 'a great honour' to be given 'wine with sugar'.

From other sources over the centuries we learn of pubs being used for political rallies, lectures, horse sales, for military recruitment, flower and vegetable shows, and even as the place where barbers set up for business.

In short, pubs have long served a multitude of functions that go far beyond the consumption of alcohol, and it is in this context that we should view pub games – as just one aspect of a rich social and cultural phenomenon that has not always been portrayed in the best, or fairest of lights.

» marbles) and tables (an early form of backgammon), we know about. Guile bones, ten bones, noddy board, penny prick, tick tack, fox-mine-host, cross and pile, hide under hat, and main chance we can just about imagine.

However one game called 'milking cromock' remains a tantalising mystery.

Unsurprisingly, the harshest of all crackdowns occurred during the rule of Oliver Cromwell from 1649–60, a period that, according to pub historian Peter Haydon (*see* Links), witnessed 'an unparalleled destruction of popular culture'.

No admirer of the pub, Cromwell, it was said, took 'special note of the mischiefs and great disorders which are daily committed in Taverns, Inns and Alehouses', reserving particular ire for those licensees who 'broke Sabbath observance by allowing swearing, drunkenness, tippling, gaming or playing at Tables, Billiard Table, Shovel Board, Cards, Dice, Ninepins, Pigeon Holes, Trunks, or keeping of Bowling Alley or Bowling Green or any of them, or any other games'.

Note the catch-all phrase at the end of this list.

The Puritans were not alone in imposing restrictions on Sunday games. In some parts of the country these would persist until well into the 20th century.

But for the most part, the Restoration in 1660 heralded a new era of freedom and licence that saw sports and games, and entertainments generally, flourish with a wild intensity.

As historians such as Dennis Brailsford have noted (*see* Links), this 'taste for diversions' was fuelled as much by the nation's propensity towards gambling as it was by any intrinsic love of play.

SMITHFIELD SHARPERS

or

The COUNTRYMEN DEFRAUDED

Old Trusty with his Sons made friends,
To gentle Sleep himself commends ;
With Priv upon his knees ;
Whilst Tom his Son, all eager gaping,
Expects each moment, he'll be scraping ;
The treasure up, he sees . . . . .

Mean time the Harpy-Tribe are plotting,
By forcing liquor, winking, nodding ;
To cheat the Youth unlearn'd :
Who to his cost will quickly find ,
No Watch, nor Money, left behind ,
And friends to Sharpers turn'd .

Publish'd by E.Palser, Surry Side, Westminster Bridge.

Indeed for much of the 18th and 19th centuries the word 'sport' denoted betting, rather than physical activity.

Personifying this licentiousness was the 'gamester' a character who would put bets on anything, and was either admired or despised, depending on whom he fleeced, and how. Sir John Suckling, whom we shall encounter in Chapter

Nineteen, was one of the worst, but as the illustration above shows, they were everywhere.

There was even a book advising how to deal with them.

Focusing on dice and cards, *The Nicker Nicked, or, the Cheats of Gaming Discovered*, was published in 1669, and then five years later re-released in an expanded form entitled *The Compleat Gamester*.   »

Dating from c.1787, Thomas Rowlandson's 'The Smithfield Card Sharpers, or the Countrymen Defrauded' chose a theme familiar in 17th and 18th century literature, that of innocents being plied with drink in a London tavern and then lured into a rigged game of cards. But this was no London monopoly. Gamesters all over the world have always preyed on outsiders.

» Although neither book was credited, the writer and poet Charles Cotton is assumed to have authored both. This is largely because in 1676 Cotton also completed an expanded edition of that other great opus, *The Compleat Angler*, which had been written two decades earlier by his close friend and Staffordshire neighbour, Izaak Walton.

The content of *The Compleat Gamester* is best summed up by its subtitle, 'How to play at Billiards, Trucks, Bowls and Chess, together with all manner of usual and most Gentile Games either on Cards or Dice, to which is added the Arts and Mysteries of Riding, Racing, Archery and Cock Fighting.'

(Trucks, incidentally, was a form of Italian billiards, from which was derived the name *troco*, later applied to lawn billiards, as featured in Chapter Twenty Four.)

Cotton, if it was he, emphasised in the introduction to *The Compleat Gamester* that, 'Mistake me not, it is not my intention to make Gamesters by this Collection, but to inform all in part how to avoid being cheated by them.'

'Furthermore,' he added, 'Recreation is not only lawful, but necessary.'

In 1742 *The Compleat Gamester* was superceded by Edmond Hoyle's *Short Treatise on the Game of Whist*, a work that has since been revised and expanded in numerous editions, and remains the seminal reference on card games. Hoyle also wrote on backgammon, picquet, quadrille, brag and chess.

But to return to Cotton's era, another writer from the Restoration period whose work forms a vital source for our endeavours is Francis Willughby.

Willughby's *Book of Games* remained unfinished when he died, at the age of 36, in 1672. But to the delight of sports historians, over 300 years later his notes and papers were finally collated and published in 2003 (*see Links*).

Although, like Charles Cotton, he was a member of the landed gentry (the family seat was in Middleton, Warwickshire), Willughby approached his subject not as a gamester but, as befitted his membership of the Royal Society, with systematic observation, description and classification. (Indeed he was first and foremost a naturalist.)

Willughby's range was impressive, providing modern historians with what is by far the earliest and most comprehensive of compendiums yet discovered.

Several of his 'games' we would now classify as 'sports', such football, stoolball, hurling and tennis. In common with Cotton, he also tackled cribbage, a pub favourite to this day, and other such forgotten card games as 'Hanikin Canst Abide It' and 'Laugh and Ly Downe'.

But in the context of this book, Willughby's most precious legacy are his notes on games most closely associated with pubs.

These include boules, long laurence, nine men's morris, nine holes (or Trou Madame), quoits, shovel board and backgammon.

Another prime source not published until many years after its author's death are the diaries of Samuel Pepys, which ran from 1660–69, but did not see the light of day until 1825.

Besides being Secretary to the Navy, Pepys loved a good pub, and pub games too, playing with varying degrees of success cribbage, bowls, nine pins (a form of skittles) and shuffleboard. Pepys was also a vital witness

to the game of pall mall, or pell mell, and to more unsavoury activities such as cock fighting, bull and bear baiting, and that great favourite of boys on Shrove Tuesday, throwing at cocks.

Such bloodsports are not covered in detail in later chapters, not out of any squeamishness, but because, rather like boxing, football and cricket, they were activities that often took place *at* or *near* pubs, but were not pub games as such.

However, it important to add that, in common with boxing, football and cricket, cock fighting and animal baiting, together with dog and rat fighting, were events frequently organised and promoted by publicans.

Moreover, while bloodlust undoubtedly formed part of their attraction, gambling on the outcome was the prime motivation (although there was for many years also a genuine belief that beef tasted better if the bull had been baited before slaughter).

Although in several parts of Britain bull baiting had been suppressed by moral crusaders in the late 18th century, it was only finally outlawed in 1835, followed by cock fighting in 1849.

But of course their association with pubs has lived on in pub names, such as The Cockpit in London's Blackfriars (said to have been built around an actual pit), and the Bull Ring Tavern in Digbeth, Birmingham.

Joseph Strutt – whose name, as noted earlier, crops up in the chapters that follow more than any other writer on games – made his feelings on animal baiting and cock fighting quite clear in his invaluable study, *The Sports and Pastimes of the People of England*, first published in 1801.

Bull and bear baiting, he wrote, were 'attended only by the lowest and most despicable part of the people'. Cock fighting was a 'barbarous pastime', and throwing at cocks a 'wicked and wanton abuse.'

But then many of Strutt's opinions were as scathing as this. For impressive though his work was, and remains, it cannot be denied that he was essentially a desk-bound researcher who lacked the common touch.

What he did not lack was curiosity. As the 'father of English antiquaries' he devoted his life to the study of ecclesiastical antiquities, medieval manuscripts, customs and habits, and, in the period before he turned his attention to sports and pastimes, published a mammoth two volume history of English dress.

Any modern qualms we may have about his snobbishness and distaste for 'common pot houses' must therefore be put in context.

In addition to which, since his death, there have been a number of updated and improved editions of *Sports and Pastimes*, the last and best of which, edited by J Charles Cox and published in 1903, is the source from which many of the references in *Played at the Pub* have been taken.

Strutt's work, it should also be noted, predated the main thrust of 19th century industrialisation, a period in which, as the urban population grew ever larger and denser, the number of pubs multiplied, and with it, pub games became ever more popular.

As told by Geoff Brandwood and Andrew Davison in *Licensed to Sell*, their history of pub buildings, (*see Links*), a turning point in this trend was the passing of the 1830 Beer Act. »

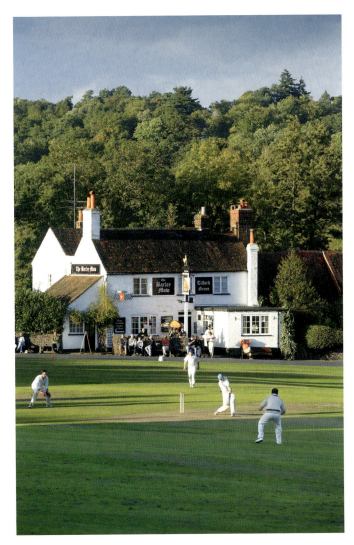

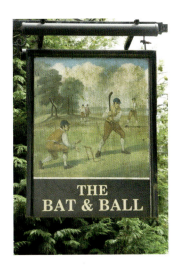

▶ A quiet rural inn on a crossroads in Hampshire, **The Bat and Ball** at **Hambledon** seems an unlikely place for the game of cricket to have taken a great leap forward, as it did between the 1760s and the 1780s, when the Hambledon Club – as much a gentlemen's drinking club as a sports club – dominated the game. Broadhalfpenny Down, its ground, lay across the road, while the club's prime mover and one of its regular players was John Nyren, the Bat and Ball's landlord.

In 1994, to the horror of purists – questions were even asked in Parliament – Allied Breweries mothballed the Bat and Ball's collection of artefacts and turned the place into a restaurant. It took the next owners two years to repair the damage and restore the pub's status as a shrine to cricket lovers.

Among many fascinating artefacts on display is this late 18th century curved bat (*right*). When a batsmen from Reigate turned up one day in 1771 with a much wider, flat bat, Hambledon declared that no bat should be wider than 4¼ inches, a rule that, remarkably, survives until the present day.

Incidentally, cricket's first printed rules were drawn up at a pub, the Star & Garter on Pall Mall, in 1774, while Thomas Lord, who laid out the famous MCC ground that bears his name, was himself a wine merchant and licensee.

▲ Cricket is hardly a pub game, but village cricket without pubs would be unthinkable. Hence 'England as you expect it to be' is the slogan of the Grade II listed **Barley Mow** in **Tilford Green, Surrey**, a pub whose setting opposite the village green made it perfect for the cricketer 'Silver Billy' Beldham's first foray into the licensing trade in 1822. Known for his flowing silver locks and beard, Beldham made his name as a batsman for Hambledon (*see right*) and later played for the MCC, who still display his portrait in the Long Room at Lord's.

Pubs with cricketing connections are common, but few enjoy an aspect like the Barley Mow. Even rarer are pubs like the Poplars Inn, Wingfield, in Wiltshire, which has its own pitch and resident team.

▲ Intricately painted balls hang out in the **Coach and Horses**, one of several pubs in **Ashbourne, Derbyshire**, where similar displays are held to celebrate the annual **Royal Shrovetide Football** game.

Contested between the massed ranks of the town's Up'ards and Down'ards in the streets, across fields and a river – the goals being three miles apart – Ashbourne's game has been played since at least 1821 (although a poem by our gamester friend, Charles Cotton, suggests that it may date back even as early as 1683).

As Hugh Hornby has detailed in *Uppies and Downies*, part of the *Played in Britain* series (*see Links*), pubs have long played a role in Britain's festival football matches.

In Ashbourne, for example, the proceedings start with a celebratory lunch at the The Green Man and Black's Head Royal Hotel, whose pub sign, the longest in the world, spans the width of St John Street.

Every January in Lincolnshire, four pubs, three in Haxey and one from the neighbouring village of Westwoodside, compete across ploughed fields and narrow lanes to win possession of a leather 'hood'.

In order to win this epic struggle, the hood must be brought close enough to the pub's front door for the landlord to be able to touch it with his feet inside the threshold.

Pubs are equally entwined in the histories of rugby and association football. The Northern Union (later the Rugby League), was formed in 1895 at the Grade II listed George Hotel in Huddersfield, where there is now a small museum. The Football Association formed in 1863 at the Freemason's Tavern on Great Queen Street in London.

At grass roots level, pub teams remain a intrinsic part of the national game, whilst many a major club, Manchester United included, would not exist had it not been for the support of brewers in their early years.

And yet, although a dozen or more senior league clubs actually formed at pubs, only one started out life as a genuine pub team. Formed by the landlord of the Featherstall & Junction Hotel in 1895, Pine Villa went on four years later to become Oldham Athletic (which, by a happy coincidence, happens also to be the beloved club of your author).

» Passed in an attempt both to boost the economy and the Tory government's flagging popularity, the Act allowed anyone to sell beer for an annual Excise fee of £2.

The result was a sudden and massive rise in the number of licensed premises – or public houses as they were now often called – of which a growing number were able to offer different levels of service in different parts of the building to a broader range of customers.

Running in parallel with this boom were the beginnings of a games manufacturing industry. Thomas Jaques' company, established in London in 1795, pioneered the mass production of sets for chess, backgammon and several other pub staples. In the early 19th century cabinet maker John Thurston started to supply pubs with billiards and bagatelle tables. They were so popular that the two games were specifically targeted for licensing restrictions by the 1845 Gaming Act, which otherwise set out to end abuses in the settlement of gambling debts.

Indeed for the next century the authorities played a cat and mouse game with publicans over what games could, and could not, be played in public houses.

Supposedly a distinction was made between games of chance, such as dice (which would obviously be played only for stakes), and games of skill, such as billiards, that could be played merely for pleasure.

But as was shown in a landmark court case in 1889, involving a Norwich publican who had allowed customers to play a game of life pool on his billiard table (*explained further on page 97*), the authorities main intent was to clamp down on any betting activity

at all in pubs, whether for a few pence per round of cribbage, or for £50 on the winner of the Derby.

As a sympathetic editorial in *The Times* commented, the modern publican 'would probably have as soon believed, until he heard these learned Judges' decision, that it was as wrong to permit smoking on his premises as a quiet game of billiards for moderate sums.'

This ongoing ambiguity, combined with growing pressure from the temperance movement, made pubs an easy target for magistrates and moralists alike.

And yet in the rapidly expanding cities, in particular, pubs offered a range of communal activities that, in the years before works-related sport and recreation started to become available (from the late 19th century onwards), were hardly on offer for working class people elsewhere, and in some cases would seem hardly less respectable than one might find at any local church.

Just as in field sports the Victorians demonstrated a terrific flair for innovation, so too did publicans and their regulars when it came to games, competitions and general merriment.

One useful source for this barely recorded aspect of social history is a series of studies of Victorian pubs in the Greater Manchester area, commissioned and published by Neil Richardson in the latter decades of the 20th century (*see Links*).

As we might expect, his team of local historians found that the playing of cards, dominoes and dice figured prominently, as did billiards and bagatelle.

Ringing the bull was common, as was puff and dart (a curious forerunner of the modern game of darts).

Amongst the many inevitably caught out by local magistrates, Sarah Bottomley, landlady of the Puckersley Inn, Royton, was fined for allowing 'trotting the horse' to be played in her pub.

Frustratingly, however, no-one has ever been able to find out what this game actually was.

Illicit cock fights and ratting contests persisted well after they were prohibited in the 1840s. In 1858 there took place cat baiting at the Devonshire in Lees, while three years later the same venue held a sparrow shooting contest.

But equally there were perfectly respectable bowling matches, skittles and quoits competitions, for which prizes such as copper kettles and teapots were offered.

At the Bees Wing, a pub in Alt, Oldham, the landlady, Dolly Greenwood, organised annual foot races for her female regulars. (In 1860, the runner-up complained that she had been pulled back by a rival, so the race was re-run, after dark, with the men holding candles to light the route.)

Lark singing contests were common. At the Grapes Inn at Lees in 1860, the winning bird kept on singing for 24 minutes.

There were also competitions for the growing of prize leeks, onions, celery and rhubarb, while in Stalybridge, the Old Brown Cow staged a pigeon show in 1889, at which owls were exhibited too.

We also learn that the Blazing Rag in Mossley got its name because there was a tradition of starting hound trails from the pub. In this, a circular trail was laid with a rag soaked in aniseed, which was then, on its return to the pub, thrown onto the fire.

And if ever there was a lull, one could always rely on someone to issue someone else with a

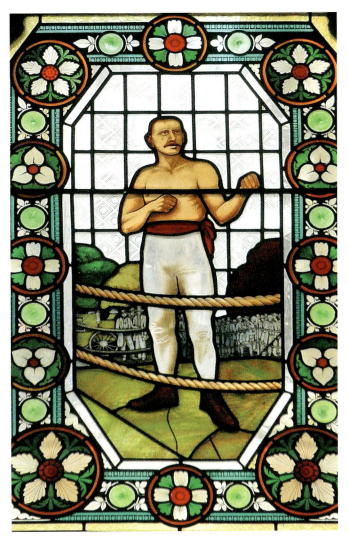

challenge. (Many of our finest and most popular pub activities have started in just this fashion.)

Typical was the proprietor of the Commercial in Shaw who bet his customers two guineas that he could run from his pub to the North Star and back in under fifteen minutes. Some even placed side bets at 60-1. But he managed it, with two minutes to spare.

Doubtless these Lancashire pubs were no different from those in any other region of England. It just happens that Neil Richardson, a stalwart of the local branch of CAMRA, was determined that this 'submerged tradition' on his doorstep should gain the airing it deserved.

Two other aspects of pub life in the 19th century were to »

◀ This is boxer **Bob Fitzsimmons**, one of seven Victorian sporting heroes depicted at **The Champion**, in **Wells Street, London**. Although the Grade II listed pub is itself Victorian, the stained glass portraits were created in the 1990s by York artist, Ann Sotheran.

In 1868, at around the time The Champion opened, the boxing annual *Fistiana* counted 114 prize-fighting pubs in England. Most were run by ex-boxers with gyms in a back room. By then boxing was becoming respectable, having adopted the Marquess of Queensbury Rules the previous year. But in the heyday of bare knuckle pugilism, when pubs like the Lamb and Flag in London earned the nickname Bucket of Blood, pubs formed a vital network, imparting intelligence as to where and when fights were to take place (usually in rural outposts, out of range of the local constabulary).

One such pub was the Winchilsea Arms (now the Ram Jam Inn) in Rutland where in a nearby field in 1811, 20,000 gathered to see one of the last bare knuckle fights in Britain, between Tom Cribb and a black American, former slave Tom Molineaux.

Cribb went on to run the Union Arms in Panton Street, London, and though he later had to relinquish it to pay off gambling debts, the pub has since been renamed after him.

≫ influence the way games were played, and the type of games being played.

Firstly, the increased availability of transport links gave rise to inter-pub matches, particularly in the worlds of bowls and quoits. Organised trips for pub regulars to attend these matches, for example at resorts such as Blackpool, were often paid for by savings clubs set up within the pubs themselves.

Secondly, in the late 19th century the licensing authorities cracked down hard on smaller alehouses, thereby presenting the larger breweries with a ready incentive to snap up licences and build ever larger replacements.

With their imposing exteriors, high ceilings, ornate tiling, wooden panelling and etched glass, this new generation of pubs gained the oddly inappropriate tag of 'gin palaces'. But they were also, in modern day parlance, multi-entertainment and sporting venues. In addition to the usual range of snugs, saloons, dining rooms, smoking rooms, ladies rooms and club rooms, games rooms were well stocked with all the latest games and accessories, while billiard rooms reached levels of sophistication that, in hindsight, never had a hope of showing a return on the outlay.

Hundreds of pubs, particularly in the Midlands and north west,

were adjoined by beautifully appointed bowling greens. Skittle alleys and quoits grounds proliferated too.

In London especially this led to multiple bankruptcies. In Birmingham, next door to the new stadium of Aston Villa, the lavish Holte Hotel, completed at great expense in 1897, with not one but two bowling greens, was put up for sale by the brewery only a year later, and still failed to find a buyer at a knock down price.

But where moderation prevailed, pub games that were cheaply provided and required nothing more than a table or a few feet of clear space, offered immense value. Just as long as no-one was ever caught playing them for money.

Hence in 1903 the *Licensed Victuallers' Gazette* collated into book form a series of articles it had run offering guidance to publicans.

Entitled *Lawful Games in Licensed Premises (and their Grounds and Outhouses)* the list of games ran from Aunt Sally through to wall quoits (also known as 'hook it').

Bagatelle, it explained, had been legal since the 1845 Gaming Act. Dominoes had been legitimised in 1852. Games could be played not for money, it stressed, nor even for 'money's worth', and Sunday play was out altogether.

Even with these restrictions in

place, however, pubs continued to be seen as a negative presence, reaching a low point during the First World War when licensing hours were cut to prevent munition workers from over-indulging.

This state intervention notwithstanding, pub games enjoyed an upsurge during the inter-war period.

Four trends fuelled this boom.

The first was that manufacturers now latched onto pub games as a lucrative source of business, especially darts, but also shove ha'penny, rings, table skittles and the newly introduced bar billiards.

The second was that, at a local level, there appeared on the scene hundreds of thriving leagues, often with backing from breweries; for skittles in the West Country and London, for bat and trap in Kent, for Aunt Sally in Oxfordshire, to name only a few.

National competitions caught on too, also as the result of sponsorship. As we later report, the *News of the World* in particular played a vital role in promoting darts, snooker and quoits.

A third factor was the move towards family-friendly pubs for the newly expanding suburbs, a process begun before the First World War by the movement for 'reformed' public houses. In the 1920s and '30s this resulted in some of the finest pub designs of

the 20th century, for example in Carlisle and Birmingham (where the reformers adopted the slogan 'fewer and better'). Again, the provision of games formed a vital component of this endeavour.

The fourth inter-war trend was that at last pubs started to be portrayed sympathetically.

The Independent politician and keen skittler, AP Herbert, was one voice, espousing the virtues of pubs and pub games in his popular 1930 novel *The Water Gipsies*, and in articles and House of Commons debates. Pathé News, providers of newsreel clips to mass cinema audiences, also conveyed a positive message by filming numerous traditional games from around the country. Gloriously, many of these clips are now free to view on the British Pathé website.

Then in 1938 researchers working for the Mass Observation unit descended upon Bolton – which they called Worktown in their subsequent report *The Pub and the People (see Links)* – with the aim of closely observing ordinary people in ordinary pubs.

Within this world, as well as the usual darts, dominoes and card players, Mass Observation found a myriad of interest groups; pigeon fanciers and dog lovers, anglers and bowlers, each forming sub-cultures within the town's dense network of pubs. ≫

Darts at 'the local', as portrayed by the aptly titled *John Bull* magazine in July 1946. Throughout the First World War the public house was vilified as a threat to the war effort, whereas during the Second World War its role in communal life was celebrated in government propaganda. This is what we were fighting for. A pint and a game of arrows.

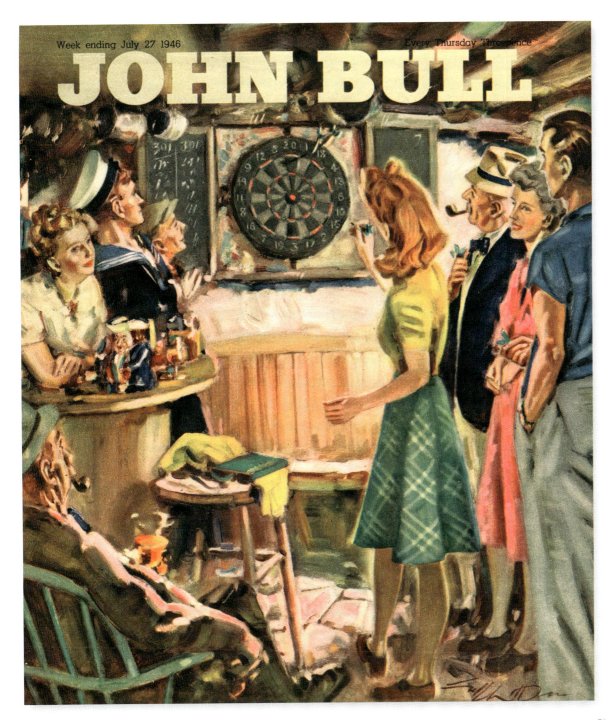

Week ending July 27 1946

JOHN BULL

Every Thursday Threepence

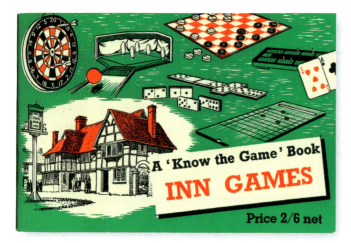

A 'Know the Game' Book
INN GAMES
Price 2/6 net

▲ Published in 1955, this booklet – the first of its kind to treat pub games as an entity in themselves – conveys on its cover the nostalgic warmth that coursed through a number of publications in the post war period.

Strictly, the word 'inn' should apply only to licensed premises that offer accommodation (in the same way that a 'tavern' is so-called because it serves more wine than beer). But after years of war and rationing, how much more comforting was an 'inn' when compared to a pub.

This pining for the Olde English inn first surfaced in book form in a series of paeans to all things ale-related, sponsored by Whitbread.

In *Your Local*, published in 1947, darts, dominoes, shove ha'penny and skittles were all praised, tempered by caution at the arrival of electric pinball machines, in which 'flashing bulbs shoot up and down… in aimless fashion'.

No doubt, noted the anonymous author, American servicemen were delighted to find these colourful reminders of home. 'But it was not long,' he added, 'before they were converted to darts.'

Within the same Whitbread series, in 1948 *Inns of Sport* offered a splendid romp around pubs most associated with such pleasures as fox hunting, duck shooting and steeplechasing, and concluded with author J Wentworth Day asserting that 'In the heart of every Englishman you will find a secret inn, a temple of memories, a shrine of sport.' He then went on to reveal that his own favourite inn was in the Scottish Highlands.

Published in 1951, this time by Odhams, *English Inns* echoed this tone, featuring page after page of beautifully unspoilt rural inns and charming 'hostelries' (the word pub is hardly mentioned), almost as if offering an antidote to all that steel and glass modernity readers may have encountered at that year's Festival of Britain celebrations.

Games like ringing the bull, knur and spell, and bat and trap were described in the introduction (by the much decorated General Sir Henry Colville Wemyss) as old English games, 'faithfully preserved by the villagers'.

'In no other country has the inn produced so many different things of value to the community.'

» They heard straight-faced publicans insist that no betting was allowed, while clearly low level betting took place all around them. 'The pub spirit,' the report deduced, 'is not the team spirit. It is the freedom of each individual to do as he wants, an unregimented, individual "democratic" spirit…'

In common with Strutt, much of the report's tone is patronising, many of the observers being middle class Oxbridge students. But if nothing else they did confirm that people who played games drank more slowly, and therefore less.

This finding was particularly aimed at those local authorities, Liverpool and Glasgow included, who chose – *ultra vires*, argued AP Herbert – to ban pub games altogether, on the grounds that 'games encourage drinking'.

Mass Observation was able to demonstrate that in fact the opposite was true.

This gradual change in how pubs were perceived was to have a profound effect on their portrayal both during and after the Second World War. Far from being anti-patriotic, the 'local', as depicted on film and in print (in *Picture Post* for example), was now seen as an inherently British construct, while darts, dominoes and cribbage, that holy trinity of pub games, were considered true games of the people, their roots lying deep within folk tradition.

Hardly surprisingly, such beliefs were rarely subject to critical or historical analysis, particularly when it came to the origin of darts, in truth a relatively recent, late 19th century invention.

Which is why the publication in 1966 of the *Watney Book of Pub Games*, by Timothy Finn, may be considered a vital stepping stone

for the modern research that was to follow.

Finn, an Oxford history graduate with a self-confessed thirst that extended beyond the quest for knowledge – for it is axiomatic that no pub historian should take himself too seriously – devoted a year to field work 'from the Tyne to the Tamar'.

He then went on to complete an expanded edition in 1975, entitled *Pub Games of England*.

A year later your present guide followed this up with *Pub Games*, which, as explained in the Foreword, was itself updated and expanded into *The Guinness Book of Pub Games* in 1992.

These were years of tremendous change, not only in pubs but in the range of games being played.

Contrary to what many outside observers might have imagined, even at the time, certain traditional games reached astonishing peaks of popularity during the 1980s, for example skittles in the West Country.

The unexpected success of new imports pool and pétanque, starting during the 1970s, also showed that one could never predict what lay round the corner.

These developments, and numerous others from the latter years of the 20th century – the sale of bowling greens for development, the decline of dominoes and cribbage, and of dozens of once mighty district leagues in a host of other games – are themes that permeate whole swathes of the text that follows.

Readers should also note certain other underlying themes from recent years.

Not least, the last few decades have witnessed a massive increase in the numbers of women participating in pub games, and of mixed teams generally. If it is true, as some social commentators have commented, that 'girls are the new boys', from our own observations that bodes well for the future of skittles, hood skittles, Aunt Sally, bat and trap, darts and table football.

The contribution of women to the running of pubs has also been marked by the publication in 1984 of an autobiography by Edie Beed (*see Links*), telling of her 70 years of work in Kent and Devon.

Best of all are her recollections of a lost world of concert parties and Christmas clubs; of the fishermen from Whitstable who, in order to satisfy the archaic requirement that on Sundays only *bona fide* travellers could buy beer, used to walk the minimum statutory distance of three miles to her pub; and of billiards and bagatelle tables having to be covered up every Sunday, Good Friday and Christmas Day, while her regulars played tippet, a game that could be hidden in a flash should any licensing official call by.

We can only hope that there are more publicans out there who will record their own experiences with equal candour and detail.

As for research, at an academic level there has been a wealth of material since the 1980s; from Neil Tranter on Scottish quoits, Alan Metcalf on potshare bowling in the north east, Alan Tomlinson on knur and spell in Yorkshire, Tony Collins on the relationship between sport and pubs, and Collins again, together with Wray Vamplew and John Martin on traditional games generally.

We are further indebted to Patrick Chaplin, who has devoted years to the distentangling of all the myths and nonsense that has passed for darts history in the past

(and in doing so has added hugely to our understanding of pub games generally).

But we end this introduction on perhaps the most significant development of all, the internet.

As a repository of wisdom readers will not, we trust, need reminding that a good deal of what purports to be historical fact on the internet is suspect. As far as pub games are concerned, there is much that has either been copied unquestioningly or – as is true of bar room tittle tattle generally – placed there deliberately in a boisterous spirit of mischief.

That said, there are numerous websites of great worth.

James Masters' traditional games site is worthy of particular mention, as is John McLeod's site on card and tile games. The Old Bailey Proceedings Online Project forms another invaluable resource for research in this field, for reasons which should be obvious.

But by far the most valuable contribution of the internet has been in benefitting players and games organisers.

It is the very nature of pub games that many do not lend themselves well to controls or governance that extends much beyond the local. There are no national bodies governing skittles or dominoes, and no 'official' rules for cribbage or bat and trap.

Indeed, as stated in the Foreword, one of the most endearing aspects of pub games is that those who play in one village, even today, can often be blissfully unaware that the same game is also being played in a village only a couple of miles away, perhaps with different rules and equipment.

It would of course be deeply regrettable if the advent of the internet were to result in the

loss of all local variations, as has almost happened in darts.

On the other hand, that players can now see, via the internet, that they may not, after all, be alone in enjoying a particular game, is of incalculable value, in terms of sharing knowledge, and in widening contacts between likeminded clubs and individuals.

It is no exaggeration to state that several games, such as quoits and rings, have recovered considerably as a result of these closer links.

There is further evidence that the easy availability of knowledge has also led some pubs to take up games that they had hitherto not known about.

So the 'submerged tradition' is no longer hidden away.

But as to where all this will lead is anybody's guess. At a time when pubs are closing in record numbers, and pub activities in general are becoming subject to ever tighter regulation, no-one is in a position to predict the future.

All that can be repeated is that so long as there are pubs, for sure one game or another will always be played in them.

▲ As games topple like nine pins, the fight back has begun. At the **Kings Arms** in **Taunton** in February 2008, John Mills of Blackthorn cider and local MP Jeremy Browne launched the **Save Our Skittles** campaign in an attempt to halt the closure of skittle alleys.

Meanwhile, the Pub is the Hub campaign reports that the installation of an alley at the Jack Russell Inn at Swimbridge in Devon has not only brought skittles to the village, but has provided a venue for hugely popular pub quizzes.

Skittles has been around for centuries. Pub quizzes are rather more recent. But whatever the game, the result, argue the campaigners, is the same. Busier pubs and closer communities.

Chapter Two

Darts

Called variously the London or Trebles board, or sometimes simply the 'Clock', the standard dartboard is one of the world's most instantly recognisable graphic images. And, what is more, its design – a clever amalgam of earlier boards from around the country – is a thoroughly British invention. This particular board was made by Winmau, a Suffolk-based firm founded in the east end of London in 1945. In 2002 it was bought by its rival, Nodor, also formed in London (in 1919) but now based in Bridgend. All Nodor dartboards are made from Kenyan sisal. To date the company has sold nearly 40 million boards.

In June 2005, after years of lobbying, the British Darts Organisation and the Professional Darts Corporation finally managed to secure the recognition of darts as a *bona fide* sport from the combined sports councils of Great Britain and Northern Ireland.

Truly it was an historic moment, for the line that distinguishes a 'game' from a 'sport' has long been a fine one. Chess, for example, is recognised by the International Olympic Committee, but has never been contested at an Olympics, while Sport England recognises ten pin bowling but, for administrative reasons (mainly the lack of a governing body), not its doughty old precursor, skittles.

As for darts, its champions were able to argue successfully that high levels of skill are required, but also levels of physical exertion that are no less demanding than for other accredited sports such as archery or shooting, both of which *are* contested at Olympic level.

But whether we call it a sport or a game, to many people darts will always be associated with pubs, and with good reason.

It is the one pub game that everyone has heard of, and the one that most people will have tried, at least once. According to the General Household Survey of 2002, one in ten British males plays the game at least once a year.

Which makes it all the more frustrating that, until recently, a great deal of what has passed for darts history in this country has been palpable nonsense, and nonsense that has gained even wider circulation via the internet.

There are various reasons for this, but chief amongst them is the perhaps understandable reluctance of darts enthusiasts to accept that their game, or sport, is not of ancient lineage, but is, in truth, barely more than about 120–150 years old.

The first of the daft darts stories goes something like this.

Darts is descended from archery because darts themselves are often referred to as arrows (or more colloquially 'arrers'). The most famous archery event in English history was the battle of Agincourt in 1415. Therefore, darts was born after the battle, when archers

whittled down their arrows and threw them at targets.

Suffice it to say that there is no historical record of this momentous event.

We are then told that in 1532 Anne Boleyn presented Henry VIII with 'certain dartes of Biscayan fashion, richly ornamented'.

But these were not darts as we know them. Rather, they were javelin-like projectiles, thrown underhand, for hunting wild boar and the like. As shown opposite, the French still play a game using similar projectiles, called *Javelot Tir sur Cible*.

Another myth often cited is that the Pilgrim Fathers, no less, played darts aboard the Mayflower as they headed to the New World in 1620.

An interesting idea, this; puritans playing a pub game.

Sadly, however, darts historian Dr Patrick Chaplin – to whom we are indebted for much of the material in this chapter (*see Links*) – can find no evidence for this. Nor can the Pilgrim Society in Plymouth, Massachusetts, nor the American darts historian, Dan William Peek.

Next we are told that Royalist troops invented darts in Oxford during the Civil War, by throwing shortened arrows at the end of wine barrels.

It is a seductive tale, especially as the earliest known dartboards (in the 19th century) were indeed log ends (though they might equally have been barrel ends too).

The Cavaliers have also been accredited with the invention of Aunt Sally (*see page 62*).

But again, alas, there is not a scintilla of evidence to back up either of these stories.

So, if not in the 'mists of time', when did darts as we know it today first come about?

In July 1993 in Torquay, the darts team from the Railway Inn turned up for a match at the Little House, equipped with miniature darts and two-foot long blowpipes.

They won, handsomely.

The Secretary of the Torbay Darts League admitted later that although the Railway team had acted contrary to 'the spirit of the game' there was nothing in the rules to say that blowpipes could not be used.

Whether they knew it or not, the lads from the Railway were the last of a long line of dart blowers, rather than throwers.

For it could well be that the game of 'puff and dart', as it was known in the 19th century, was the true forerunner of darts as we know and play it today.

In his study of the sports and pastimes of the English people, published in 1801, Joseph Strutt (*see Links*) mentioned darts only in the context of the French court game; the form Henry VIII played.

But he did refer to 'blow point', which he had seen described, in a 16th century manuscript in the Harleian collection, as a children's

game. Not having seen this game played, Strutt surmised that it was 'probably' played by 'blowing an arrow through a trunk at certain numbers by way of lottery'.

The earliest known reference to a game such as this being played in a pub appears in the London-based *Literary Gazette* of 1819.

This described puff and dart as 'a provincial game... a vulgar game, in which a fellow is blowing a dart through a tube at a mark in the wall of an alehouse'.

Echoing this lowly status was a report in the *Norfolk Mercury* in April 1837, describing how three men accused of murdering a local woman had been apprehended in a 'common tippling house' in Doncaster while 'playing a match at puff and dart'.

◀ Whenever darts is mentioned in pre-19th century English sources, almost certainly this is the sort of game to which the writers were referring; a French throwing game that, as far back as the 13th century was, in common with archery in England, officially encouraged as part of men's military training.

Originally associated with the Champagne region and banned briefly as a result of the French Revolution, **Javelot Tir Sur Cible** (literally 'javelin shooting on target') became popular amongst coal miners in the late 19th century, and is nowadays played mainly in Nord Pas de Calais and Picardie.

The javelot itself weighs 250–400 grams and is like a short spear, with a steel tip and distinctly coloured flights made from goose or turkey feathers.

Each player throws two javelots for his turn, underarm, from a distance of 8m, at a wooden target (or *cible*) made usually from blocks of poplar, and marked with two concentric rings. The outer ring, painted red and measuring 210mm in diameter, scores one point. The inner ring, measuring 60mm is worth two points.

Although once commonly played in rooms above *estaminets* or in the yards alongside, the game is now mostly played in *javelodromes* set up in communal halls.

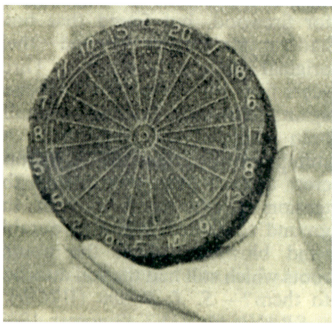

▲ Derided as vulgar by the *Literary Gazette* in 1819, **puff and dart** was depicted more favourably in the 1870 edition of **The Boys' Own Book**, subtitled *A Complete Encyclopaedia of All the Diversions, Athletic, Scientific & Recreative of Boyhood & Youth*.

Described as an 'old fashioned tavern game,' puff and dart, noted the book, 'has lately found its way into private houses, where it enjoys a certain kind of popularity under the name "Drawing-room Archery."'

It was played with a brass tube and 'needle-pointed' darts, using a target consisting of concentric rings.

However, in her *Glossary of Northamptonshire Words and Phrases* of 1854, Anne Elizabeth Baker described a target that appears to have been closer in design to the modern dartboard.

Puff and dart, wrote Baker, was 'a game played by puffing or blowing a dart through a long narrow tube, aiming to strike the numbers painted on a circular board hung against a wall; the various figures are arranged like those on the face of a clock, and he who strikes the three highest numbers wins the game, which is played by two or more persons'.

This configuration of numbers arranged like the face of a clock is of course the essence of the modern dartboard.

In 1868 the catalogue of a games supplier called WH Cremer, of New Bond Street, London, described puff and dart as, 'An Old English game'. It consisted of 'a Target with Bell attached to the Bull's Eye; on each side of the target are certain numbers'.

▲ A persuasive, if frustratingly indistinct piece of evidence that **puff and dart** provided a model for modern darts is this photograph of a tiny board (of perhaps seven inches in diameter) that appeared in **The Countryman** magazine in its winter edition of 1947.

Described as a board used for puff and dart in Sussex pubs 'about sixty years ago (that is, around the 1880s), it is in both form and construction immediately recognisable as an early version of the modern dart board.

That is, the numbers are arranged around the board like the face of a clock, and in segments rather than concentric rings, each number and segment being delineated by wire nailed onto a piece of wood, perhaps a log end.

Moreover, the ordering of the numbers, from 1–20 around the board, plus the provision of a doubles ring around the outer edge,

mirrors exactly the design of the later Manchester dartboard (ten inches in diameter) to which we shall return (*see page 34*).

Whether or not the design of this truly remarkable Sussex board preceded that of the Manchester board is impossible to say on the evidence available. But it certainly is an important piece of evidence.

One reason why puff and dart did not survive may well be the availability of cheap French darts, which, as explained opposite, made the throwing of darts more common, in pubs and fairgrounds.

But puff and dart also had its scare stories. In Edgar Allan Poe's 1844 tale *The Angel of the Odd*, the protagonist reads a London newspaper story about a man who dies from inhaling a dart. A similar case, in which the player survived, was reported in the *Provincial Medical and Surgical Journal* of July 1849.

» In 1870, Abraham Buckley, farmer and publican of the Beaver Inn, Crompton, near Oldham, was accused of offering a quart of beer to the highest scorer from three darts in a Saturday night game of puff and dart.

He was at it again in 1871 and this time was fined a punishing 20 shillings plus costs and had his licence suspended.

By this time puff and dart was deemed sufficiently respectable to be played in the parlour (see opposite), where it was joined by a new indoor game, dart and target, that appeared even closer to the modern form of darts.

As described in the 1881 edition of Cassell's Book of Indoor Amusements, Card Games and Fireside Fun, this too used a board with concentric circles of different colours and worth different scores, with a bull's eye in the centre. But now the darts were to be thrown, rather than blown.

For those readers not dextrous enough to make their own darts – as instructed, using sticks, pins, sealing wax or twine, and paper flights – Cassell's also referred to a manufactured version of the game, known as Dartelle.

That both puff and dart and dart and target were still played in pubs by the turn of the century is confirmed in a 1903 publication, Lawful Games on Licensed Premises (And their Grounds and Outhouses). This was a compendium of articles previously published in the Licensed Victualler's Gazette.

Both games, it explained, had 'three or four concentric circles of different colours with a bull's eye in the centre'.

But there was a warning. 'On no account may any game be played on licensed premises for money or money's worth'.

The French connection

It is at this point in the story of darts that we must re-cross the Channel, where versions of dart and target were already popular in northern France and Belgium, under the respective names of fléchettes, or 'small arrows', and vogelpik, meaning 'bird dart'.

(Researchers at the University of Leuven believe that this latter name derives from an older game called striufvogelspel, or oiseau piquer in French, in which a large wooden bird was suspended on a cord, with a detachable beak. Players had to swing the bird so that its beak stuck in the board. Apparently this bizarre game is still played in Lier, near Antwerp, and in Kappelle-op-den-Bos.)

In both fléchettes and vogelpik each player threw four, rather than the three darts that became standard in Britain, while the boards, all with concentric rings, varied in size. One was even triangular, following the shape of the famous Bass red logo (Britain's first official trademark, registered in 1876).

A typical vogelpik board can be seen at the Bruges Folk Museum, as part of a reconstructed 19th century Flemish pub called De Zwarte Kat, or the Black Cat.

But the significance of fléchettes and vogelpik lies not so much with their boards or their rules as with the fact that it was also in northern France, and more specifically in the village of Hasnon (south east of Lille), that mass production of cheap darts for these games started in the 1880s.

It was these same French darts that helped the development of darts as we know it today, on this side of the Channel.

French historians have traced the origins of this remarkable

▲ French dart makers in the village of **Hasnon**, the main source of cheap darts for the British market from the 1880s until 1939.

industry to a Monsieur Viloquet, a bobbin maker in Hasnon.

As was common in this part of France, colliery workers played javelot during the summer months, hanging a target on a tree in the backyard of their local estaminet.

In order for them to be able to play on during the winter, Viloquet set about making a miniaturised indoor version. For a board he made a target with six concentric circles (compared with only two as used in javelots).

He also started making fléchettes, so successfully that they were soon on sale in the nearby town of Lille, where there happened to be at the time a swarm of British engineers (particularly from Lancashire), helping to set up weaving and spinning machinery in textile mills around the Lille-Tourcoing-Roubaix conurbation.

Inevitably these visitors frequented local estaminets, came across fléchettes, and took examples of the darts home with them as souvenirs.

In time, Hasnon darts became commonplace in Britain. They were sold, loose in bins, in »

According to the village's own figures, by 1932 thirty different makers in the area were turning out an astonishing 100,000 darts per day, for Britain alone.

Foreign competition after 1945 ended this dominance, with the last factory finally closing in 1968.

Even so, it seems a shame that Hasnon's extraordinary contribution to the worldwide game is today marked only by an oversized dart and target on display in the village, and by a brief summary on the village website, rather than by a dedicated museum.

» hardware stores and, later, in shops such as Woolworth's.

They appeared in pubs, at fairgrounds ('throw a dart and win a prize') or were used by showmen to display tricks.

Meanwhile, paper flights (as opposed to feathered flights) were introduced from the USA in 1898, while in 1900 a British inventor took out the first darts-related patent for an improved dart using metal ferrules and clips.

However the next stage in the evolution of darts concerned the dartboard, and more specifically the transition from the concentric ring, or archery-style target, to the numbered, segmented board, marked out by a wire frame, or 'spider' as it became known.

Evolution of the dartboard

The iconic design of the modern dartboard emerged in the London area some time between 1900–24.

As illustrated overleaf numerous regional versions predated and subsequently co-existed with this London board, but only a handful survive, all in small numbers.

Inevitably there has long been speculation as to who might have been responsible for devising the board's tantalising numbering system of one to 20 (especially given that, according to various mathematicians, there are literally billions of possible permutations).

The most oft-quoted candidate for the honour was first mentioned in 1979 when a journalist was ghost writing the autobiography of darts player Leighton Rees. This version, repeated in the *Daily Mirror* in 1992, stated that the credit lay with a Lancashire carpenter in 1896.

Supposedly based in Bury, Brian Gamlin is said to have died in 1903, before he had a chance to patent his idea.

But no trace of a Brian Gamlin has been found in any of the usual records, and although some have since claimed that he must therefore have been of no fixed abode – a showman perhaps – more likely is that the story was, at best, based upon some idle boast once overheard or misheard.

On the other hand, who better than a showman to come up with a format that would make it so difficult for punters to win a prize?

Another tale from these formative years in darts comes from Nigel Thompson, whose family started making dartboards in Manchester, soon after they arrived from a village in the French Dordogne in the 1880s.

Thompson's grandmother, Phyllis Perrigo (originally Perigueux), claimed that the Manchester board's sequence of numbering was brought over from France by her grandparents.

Intrigued, Thompson went back to his ancestral home to see if he could discover any trace of darts or of any darts-related culture at all.

'They were all playing *boule*,' he later recalled, wistfully.

For his part, darts historian Patrick Chaplin believes that the origins of the now standard numbering system are more likely to lie in Yorkshire.

In 1992 he interviewed Thomas Edward Buckle, who claimed that his father, Thomas William Buckle, had devised the numbering sequence used on Yorkshire boards in 1913, or thereabouts, in Dewsbury.

Why was this claim so important? Because the Yorkshire sequence of numbers was later adopted by the London board, which in time became standard.

Thomas William Buckle, Chaplin learnt, began making dartboards commercially in Leeds after he was invalided out of the army in 1915. Indeed his 'Hex', 'Club' and 'Star' boards became well known across west Yorkshire.

Yet he never took out a patent on any part of his work and, regrettably, shunned all publicity, even refusing a chance to explain his work on BBC Radio.

This was a shame, for whoever did work out the numerical sequence of the Yorkshire board, did the world a very great service.

▶ Often reproduced by the *News of the World* in publicity material for their national darts championships, this rare, early image of a darts team, thought to date from around 1900, has fascinated historians for years. Not least this is because it provides a unique glimpse of a home-made, regional dartboard from the period before the commercial manufacture of boards heralded a new era of uniformity, from the 1920s onwards.

The **Dogger Bank** in Freeman Street, **Grimsby**, was a one-room, men-only pub, popular with fishermen. Its landlord, Francis Dolan, is seen standing, second from the right.

According to the Dolan family, who held the tenancy until 1953 (shortly after which the building was demolished), Francis made the dartboard himself, which might explain why no others of this ilk have ever been recorded.

The board, it can be seen, is numbered from 1–28, has a single bull and an outer doubles ring.

But there are also mysterious double circles on each of the four quadrants, together with three runic lines. No doubt the circles formed part of the game, but the purpose of the lines is quite unknown.

The Dolan family recalled that Francis had also made a much larger dartboard which, amazingly, covered an entire wall and scored up to 1,000 points. In order to stop it from drying out in the warm atmosphere of the pub it apparently had to be regularly watered *in situ*.

As to whom the Dogger Bank team played against in order to win those two silver cups and other prizes – perhaps the Dogger Bank No.2 team? – and whether or not any rival pubs played on boards similar to this, unfortunately no records survive.

DART COMPETITIONS.

DOGGER BANK No. 1 TEAM,

Winners of 2 Silver Cups and Several other Prizes.

▶ Before the London board came to dominate British darts (from 1924 onwards), there existed an almost bewildering range of **regional dartboards**, each subtly different.

But one thing they did have in common – at least before the arrival of the 'bristle' board in the 1930s – was that they were made from wood.

Usually elm or poplar, wooden boards were relatively inexpensive, but when not in use had to be kept soaking in water (not in beer, as is often said). If allowed to dry out, the wires distorted and the wood became too hard to take a dart. Because the boards would be re-hung whilst wet, sacks were laid on the floor to catch the drips.

But even a well looked after wooden board might last only a year, since all those regular soakings caused the wire to rust, while the wooden surface itself soon became pitted from use.

The regular immersions also meant that the boards were much plainer than modern boards.

Manchester, Lincoln and Irish boards, for example, were always plain black, with only the wire 'spider' standing out against a plain black background. In contrast, the 'bristle' board, launched by Nodor in 1935 (though actually the brainchild of a Kent publican, Frank Dabbs, and made not from bristle but sisal), needs no soaking and retains its colour.

Trying to summarise all the subtle differences between regional boards is not easy. Several no longer exist or were never fully recorded. Some were produced only in small numbers, with local quirks that failed to catch on.

The most important regional variations are illustrated on the right, but there are others that should also be mentioned.

The **Grimsby** board at the Dogger Bank we have already seen on the previous page, although we have no idea if it was a one-off or a genuine regional variety.

In Essex, a **Corringham Doubles** board was essentially a Yorkshire board with an outer bull.

In Kent, the long lost **Tonbridge** board (not to be confused with a Kent Doubles board, seen opposite) was also reportedly a Yorkshire board, but with small circles or ovals in the middle of each segment counting as trebles.

In his 1936 book on darts – the first to study the game seriously – Rupert Croft-Cooke (see *Links*) mentioned a similar form of board, with circular trebles formed by nail heads in each segment; a type that has since been referred to as either a **Club, Tournament** or **No Name Board**. Where he actually saw this, sadly, he fails to record.

At the Puesdown Inn at Compton Abdale, Gloucestershire, Croft-Cooke came across another oddity that was the same design as a standard board, but twice as large.

He also found a board with three consecutive bull's eyes.

Yet he seemed not to have strayed far, for he also wrote that darts was 'played little in the North of England', and made no mention of the Manchester board at all.

Other varieties of dartboards can be seen, just, in various British Pathé newsreels, now available online. For example a 1927 clip of comedian Billy 'Almost a Gentleman' Bennett, features a small board that appears to have a double, treble and quadruple band, while a clip from 1928 portrays 'Eve the Dart thrower' using a board that looks as if it had doubles and trebles, plus bull's eyes by each number, just outside the normal scoring area.

The Manchester board, believed to date from the 1880s, is the smallest still in use, is the only one not to have adopted the standard sequence of numbering (only the position of the number 19 segment corresponds with standard boards), and is the only board that is still made from wood (hence it is also known as the 'log end' board). It measures just ten inches in diameter, with an outer doubles ring a mere one eighth of an inch deep, no trebles ring, and an inner and outer bull (which can be altered to form a single bull). For more details on its manufacture and use see pages 34-35.

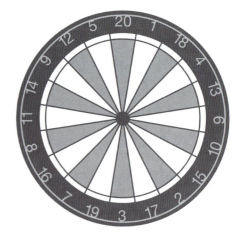

The Yorkshire board, supposedly first produced by Thomas William Buckle in Dewsbury in 1913, was the first board to feature the numbering sequence that would become the national standard, with the 20 at the top. It has an inner but no outer bull, and a doubles ring, but no trebles. Lincoln and Irish boards followed the same format as the Yorkshire design, but had an outer bull, and were usually all black. Both the Kent and Burton boards (*opposite*) were also variations of the Yorkshire board.

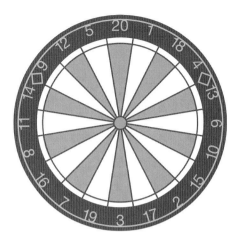

The Burton or Staffordshire board was almost identical to the Yorkshire board but had two boxes, one inch square, outside the scoring area, between the 14 and 9, and between the 4 and 13. Each box scored 25, the equivalent of the outer bull on a standard board. After production of Burton boards ceased in the mid 1970s similar boards were made in nearby Tutbury, but it is not known if any remain in use.

The Kent Doubles board is another variation on the Yorkshire board, which was thought to have arrived in Kent when Yorkshire miners found work in the local coalfields. Uniquely its outer ring counted for trebles, while the triangular areas coming inboard counted as doubles. The difference between a double and treble was thus a wire's breadth, which may explain why no examples are known to have survived.

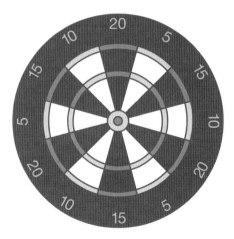

Predating the standard London board and originallly known as the East London Fives board, there are two versions still found in a dozen or more east London pubs and clubs: the Wide Fives board (*as above*), also politely called 'the Ladies' board, and the much trickier Narrow Fives board (which has narrower doubles and trebles rings, said to have been measured to the depth of three old pennies). The throwing distance for this board is nine feet (14¾ inches longer than the standard), and because there is no number 1 segment, games are 505 up.

This is the now internationally accepted standard dartboard, known in its early years as either the London board, the Trebles board or simply 'the Clock'. Measuring 18 inches in diameter, it is in essence an attractive and challenging amalgam of the Yorkshire board (in its numbering sequence) and the East London Fives board (with its inner treble ring and both inner and outer bulls). No one is sure when it first appeared – some say the 1890s – but once it was adopted by the newly formed National Darts Association in 1924 its dominance was assured.

NINEPENCE NET
HOW TO PLAY
DARTS
& NEW GAMES
FOR THE DART BOARD

HOW TO BECOME A SKILLED PLAYER
A GREAT INDOOR GAME
FOR PARTIES & SOCIAL EVENINGS
LONDON: W. FOULSHAM & CO., LTD.

In his study of London pubs for the Church of England Temperance Society in 1934, Basil Nicholson described the game of darts as 'a growing rage'. Dartboards and darts, branded items and instruction books, such as this 1938 publication by John Young, sold in their millions. 'To many people,' wrote Young in his introduction, 'the mention of the word "darts" conjures up a vision of an ill-lit public bar in which a rowdy crowd enjoy their somewhat plebeian pastime to the accompaniment of oaths, and a strange language peculiar to darts players.' But now, the game was respectable, for both men and women of all social classes.

Darts in the 20th century

So little of early darts history is recorded that almost all references to the game are of some interest.

Two from the Edwardian period stand out in particular.

Firstly, in *The Flower of Gloster*, his account of a canal trip around Oxfordshire, published in 1911, author and playwright Ernest Temple Thurston described coming across darts at the Red Lion, Cropredy (now a Grade II listed, real ale pub where the game is still played).

This snippet is telling if only because Thurston clearly felt that most readers, like him, might not have come across darts before.

'Upon the wall opposite the open fireplace, there was a board, marked out as a sundial, each division bearing the value of some number. A ring in the centre marked the highest number of all. The board was painted black, and all about the face of it were little holes where darts had entered.

'It was a game they played to while away a lazy hour.'

Thurston provides no further details, other than to add that he and his boatmen played against the locals for 'four glasses of ale'.

Again, this is of interest for, strictly speaking, to play darts, or indeed any pub game, for a bet or even just for a round, would have been regarded by many local magistrates as an illegal act.

A second Edwardian tale, from Leeds, suggests that one of the means by which magistrates tried to suppress darts in pubs was to classify it as a game of chance.

The story has been repeatedly embellished over the years, but the essence, as investigated by Patrick Chaplin, is this.

In 1908 Jim Garside, landlord of the Adelphi Inn, Kirkstall Road, was summoned to appear at Leeds magistrates court for allowing darts to be played in his pub.

In his defence, Garside called as a witness the Adelphi's best darts player, William 'Bigfoot' Annakin, whose skills he showcased by requesting him to hit specific numbers on a dartboard.

Which of course Annakin did, with consummate accuracy.

Some versions of the story then have the Clerk of the Court attempting to do the same, and failing even to hit the board. But whatever the details, the alleged outcome was the same.

Darts, it had been proven, was indeed a game of skill, and not one of chance.

Chaplin heard this story from Annakin's grandson in 1986, and has no reason to disbelieve it.

Yet he could find no reports of the case in contemporary newspapers, and even more frustratingly, discovered that all records from Leeds Magistrates Court from January 1908 to December 1911 had been lost.

Whether or not the Leeds case was a genuine turning point, with the exception of those places where bans remained in place until the Second World War (usually on all pub games) – including Liverpool, Glasgow and Huddersfield (*see Chapter One*) – from the 1920s onwards there can be no doubt that darts did start to gain respectability.

Indeed that same decade saw three other sports and games catch the British public's imagination.

Greyhound racing and speedway emerged thanks to advances in technology. Darts, together with snooker, owed its new-found popularity to the joint efforts of manufacturers, publicans and the popular press.

In the case of darts the turning point came in 1924, when an industrial chemist turned dartboard manufacturer, Ted Leggatt, wrote to the publicans' newspaper, the *Morning Advertiser*, to suggest a meeting at an office in Holborn between all parties interested in the game.

(Leggatt had, the year before, brought out an experimental dartboard made from plasticine. It did not catch on, but the tradename Nodor that he gave to his new form of odourless plasticine lived on as the name of his dartboard company.)

Attended by publicans, brewers and representatives of existing darts leagues, the result of the Holborn meeting was the formation of the National Darts Association, with Leggatt as its first chairman.

The NDA's first, and perhaps most far reaching decision, was to adopt as standard the London, or Trebles dartboard, thereby sounding the eventual death knell for several regional variants.

The NDA also established a set of clear rules. Three darts constituted a throw. The game was to be 301 up (which was five times around a cribbage board), starting and finishing with a double. Each match was to be the best of three.

Again, brilliantly simple and concise (although the target has since been upped to 501).

The first ever NDA tournament to be played under these rules was the Licensee's Cup, staged at The Red Lion, Wandsworth, in London on June 1 1926. So impressive was this that within months the *News of the World* newspaper had decided to sponsor another competition for the London area in 1927–28.

From that point onwards, darts took off.

A series of books on the game appeared, each emphasising how respectable darts had become.

Typical amongst these was *The Various Dart Games – and How to Play Them* (1939), by A Wellington, with a foreword by Aneurin M Davies of the *News of the World*. This featured on its cover an elegant couple, he in dinner jacket, she in backless evening gown, throwing darts.

'Darts has long been an honest game of the tavern,' wrote Wellington, 'but now it has invaded Mayfair and, as a consequence, everybody is playing it. Therefore, when you receive a printed invitation marked "Darts and Dancing", do not be surprised.'

Wellington was not entirely wide of the mark. In December 1937, George VI and Queen Elizabeth (the Queen Mother) visited a community centre on a trading estate in Slough, and were persuaded to throw a few casual darts. A photographer captured the scene and suddenly darts became fashionable.

As the *Sunday Chronicle* headline put it, 'Women Flock to Follow The Queen's Lead At Darts.'

The *Chronicle* also revealed that darts was played in the servants' quarters at Buckingham Palace.

Not everyone was happy with this trend. In his 1936 book on darts, the prolific writer and now gay icon Rupert Croft-Cooke bemoaned the creeping uniformity of the game, and begged, 'Let this one pastime at least escape the modern passion for drilling men through their lives, surrounding them with regulations and officialdom, and making even their sport conform to a thousand dreary rules and trite conventions.'

Also in 1936, novelist TH White wrote in *England Have My Bones*,

that he had no wish for darts to be run by an 'Affiliated Co-Operative Limited Gilt-Edged Ultimate Wenman's Exclusive Divinely Inspired Dart Association in London...

'These cockneys issue an authoritative booklet of their own rules to any degenerate publican who chooses to observe them.'

But London did, more or less, hold sway. When researchers for Mass Observation descended on Bolton in 1938, gathering material for what became *The Pub and the People* (see Links) they noted, 'At one time in the north of England darts were played on a comparatively small board...'

Measuring 'about nine inches across' this was what is known as the Manchester or log end board.

(The observer added that a century earlier even smaller, six inch boards were in use, with darts blown through an 18 inch blowpipe.)

By 1939 however, Bolton's local board was being 'replaced by the larger type used originally in the south'.

The London game not only usurped regional boards. Its popularity in Bolton also drove out rings (see page 84), which Mass Observation for some reason insisted on calling quoits.

Even darts enthusiast Croft-Cooke noted ruefully, 'The long competition is breaking down, and everywhere the Shove Ha'Penny boards have been shuffled into corners, while the moon-face of the dartboard shines behind its specially arranged electric light.'

This colonisation of Britain's pubs continued after the Second World War. As recalled by the landlady of a pub in Kent, where daddlums had been popular (see page 68), 'A little fellow from the

▲ A packed house at the Palais de Danse in **Ilford, Essex**, watches heats in the **News of the World Individual Darts Championships** in April 1937. How many in the audience, one wonders, sang the tournament's signature tune, written that same year (see below)?

The *News of the World* had once supported quoits and by then also sponsored snooker. But its darts tournament dwarfed them all. In its first year, 1927–28, held only in London, a thousand or so players entered. The winner was a Boer War veteran from West Ham,

whose average for three darts was 71, which would get him nowhere today (but was from nine feet, longer than today's distance).

Rival competitions soon emerged, but the *News of the World* was by far the most coveted.

In its first season as a national tournament, in 1947–48, a total of 289,866 players entered.

The logistics were mind-boggling. Every player had to be attached to a pub or club. Following local heats, 4,096 winners went into 512 sub-area finals, and from there to 64 area finals, the venues for which grew larger at each stage.

There were then eight divisional finals, leading at last to the Grand Finals in London, held at venues such as Alexandra Palace or the Agricultural Halls in Islington. The 1939 finals at the latter, in which Marmaduke Brecon of the Jolly Sailor in Hanworth triumphed, drew a record crowd of 14,534.

Although television later stole the competitions' thunder, the *News of the World* tournament continued until 1990, and was briefly resurrected in 1996–97, when its final male winner was Phil Taylor.

NEWS OF WORLD
DARTS SIGNATURE TUNE
NOW! JOIN IN THE CHORUS

'LET'S HAVE A JOLLY OLD GAME OF DARTS, BING.
LET'S HAVE A JOLLY OLD GAME OF DARTS, BING!
FIRST YOU GET A DOUBLE, THEN RIGHT OFF YOU GO:
BUT YOU NEEDN'T TROUBLE IF YOU DON'T KNOW
HOW TO THROW.
SO LET'S HAVE A JOLLY OLD GAME OF DARTS, BING!
PUT A LITTLE GLADNESS IN YOUR HEARTS.
ON ANY KIND OF DAY, IT'S A LOVELY GAME TO PLAY.
SO LET'S HAVE A JOLLY OLD GAME OF DARTS, BING!

▲ In about 1975 the British Darts Organisation (BDO) started using the word **oche** instead of **hockey** to denote the line behind which players must stand when throwing (as shown here at **The Alliance** in **West Hampstead, London**).

In the absence of an explanation for this, sundry theories emerged; that oche derives from an Anglo Saxon word (or was it Norman or Flemish?) for the 'notch' in the ground from which archers drew their bows; that it comes from *hocken*, meaning to spit (so that oche signifies the distance a man could spit); or that 'hock' was 19th century slang for a foot.

One hoaxer claimed that 'hockey' was used because the throwing distance equalled three crates of beer as brewed by a firm called Hockey & Sons. Needless to add,

no such brewery ever existed.

But whatever its origins, this still does not explain why hockey had to give way to oche. Unless it was merely an attempt to legitimise the Cockney pronunciation of 'ockey?

As to the actual distance, in the early years of its darts tournament the *News of the World* set this at 9', but in 1947 reduced it to 8'. Meanwhile the National Darts Association of Great Britain (formed 1954), set their distance as 7' 6".

Finally, in the 1970s the BDO decided to split the difference.

Yet instead of opting for 7' 9" (or 236.22cm), as Britain was then going metric they added an extra quarter inch, so it would correspond closer to 237cm.

And 7' 9¼" is how it remains (even though 7' 10½" would have made a much easier 2.4m).

» East End of London came round in an Austin 7 with a boot full of dartboards in 1947 or 1948, and that was that.'

By 1948, when the *News of the World* Championship went national, it was claimed that eleven million people were playing darts regularly in Britain.

Top players became media stars of the day. Jim Pike, who won 37 major titles, embarked on a tour of music halls, only to find himself banned from the *News of the World* contest for being deemed to have turned professional.

Instead, Pike stayed on the road, playing challenge matches and performing tricks, one of which – nicking the usual cigarette from someone's mouth – was captured on a Pathé newsreel in 1946 (but only at the third attempt).

Pike's great rival, Joe Hitchcock, also appeared on Pathé, in 1948, in a clip entitled *A Modern William Tell*, in which he too knocked a cigarette out of an assistant's mouth, using a six-inch nail instead of a dart. He then knocked out a match held between the assistant's lips before his final trick, which was to knock a sixpenny piece out of the assistant's hand, then ricochet the nail into the bull on a dartboard.

Another *News of the World* winner in 1964 and 1965, Tom Barrett, from the Odco Sports Club in Long Acre, London, went further by making a triumphal tour of West Germany, Sweden, Canada, Australia and the USA, where he appeared on *The Tonight Show* with Johnny Carson. Back home he also appeared on the BBC's *Blue Peter* and helped with stunts filmed for *The Saint* (with Roger Moore) and for the Beatles film, *Help!*.

By the late 1970s, when television finally embraced the

game on a regular basis, an estimated seven million people were playing darts. Though still a phenomenal number, that was four million down on the immediate post-war years.

Yet television brought about another huge surge in interest.

As darts technology itself improved and the leading players grew ever more professional under the auspices of the newly formed British Darts Organisation, a new elite emerged; the likes of John Lowe, Eric Bristow, Leighton Rees and Jocky Wilson.

These characters, and no doubt the fact that in the long tradition of pub games most of them drank (some of them copiously), and smoked in between throws, helped to attract huge television audiences. In 1983, ten million, a quarter of the adult population, watched a world championship match. In 1988, there were 14 separate darts events on television.

But as was the case with wrestling, bowls and snooker, this love affair did not last, and in 1993 ITV pulled out of darts.

As noted previously, the *News of the World* also dropped their event in the 1990s.

A national institution for over half a century all but disappeared from the limelight with barely a murmur of protest.

'You have only to go into your local pub these days to see the dartboard empty in the corner,' sighed a spokesman in *Darts World* magazine, in early 1991.

'The youngsters are all playing pool instead.'

There followed a storm of acrimony and a blizzard of acronyms, as various factions fought to control the game. The top sixteen professionals and several companies and promoters

formed the World Darts Council (WDC), and later the Professional Darts Corporation (PDC).

This, however, put them on a collision course, both with the British Darts Organisation (BDO), the then ruling body of the game nationwide, and the World Darts Federation (WDF).

The result is that two world championships are now staged every year, transmitted within a month of each other on rival television channels.

The BDO stages theirs at the Lakeside Leisure Complex in Frimley Green, Surrey, covered by the BBC, while the PDC World Championships – covered by Sky Television using a whole panoply of tiny cameras and slow motion effects – have been staged amidst frenetic razzmatazz at the Circus Tavern, Purfleet in Essex, and in 2008 at Alexandra Palace.

PDC players have nicknames such as 'The Iceman', 'Bravedart' (a Scot, naturally), 'Hawaii 501', and last, but by no means least, Phil 'The Power' Taylor.

Burslem-born Taylor is without doubt the greatest darts player the world has yet seen. In the 2006 final he averaged 106.74 points per three dart throw, to clock up his 13th world title.

According to Barry Hearn, promoter and now chairman of the PDC, 'the umbilical cord between

darts and the pub has been broken and what you are seeing is a classless sport.'

Others would argue that darts remains a pub game at heart, not least as a focus for drinking and betting, if no longer for smoking.

In fact according to a survey, carried out in 2006, there were still dartboards at some 53 per cent of Britain's 58,000 pubs, making it still by far the most popular pub game in the country.

And although the figures for participation are much reduced since the 1970s, the BDO reckons there are about three quarters of a million registered players, with another three million playing on a regular basis.

But in common with so many British games, the success of darts is no longer measured by what is happening purely on these shores.

The World Darts Federation now has over 50 countries under its wing, the latest of which to join, Iran, is estimated to have 600,000 players, many of whom regard Phil Taylor as their hero.

If only we could be sure that the version of darts history that we might pass on would be as reliable as 'The Power'.

And that darts' heritage in its mother country will be as carefully nurtured in the place where it is surely best suited, and most at home – the pub.

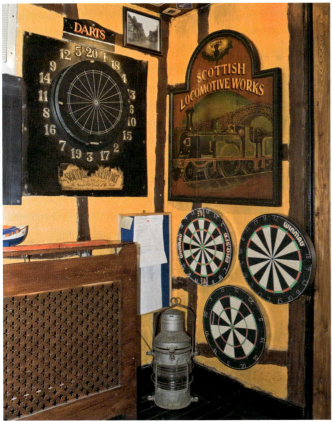

Keeping the faith – a Wide Fives board is still first choice on ladies night at the Greyhound pub at Claydon, in Ipswich (*top*), while at the Cock Inn in Luddesdowne, Kent (*left*), a black, wooden Kent board is set up for play, leaving in reserve a standard Trebles board, a London Narrow Fives board and, on the right, a Yorkshire board.

Craftsman David Mealey still uses traditional methods to make Manchester dartboards in his Denton workshop, where he also makes dominoes. Each number and spoke of the wheel is hand cut from aluminium sheets, then hammered into the poplar log end, before a black dye is applied. For added value, the boards are also two-sided.

The Manchester dartboard

John Gwynne, journalist, darts promoter, television commentator and Mancunian, once described the Manchester dartboard as being as important to the city's culture as both City and United, Lancashire Cricket Club and the Hallé Orchestra.

But in darts terms it is also of importance nationally, for since the development of 'bristle', or rather sisal boards in the 1930s, the Manchester board – often also called a log end – is the last in Britain still to be made from wood.

Originally the cross section of an elm tree was favoured. Since the spread of Dutch Elm disease from the 1970s onwards, however, poplar has been used instead.

Otherwise, this is a design that has barely changed in over a century. It remains a mere ten inches in diameter, with almost microscopic doubles, only one-eighth of an inch deep.

Also, as illustrated on page 28, it retains its unique sequence of numbering, with only the number 19 segment being in the same location as a standard London or Trebles board.

How the Manchester board came to be numbered this way, no-one is sure. Nor can we know why the Sussex puff and dart board we saw on page 24 had exactly the same numbering.

But what can be said is that commercial production of the boards began in 1885 at the workshops of a Manchester firm known as Perrigo (run by a French immigrant family called Perigueux).

Between the wars and until the late 1940s and 1950s the Manchester board remained extremely popular in the Greater Manchester area, even if at many pubs it was kept in tandem with the standard London board.

A local supplier called W Sweet claimed in a 1928 advert that 99 pubs out of a 100 in Manchester had one of its boards.

Inevitably there were also local tournaments using the boards, such as one run by a Johnny Barrow in the late 1940s, for which the prize was cash, plus a cup worth £200.

But as useage of the boards faded in the latter part of the 20th century, a crisis point was reached in 2003, when, to the dismay of enthusiasts, the last known main manufacturer decided to stop making the boards.

It was at this point that John Gwynne rallied the troops, and in 2004 the Manchester Dartboard Federation was formed.

Twenty local leagues affiliated to it, their geographical spread stretching, according to Gwynne, from Glossop in the east to Cadishead in the west, and from Middleton in the north to Wythenshawe in the south.

The Manchester cause was further helped by David Mealey offering to take over production of the boards (see left) and by sponsorship of a Log End Team Championships by the Manchester brewers Holts (in which 16 teams of seven have competed).

Organising these events has not proved easy, particularly as each league tended to play under its own interpretation of the rules.

Also, several leagues, many of them for women, have opted not to join the Federation, preferring to maintain their independence.

Hence one observer reckons that between the Federation and other non-affiliated leagues, there may be as many as 50 log end leagues as of 2009.

Even so, casual visitors to the Manchester area might struggle to spot one of the boards. This is because, as shown right, when not in use the boards are stored in water, with standard boards hung up in their place.

One therefore has to be in the right place, at the right time of year and on the right evening to catch a game in progress.

But if successful, the main game likely to be seen is Slip Up, the Mancunian version of Round the Board. In this, every player has to land one dart into each number, consecutively from one to 20.

However, if you hit a double, say double one, your next shot is three. A double nine takes you to 19, and so on.

A player finishes by repeating the first double he scored in that round, followed by a bull.

Theoretically that means a round can be completed in just seven throws: that is, double one, single three, double four, single nine, double ten, double one (again) and bull. But any round that takes less then twelve throws is a feat that will guarantee a mention in the local newspaper.

(If a player fails to land a double, some leagues require a double one for his penultimate throw, some prefer a double 20.)

Slip Up is mainly a men's game, whereas most ladies' leagues play the usual reduction game, going in at 301 and finishing on a double.

For this game, an additional inner bull – known fondly as 'Little Audrey' – is fixed into the larger one. Thus in some Manchester pubs one hears that Monday nights are for 'the Big Girls' Board' (meaning the much easier London board), while Tuesday nights see Little Audrey emerge from her bath.

◀ When not in play a **log end dartboard** has to be kept soaking, as shown here in the hands of landlord Paul Robson, at the **Railway Hotel, Fairfield, Manchester**.

Some landlords add black dye to the water to retain the colour.

On the evening of a match the board is rinsed off and then carried to its mounting point, where, as here, it will usually take the place of a standard board.

Being eight inches smaller in diameter than the standard, Manchester boards are hung at a height of 5 feet 3 inches from the floor to the centre (compared with 5 feet 8 inches for the standard).

The throwing distance is also shorter, being 7 feet 6 inches.

Pubs offering both boards therefore need to have adjustable mounts and two oches.

As soon as a game is over the board must be returned to its tub to avoid it drying out. If not kept soaking the numbers and wires can spring out and even snap.

One dartboard maker used to say that Christmas was the worst time.

'They play the last league match, close the door on the cabinet and forget to take the board down. By the time someone remembers, the board's dry as a bone, cracked up and done for.'

But even if well looked after a log end board will typically last only a year; that is, six months per side.

▲ World darts has evolved largely thanks to the efforts of British designers and entrepreneurs: Ted Leggatt of Nodor; Frank Dabbs, inventor of the 'bristle' dartboard, and the Kicks family of Winmau, the company that in 1997 launched the first 'no bounce', staple free dartboard. But in the design and manufacture of actual darts, the one name that stands out is **Frank Lowy** (1901–69) of **Unicorn Darts**.

Born Ferenc Lowy in Budapest, Lowy trained as an engineer, but could only find work translating for a patents agency. This led him to London in 1928, and to a chance encounter with darts, recalled on this page by his son and successor at Unicorn, Stanley.

Lowy is the only English manufacturer to have been elected to the USA's National Sporting Goods' Associations' Hall of Fame.

Frank Lowy and Unicorn darts

'My father was brought up in very straitened circumstances,' recalled Stanley Lowy in 2009.

'His own father had abandoned the family by going to America. There were no jobs in Budapest, so he used his language skills to pay the bills. One day he'd have an English lesson, the next he would recoup the fees by teaching someone else what he'd just learnt.

'He was still on a tight budget by the time he sent for the family to join him in London – we later settled in West Norwood – so every summer we lodged with the Gatters, a family of farmworkers in Littleham, near Exmouth. It was cheaper than being in London, and although the Gatters were poor, we had lashings of Devon cream.'

Stan's father, meanwhile, secured a desk in a Chancery Lane patent office in return for translating documents.

'My father had never been in a pub. Didn't have the money or anyone to invite him. Then one summer, 1936 I think, I was about four, Mr Gatter took dad for a glass of Devon cider at his local, the New Inn. An old pub with low ceilings.

'He said to Mr Gatter, "What are those people doing, throwing things at the wall?"

'Mr Gatter replied with some incredulity, "Well that's darts. Everybody knows what darts is."

'So he asked Mr Gatter to tell him all about it. Father was always interested in things.

'Anyway at that time Gatter's son Ernie was desperate to play darts but as he was only 16 wasn't allowed in the pub. So being good with his hands my father made Ernie a dartboard out of an old orange box, bought three darts from Woolworths and hung the dartboard on the chicken coop so they could all play outside.

'When we returned to West Norwood after the holiday Dad was so taken that he bought a dartboard, hung it over the back of the front door and played with our neighbour, Harry Taylor.

'But he was irritated by several deficiencies with the darts, like when a following dart might stick in the cane shaft of the first one. That was called 'Robin Hooding'. Or that in a dry atmosphere the cane would fall out, or the paper flight would fall out...

'So my father drew up a design for a slotted aluminium shaft and a cap that screwed on to keep the flight in place, the first time this had been done. Being more slender, it also offered less obstruction for the following dart.

'Also, instead of paper he used vulcanised fibre for the flight.

'Harry Taylor had a workshop where he made paraffin stoves, so he made up a set of Dad's designs

for £6. And of course being in the patent business Dad applied for a patent, on November 4 1937.

'In those days to buy darts you went to a hardware shop and picked out three from a bin, say three brass or three wooden French darts, and tried to match them up as close as you could.

'My father decided to sell his darts as a matched set of three in a box. He said, "Well you buy shoes and there are always two in a box," so why not sell darts that way?'

Lowy called his dart the Silver Comet, to reflect the fact that it was chromium plated. But the sports equipment manufacturers John Wisden objected and sent someone around to see him in Chancery Lane. Their Silver Comet was a tennis racket, however, and so once they saw that his Silver Comet was a dart they realised they could not stand in his way.

'And then they asked, "How are you going to sell them?" Dad replied that he'd only just started and hadn't really thought that far, so Wisden's people said that as their reps called on all the sports shops they'd sell them for him.

'So he had a firm in Clerkenwell make up the first consignment, sold them to Wisden for a shilling a set, and they sold them onto shops, who retailed them at 2s 6d.

'In the first year I think he sold 170,000 sets...'

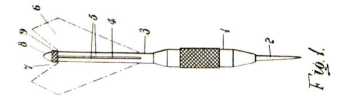

A detail from the 1937 Silver Comet patent application, showing the screw cap to secure the flight and the slender aluminium shaft.

UNICORN DARTS

ALEC ADAMSON 1961

TOM REDDINGTON 1960

ALBERT WELCH 1959

TOMMY GIBBONS 1958

ALWYN MULLINS 1957

TREVOR PEACHEY 1956

—the consistent choice of champions!

UNICORN The World's Greatest Name in Darts

Unicorn darts have been consistently chosen by every winner of the News of the World individual darts championship since 1956. The champions all agree that Unicorn darts with their elegant design and perfect balance always give the superb performance necessary for tournaments. Call in at your sports dealer and inspect these darts today. With over 300 scientific patterns to choose from you'll find exactly what you want in the Unicorn range.

UNICORN PRODUCTS LIMITED, 119-121 STANSTEAD ROAD, LONDON S.E.23   Phone: FORest Hill 7688 (5 lines)

▲ In 1939 John Wisden went into receivership, owing Frank Lowy around £1,000 and leaving him determined to set up his own firm. This he named **Unicorn**, after spotting the beast on the Royal Crest that Wisden had featured 'By Appointment' on all their products.

Unicorn were, and are, by no means the only manufacturers of darts in Britain, but they were the first to specialise in dart production, and soon grew to be the largest.

Moreover, thanks to Frank Lowy's meticulous record keeping, and the subsequent efforts of his son Stanley (who took over the business in 1961) and Stanley's sons Richard and Edward (who followed suit in 1997), Unicorn's archives, parts of which are available online, offer historians an invaluable resource.

As this advertisement from the early 1960s shows, one of the key elements of Unicorn's success was both Frank and Stanley's flair for public relations; not only signing up the top players of the day but also getting them to appear and do tricks on television all over the world. As a result, Unicorn now supplies around 180 countries.

But whereas its offices are now in Edenbridge, Kent, in common with so many manufacturers of sports goods, its darts are now all made in the Far East.

▲ Frank Lowy noticed that most men dressed quite formally to go to the pub, and so a set of darts had to slip comfortably into a jacket or shirt pocket. Hence these smaller darts in a Bakelite case went on sale shortly after the Second World War. A worker on the shopfloor coined the name **Half-Pint Darts**.

They were also amongst the first darts to feature plastic flights, developed by Unicorn because French feathers were hard to source in the post war period.

Feathers remained the choice of the professionals however, and although more expensive, were so much in demand that at one point in the 1960s, Unicorn's works in Bloxwich, Staffordshire, was turning out 28,800 feather flights per day.

Lowy was forever hatching new ideas, sketching them on scraps of paper and in notebooks. He also designed sets for chess, draughts, dominoes, shove ha'penny and snakes and ladders, and of course patented every one – incidentally with the same Chancery Lane firm that had taken him in, in 1930, and which continues to act for Unicorn today.

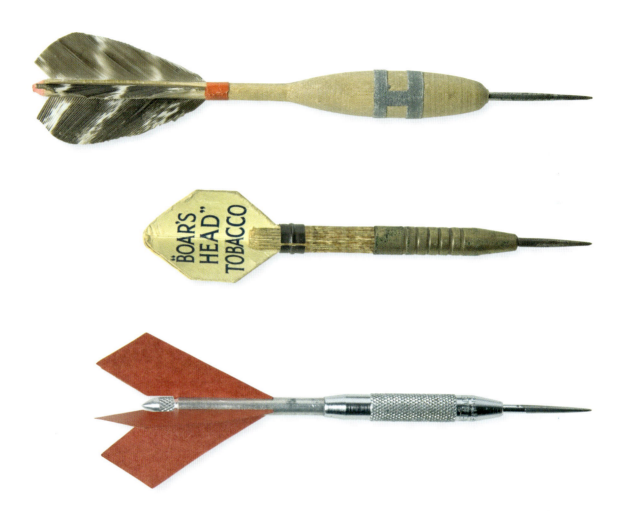

▲ The design and technology of the dart has changed dramatically over the last century, as shown by this small selection from the collection of darts historian Patrick Chaplin.

(Note all are shown at their actual size.)

At the top is an undated example of a **Hasnon dart**, as imported from France between the 1880s and the 1950s, and sold loose in bins (at three for sixpence in the late 1940s). Hasnon darts had birchwood shafts, turkey feather flights glued into slots, steel points and, to add weight (a vital component of any dart) a band of lead pressed into the shaft.

It is possible that the popular word for darts – 'arrows' – derives from these darts, which the French called *fléchettes*, or little arrows.

In the centre is a 1930s **brass and cane dart** of the sort publicans used to give away but which so annoyed Frank Lowy. It has a brass barrel and a cane shaft with slits to hold the paper flight. A sliding steel clip helped tighten the cane to keep the flight from falling out.

Lowy's response, launched in 1938, was the **Silver Comet** (*bottom*), the world's first all metal dart with its chrome-plated brass barrel, aluminium shaft, vulcanised fibre flights and its all important screw cap to hold the flight in place.

Slender and light (too light for some tastes, which is why Lowy soon introduced different weights), the Silver Comet retailed for a whopping 2s 6d for a set of three, but was deliberately aimed at the burgeoning middle class market.

▲ One of the leading professionals of his day, Jim Pike set up his own company in 1945. This typical **Jim Pike dart** (*top*) has a brass barrel, a white plastic adaptor to hold the cane shaft, and dyed turkey feather flights. Although hardly cutting edge, the design proved popular enough for it to remain virtually unchanged until the Hertfordshire-based company closed in 2000.

Also in Hertfordshire, a St Albans engineering company called C Giles & Co. produced brass and feather flighted darts under the brand name **Kwiz** (*centre*) from the 1950s until the 1970s.

But all these companies were forced to take stock when a new generation of darts appeared in the 1970s, fitted with polyester flights (which are far more durable and aerodynamic than paper or feathers and can be flat-packed in a case), and, most crucially of all, barrels made from tungsten alloy.

Because this alloy is twice as dense as brass, tungsten darts are now so slender that a skilled player can 'stack' three of them in a line within either a double or a treble ring (that is, within a depth of just 8mm).

Shown here (*bottom*) is a modern, state-of-the-art **Savage Steeltip**, with 80% tungsten, made by **Harrows**, another Hertfordshire company, founded in 1973 and now based in Hoddesdon. Others in their range go up to 97% tungsten, with the typical weight ranging from 20–30gms, and prices ranging from £15 up to £35 for a set of three.

Chapter Three

Skittles

Although nowadays confined to specific regions of England, in terms of clubs and leagues skittles remains Britain's second most popular pub game, after darts. But its history predates darts by hundreds of years. These rough hewn kyles (as skittles were known in Scotland) and ball – now held by the National Museum of Scotland – date from no later than 1650, and were discovered buried in peat outside the Galloway village of Ironmacannie in 1835. It is possible they were deliberately buried to stop them from being confiscated by the authorities.

As Thomas Hughes famously wrote in his 1857 novel, *Tom Brown's Schooldays*, 'Life isn't all beer and skittles; but beer and skittles, or something better of the same sort, must form a good part of every Englishman's education.'

Hughes may well have borrowed the phrase from Charles Dickens, whose character Sam Weller had reflected in *Pickwick Papers*, two decades earlier, that 'life ain't all porter and skittles'.

Either way, that both writers should have made the link was hardly surprising. Skittles, then as now, is a game that remains inexorably linked with beer.

So much so that for as long as anyone can remember matches have typically ended with the 'beer leg', tacked on to the end of the match in order to determine which team pays for the last round.

As to what form the skittles match itself might take, that is a rather more complex matter.

Games that require the throwing or rolling of one object to knock over a series of others are common to many civilisations and ages.

But as this chapter shows, there are subtle distinctions, essentially determined by five factors.

These are, first, the nature of the projectile (be it a ball, stick or even a wooden 'cheese'); second, the manner in which the projectile is either rolled or thrown (with or without a bounce); third, the number, relative sizes and configuration of the target objects (or pins); fourth, the type of ground or surface on which the game is played, and fifth, whether it is played indoors or outdoors.

And that is before we even get down to rules or scoring systems.

During the course of a lifetime's study, a French wood turner, Raymond Kessler, and his wife Lin, managed to collect some 600 different types of skittle pins from around Europe, and 150 different balls, many of which are now lodged in museums in France, Switzerland and the USA.

Nevertheless, as Lin Kessler wrote in her 1983 account of their findings, *La Quille Vivante*, 'We have only skimmed the surface.'

Quite so, for the Kesslers did not even get to Britain.

Had they done, they might have added at least 20 more varieties of skittles to their study.

Several of these have, inevitably, died out, but of the survivors, the four most common, pub-based versions are known generically as Old English, or London skittles, long alley skittles (played in the east Midlands), Western or West Country skittles, and Aunt Sally (played in Oxfordshire and its neighbouring counties).

Two other less common variants are the splendidly-named wallops, played in north Yorkshire, and Irish skittles.

All are featured in this chapter, with table-top versions of skittles following in Chapter Four.

Definitions of skittles

The word skittles is first recorded in England in the 1630s.

But several games of its ilk came before, each with names derived from *quilles*, the French for skittles. These included kayles, cayles, keiles, kyles (*see left*) and skayles.

In 1801 Joseph Strutt (*see Links*) explained the origin of the word skittles thus: 'Kayle-pins

As depicted in a 14th century Book of Prayers and reproduced by Strutt in 1801, kayles was an early form of skittles. When a ball rather than a club was used the game was called closh, or cloish. When bones were used instead of pins it was called loggats.

94. KAYLES.—XIV. CENTURY.

were afterwards called kettle, or kittle-pins; and hence, by easy corruption, skittle-pins'.

Unfortunately he then fails to explain the words kettle or kittle.

Strutt identified five games that we might recognise today as belonging to the skittle family, all of which are described below.

He also made a point worth restating for anyone unfamiliar with these games, that although the action involved in skittles is often, as Strutt put it, 'improperly enough called bowling', the actual game of skittles is quite distinct from that of bowls.

In most versions of skittles the aim is to knock over pins. In bowls the aim is to land a bowl as close as possible to a jack.

Yet despite this clear distinction, the terms 'bowling alley' and 'skittles alley' have long been almost interchangeable.

In 1579, for example, Stephen Gosson warned, in *The School of Abuse*, that 'Common bowling-alleys are privy mothers that eat up the credit of many idle citizens.'

The bowling that took place in Gosson's alleys would, to our eyes, almost certainly look more like what we call skittles, and involve only nine pins.

But then what is today's ten pin bowling alley if not a skittle alley, with electro-mechanical add-ons?

Nine Pins? Ten Pins? Skittles or Bowls?

But that is only for starters...

Half bowl, or rolly-polly

In situations where there was not enough room for an alley, a form of skittles emerged in medieval Britain known as half bowl (which of course had little to do with the game of bowls).

Often mentioned in those lists of games banned by the »

▲ Held at the **Strangers' Hall Museum**, **Norwich**, this is the only known surviving set of **loggats**, which shared elements of kayles, and both skittles and bowls.

Donated to the museum in 1922, the loggats date from the 19th century and almost certainly belonged to the **Hampshire Hog** pub, which stood in **St Swithin's Alley**, **Norwich**, until the early 20th century (and was otherwise famed because in c.1850 its landlord, John 'The Licker' Pratt, famously beat fellow Norfolk pugilist, Jem Mace, in an epic bout).

The Hampshire Hog is stated to have been the last pub in England where loggats was played, a statement made, oddly enough, as part of a textual analysis of Shakespeare's *Hamlet*.

In Shakespeare's time loggats was a sort of poor man's kayles, played with bones instead of skittles. Hence in *Hamlet*, as a

corpse is buried by an irreverent grave digger, the Prince asks his friend Horatio, 'Did these bones cost no more the breeding, but to play loggats with them?'

In his 1755 dictionary, Samuel Johnson thought loggats to be 'the same which is now called kittle-pins, in which boys often make use of bones instead of wooden pins, throwing at them with another bone instead of bowling'.

Another scholar declared, in 1778, 'A stake is fixed to the ground; those who play, throw loggats at it and he that is nearest the stake wins: I have seen it played in different counties at their sheep-shearing feasts, where the winner is entitled to a black fleece.'

The Hampshire Hog reference appeared in an annotated edition of *Hamlet* published in the 1870s, in which the Rev G Gould of Norwich wrote of loggats, 'The game so called resembles bowls, but with

notable differences. First, it is played not on a green, but on a floor strewn with ashes.

'The jack is a wheel of lignum-vitae or other hard wood, nine inches in diameter and three or four inches thick. The loggat, made of applewood, is a truncated cone, 26 or 27 inches in length...

'Each player has three loggats, which he throws, holding lightly the thin end. The object is to lie as near the jack as possible'.

Certainly the set at Strangers' Hall matches this description, albeit with smaller measurements; there being six wooden loggats measuring between 18–20 inches long, and two hardwood jacks of 7½ inches in diameter.

No trace of the Hampshire Hog itself remains, although a yard of that name exists behind a thatched cottage just north of St Swithin's Church, which is now an arts centre.

▲ In terms of sporting heritage, one of the most exciting archaeological finds of the 1980s was this **half bowl**, excavated from the site of a medieval hall on the corner of High Street and Blackfriargate, Hull, and now displayed in the **Hull and East Riding Museum**.

Dating from the late 13th century and thought to be Britain's oldest purpose-made ball, it was first thought to be the damaged remains of a spherical bowl.

But further inspection revealed that it had been deliberately crafted that way, probably for it to be used in the game of half-bowl, the set up for which is illustrated below.

As described on this page half-bowl was a form of skittles played in confined spaces. Because similar games were (and still are) played across Europe, and because the excavated site in Hull had monastic connections, it is possible that the game was introduced from the Continent.

» authorities from the 14th century onwards, half bowl, as the name suggests, was played with a cut-down bowl (*such as seen left*), and with not nine or ten pins, but with 15 or 16.

One of the earliest descriptions we have of the game comes from an Old Bailey court report of 1759 in which, helpfully for us, the judge asked the plaintiff exactly what, in the context of half-bowl, 'bowling' actually meant.

Explained the accused, 'In the middle of the room, there are fifteen to sixteen brass nails in the floor, and there is a bowl almost the shape of a bowl dish, which runs around and comes in anywhere... and knocks down pins which stand upon the brass nails.'

In 1801 Strutt offered further detail, and introduced an alternative name for the game that seems far more apt.

'Half-bowl is practised to this day in Hertfordshire, where it is commonly called rolly-polly; and it is best performed on the floor of a room, especially if it be smooth and level.'

Strutt then described how 15 (not 16) pins were set out (*as shown left*), with twelve forming a circle about 2½ feet in diameter.

Fully exploiting the half-bowl's 'great bias' – a challenge that required considerable practice – the aim was to 'cast' it around the edge of the circle and beyond the two furthest pins, so that it would then turn back on itself and start downing pins in the circle.

If the two outer pins were downed first the cast was forfeited.

Each pin in the circle scored one point. The other three were each distinguished by a number of small balls carved or marked on their tops, representing their value.

Thus the one furthest from the circle had two balls on top, the one just outside the circle had three, and the one in the middle had four.

The first player to reach 31 'chalks' was the winner.

Versions of half-bowl are still played today, known as *rolle bolle* in Belgium, *pierbol* in Holland and *media bola* in Spain.

But the last mention of it in a British context came in the publicans' newspaper, the *Morning Advertiser,* during the early 1950s.

Maddeningly brief it was too.

Calling the game 'rolly' the *Advertiser* reported that at The Chequers Inn, Dereham in Norfolk, 'four skittles and a half-moon shaped ball' had been found 'preserved in the flag-floored kitchen'.

Alas, since The Chequers was demolished in the late 1960s we are unlikely to find out more.

Tipping

Once considered to be one of the defining characteristics of skittles, but now a lost art, in Britain at least, 'tipping' was the name given to the second of a player's two throws.

The first, as illustrated opposite, was from a set distance, and required the biased ball to be bowled along a length of board before it curved to reach the pins.

For the second throw, the player stepped forward to a position almost overlooking the remaining pins, and then 'tipped' the ball onto the remaining pins, not willy-nilly but with the aim of achieving a specific score. If he scored more than the required amount the whole turn would not count.

Tipping has often been represented in 17th and 18th century paintings and etchings, for example the Dutch artist Jan Steen's depiction of 'Skittle

Players Outside an Inn' (held by the National Gallery in London), thought to be have been painted in the Haarlem area in c.1660–63.

Because in most variants of modern skittles no player ever stands so close to the pins, many an expert on seeing Steen's and other similar images has concluded that the artist must have misjudged the perspective or used artistic licence.

In fact, the player has been portrayed in the act of tipping.

Tipping has not been seen or noted in British skittles for well over a century, although it still features in games overseas; for example in southern France and in a street game called *brilli*, played on the Maltese island of Gozo.

Strutt and others asserted that if the game in question was played with nine pins but did not feature tipping – that is, the player bowled from a distance for both of his turns – the game must be considered either a form of long-bowling, or of nine pins.

But just to confuse matters, he also reported that tipping did occur in the version of the game known as Dutch Pins.

As readers may gather, this has never been an easy family of games to, as it were, pin down.

Speaking of which...

Pin numbers

Wherever skittles is played around the world, at ground level or on a table top, nine is the most common number of pins set up for play. But there have been, and continue to be some notable exceptions to this rule.

Writing in his *Book of Games* in the 1660s, Francis Willughby described a game called variously Ten Pegs, Nine Pegs, and Skittle Pins.

»

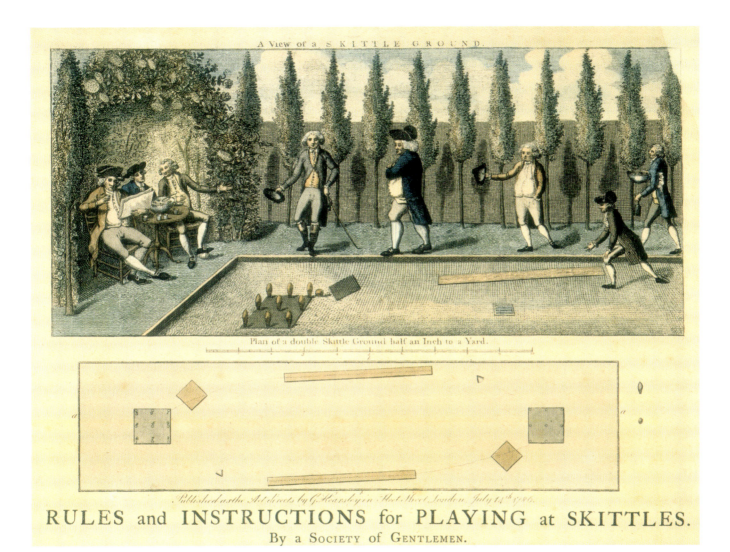

A View of a SKITTLE GROUND.

Plan of a double Skittle Ground half an Inch to a Yard.

Published as the Act directs by G. Kearsley in Fleet Street London. July 14th 1786.

RULES and INSTRUCTIONS for PLAYING at SKITTLES.
By a SOCIETY of GENTLEMEN.

▲ According to Joseph Strutt, in the 1780s magistrates tried to confiscate all skittle-frames 'in or about the City of London' in an attempt to curb gambling.

Quite possibly this set of **Rules and Instructions** was issued in the hope of making skittles more respectable.

Published by **George Kearsley** of **Fleet Street** in 1786 at 6d for a monotint or 1s for tinted, its preamble states, 'As the Game of Skittles is now a favourite amusement, a general Guide to remove doubts, and prevent Disputes, is become necessary.'

The ideal skittle ground, it suggested, was 17½ x 4 yards.

Each of the nine pins should measure 15" in circumference at its widest, and 12" tall.

The bowl was to be 18" in circumference.

To count, the bowl had to be rolled along the fixed wooden board – left-handed players were clearly not provided for – and not touch the boards surrounding the alley.

The diamonds marked to the side of each of the skittle-frames were presumably where players stood for the purpose of 'tipping'.

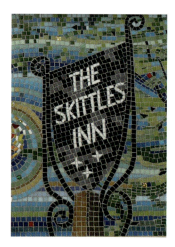

▲ Skittles but no beer – by naming their alcohol-free social centre **The Skittles Inn**, the planners of **Letchworth Garden City** were clearly influenced by the game's revival in the early 20th century.

But whereas temperance billiard halls proved comparatively successful during the same period, the Skittles Inn, designed by Raymond Unwin and Barry Parker and opened in 1907, failed to pay its way, and since 1925 the building, now Grade II listed, has served as an adult education centre called The Settlement.

It is interesting nevertheless that a game so closely linked with drunkenness became rebranded as a respectable, even quintessentially English pastime.

» A diagram in the book shows nine pins set up in a box-like shape called a 'Ruck', in the centre of which was the 'Ten Peg' (to signify its worth in points).

Between the throwers and the Ruck was the smaller Five Peg, also called the Five Madg.

No further evidence of this game has been found, although skittles games similar to it are still played in parts of France.

In 1976 Suffolk writer Norman Smedley described a game played in the backyards of local pubs in the early 20th century that he called 'three-pin bowling'.

The pins were set up within 'an iron triangle, spiked to hold it in place', while the wooden bowl was 'bound with a broad iron band'.

Unfortunately, Smedley could find no-one who remembered how the game was played.

Meanwhile the game of Four Corners has pins in each corner of the diamond, and was popular in Essex, where several 19th century pub manifests indicate the presence of a 'Four Corners alley'.

Strutt wrote, 'The excellency of the game consists in beating them down by the fewest casts of the bowl,' which hardly sounds too challenging, since two throws should surely have been enough.

Until we consider the bulk and weight of the equipment...

Strutt wrote that the bowl used was large and weighed six to eight pounds. But in a later book of 1837, called *Games and Sports* (*see* Links) Donald Walker described the Four Corners ball as weighing double that, at 'about fourteen pounds'. Walker also reckoned that the pins varied from 18–28 pounds. Heavyweight indeed.

Unsurprisingly, wrote Walker, 'This game requires a great deal of muscular power, as the players

have to throw the ball from twenty to thirty feet.'

Nowadays four pin bowling survives only in the West Country, where an annual competition is staged by the Portishead, Pill and District Skittles League in north Somerset, among others.

There, they use a much smaller ball measuring around five inches in diameter, and rather than rely on muscle the emphasis is on accuracy. The front pin has to be struck first for the player to score. He must then nominate which pin he intends to strike next.

Skittles in the 20th century

However popular nine pin skittles may have been in the 19th century, there is no doubt that the game reached unprecedented levels of popularity during the latter half of the 20th century.

This surge in interest is one of the most compelling aspects of pub games history, and offers a powerful refutation to those who would have us believe that all traditional games have been in steady decline since 1914.

In London, as detailed later in this chapter, the formation of the Amateur Skittles Association in 1900 led to a golden era between around 1920 and 1960. That, it is true, was followed by a massive decline in interest.

However, in the south west and south Wales, where two of Britain's oldest skittles leagues still in operation formed in 1902 in Hereford and in 1909 in Cardiff, the game grew steadily throughout the century to reach a high point around the 1980s and 1990s.

For example the Stroud & District League, one of several set up in Gloucestershire during the 1930s – mostly with backing from local breweries – expanded from

eight pub and club-based teams at its inauguration in 1935, to 123 men's teams and 64 ladies' teams by the time of its Jubilee in 1996.

Cheltenham's league similarly enjoyed peak membership between 1973 and 1994, running 19 men's divisions of 16 teams each.

A similar story can be told in the east Midlands, where leagues in Nottingham, Sutton-in-Ashfield and south Leicestershire all hit purple patches in the 1980s.

Thus skittles in the south west and in the east Midlands appeared to have bucked the very post war trends that put paid to so many other well established pub games around Britain.

Or at least that was the case until the late 1990s.

Numerous reasons have been cited for the recent decline of skittles, all of them familiar to pub game enthusiasts.

Skittle alleys, we are told, take up valuable room which can be more profitably converted into dining or bar areas.

Support from local breweries has diminished.

Alleys, balls and pins are costly to maintain or replace.

Skittles is a low-tech game that lacks appeal to young players.

As older players retire or die, recruiting new blood gets harder.

As fewer people find themselves able or willing to commit to regular league nights, teams find it harder to fulfil fixtures.

Beer and skittles no longer mix with driving, making it harder for teams to travel.

And, as always, the smoking ban of 2007 is blamed too.

But while there can be no doubt that the number of skittlers in Britain has declined since the 1990s, is it true to conclude that the game is therefore in crisis?

According to the Save Our Skittles campaign, launched in February 2008 (*see Chapter One*), the number of alleys nationwide fell from 4,500 to 2,500 in a decade.

That figure, the campaigners will admit, is a guesstimate, for in truth no-one has yet undertaken detailed research. And while more pub alleys are closing, the perception remains that those in working mens' and social clubs are more resilient.

There are regional variations too. Numbers are definitely down in the east Midlands, in Cardiff and Bristol, and catastrophically so in London. But in several areas, such as Clay Cross in Derbyshire and Minehead in Somerset, numbers are reported to be either increasing or holding steady.

It is often said that one of the great weaknesses of skittles is also one of its strengths, and that is the lack of any governing body.

Yet how could it be otherwise when rules and conventions differ so widely, not merely between regions or counties, but between neighbouring villages.

Skittles' diversity is thus to be celebrated, and defended.

On the other hand, the advent in 2003 of the British Skittles Championships, sponsored by Blackthorn, has undoubtedly helped to galvanise the game in the south west and south Wales.

For the first time skittlers from these regions have been able to meet, compare notes, and showcase their own particular strengths, culminating in a finals event at Weston-super-Mare each September.

Scant consolation for the few remaining skittlers in London, or for those who play a very different game in the east Midlands. But a fightback all the same.

▲ Of an estimated 2,500 skittle alleys in Britain, only a minority are purpose-built, and of those, only a handful may be said to be of architectural interest. Instead, the majority are found in anonymous function rooms, corridor-like spaces, or as here, in outhouses,

This is the **Queen and Castle**, in **Kenilworth**, **Warwickshire**, photographed c.1901, at a time when skittles was going through a revival in pubs, clubs and within the temperance movement.

The form of skittles being played appears to be that which was espoused by the Amateur Skittles Association, known as Old English, or London skittles. The two clues are the squat and bulbous shape of the pins, and the fact that the player about to throw looks as if he is holding a heavy 'cheese'. (He would hardly have needed two hands to hold a small bowl.)

Note the two men holding white jugs of beer, ready to fill up the players' glasses.

No trace remains of the skittle alley but the Queen and Castle still stands, having been turned into a Beefeater pub and restaurant during the 1980s.

▶ Wherever skittles is played the pins are set up in a diamond formation, usually 4' x 4', known as the frame. But the size and shape of pins varies from region to region.

The smallest, sometimes called Glamorgan pins and used only in south Wales, are slim and bottle-shaped, around 8-10" tall, and mostly made from moulded plastic.

Shown here (*top left*) are pins made for the **Llanbradath Social Club**, near **Caerphilly**, members of the Whitchurch & District League.

The bands on the front three pins have no significance for scoring, but are an aid for taking aim in games of Nomination or Front Pin skittles, when players have to hit specific pins first.

Elsewhere wooden pins are the rule, most being sycamore or beech, because applewood, once used widely in the West Country, has become harder to source.

In Somerset, the pins at the **Royal Oak, Street** (*top right*) are 10" tall and barrel-shaped, while Bristol pins are the same height but slimmer, which makes them harder to hit, leading to lower scores than in neighbouring counties.

Devon pins, meanwhile, are taller, at 12-15 inches, and slightly fatter, at 6" in diameter.

Note that the central pin at the Royal Oak has a ball on its top, marking it out as the **kingpin** (also known in Dorset as the **landlord**).

The scoring value and role of the kingpin varies, but it is mostly placed in the centre, as seen also at the **Rose and Crown, Thurnby,** in Leicestershire (*centre*).

For this reason the kingpin is also sometimes known as the Bird in the Cage.

But in some areas the kingpin is placed at the front of the diamond, and must be floored before any other pins are downed, in order for the shot to count. In some areas the two outermost pins, left and right, are also painted with a white stripe and are called the coppers.

At Thurnby, as in most games of long alley in the east Midlands, the skittles are slimmer and therefore need a metal ferrule at the base to ensure that they stand up straight.

Most bulbous, and heaviest of all, are the pins at the **Freemasons Arms, Hampstead**, in London (*bottom*). These measure 14–15 inches tall and are made from English hornbeam.

Because pub interiors are much warmer than in the past, landlords and skittlers have to make sure that their pins are oiled or soaked to prevent them from drying out and being more prone to splitting.

A new set of wooden pins can cost £100–170, but if kept well can last 5-6 years.

Synthetic pins are marginally cheaper and last longer, but are frowned upon by purists.

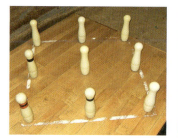

Western skittles

Western or West Country skittles are generic terms, used usually by people from outside the south west and south Wales, to describe what is basically the same game – involving nine pins and three balls – but with infinite, subtle variations in rules, techniques and scoring systems. Even team sizes vary, from six to twelve players.

To those with little knowledge of the game, the scale on which Western skittles is played is quite astounding, and far beyond the level seen elsewhere in Britain.

Skittles is in fact as much a defining characteristic of the region as, say, rugby league in the north of England, or curling in Scotland.

Travelling west from the capital, a few alleys can be found here and there in Hampshire and Wiltshire.

But once into the depths of Gloucestershire, Dorset, Somerset and Devon they proliferate, as they do in south Wales, particularly around Cardiff.

There are then further clusters of alleys in Worcestershire and Herefordshire, plus outposts in east Cornwall, Coventry, Wallingford, Canterbury, Dover and Guernsey.

Because there is no governing body for skittles, nor any magazine or periodical, nor any one website, nor even any formalised contacts between the many leagues, no-one is sure exactly how many alleys or clubs are currently active.

Some leagues are highly organised and have excellent websites. But many others operate under the radar, even of their local newspapers, and are known only to a coterie of locals who communicate using such arcane methods as landlines and noticeboards. »

◄ It may look like the corridor of a modern building but the alley at the **Horseshoe Inn** at **Bowlish** in **Shepton Mallet, Somerset** – a venue for the Mendip Farmers Skittle League – has actually been inserted into what is otherwise a Grade II listed pub, formed out of two early 19th century cottages.

One of the delights, and indeed challenges of skittles is that no two alleys are the same, no set of balls are the same – the balls at the Horsehoe Inn are made from a resin composite – and even the pins vary, not only in size and weight but in how they play in different temperatures.

Because of all these variables, in order to avoid confusion or possible disputes, in most league matches the visiting team is expected to play with the home team's equipment.

And because dirty deeds have been known – albeit rarely – this equipment has sometimes to be stored under lock and key so that no-one can tamper with it.

Nevertheless, the idiosyncrasies of each alley plainly give the home team a very solid advantage.

Most Western skittles games require the ball to be bowled, as seen at the **Shave Cross Inn, Bridport**, in **Dorset** (*left*), and from behind a base line.

In other locations the ball can be thrown, but it must hit the alley at a certain point, perhaps six feet from the base line.

An exceptional case is that of the Bath City team, who play at the Devonshire Arms in Bath, and launch the ball at head height, making sure it bounces just in front of the pins.

Bouncing is not approved of in Torquay, however, where if it does occur the opposition will invariably offer a sardonic, hummed rendition of the *Dambusters* theme.

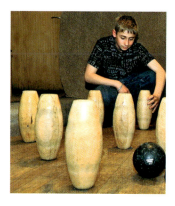

▲ In skittle alleys, unlike in modern ten pin bowling alleys, there are no automatic mechanisms for picking up and re-setting the pins.

Hats off then to the hundreds of young (and often not so young) **sticker-uppers** (or putter-uppers) who, as here at the **Horseshoe Inn** in **Shepton Mallet**, perform this arduous task, albeit in return for 'pin money', so that others can have their fun.

Many a top player has started his skittling life as a sticker-upper for his dad's or grandad's team, champing at the bit to show the old 'uns how it should be done.

Going rates vary from 50p–£3 per player, amounting to £10-20 for a typical two hour match stint.

Not in parts of Devon and the east Midlands, though, where teams are expected to stick up for themselves, as it were.

» There is however one company with perhaps the best overall view.

Set up in 1994 and based in Torquay, the Shoot Out Club lays on weekend activities for over 10,000 people a year, not only for skittles but also for darts and netball. The club also organises the annual Blackthorn British Skittles Championships.

Shoot Out Club officials estimate that in 2009 there are at least 150 organised skittles leagues in the south west and in south Wales. But they add that the real total runs much higher if one takes into account the many in-house leagues that take place within single venues, plus those that function within other organisations, such as companies, trade associations and hunts.

Some leagues have only six to a dozen teams. The majority range between 30–75 teams.

But there are maybe 15–20 other leagues that with over 100 teams split into several divisions for men and women, must sorely test the patience of their fixtures secretaries, even those equipped with the latest computer software.

Probably the largest league of all is the Cardiff Combined Clubs League. Formed in 1962, in 2009 this had 254 teams in 16 divisions. As each team must have eight players plus reserves, this means that over 2,500 individuals are registered. And that is only one of four leagues in the Cardiff area.

Across the border, Bristol is another hotbed, with an estimated 20,000 skittlers playing in at least eight leagues, while England's largest league is probably the Cheltenham Skittles League. Formed in 1938, this had 248 teams in 2008-09 (164 men's teams in twelve divisions and 84 ladies' teams, in seven divisions).

With twelve players per team, this totals 3,000 active skittlers in Cheltenham alone.

Other major leagues include Stroud & District (formed 1935), with 127 teams of 8–10 players each; Berkeley & District in Gloucestershire (formed 1957), with 112 teams of eight; Torquay (formed 1953), with 96 teams of eight; Evesham, with 72 teams of ten, and possibly the oldest league of all still in operation, the Herefordshire & District Invitation Skittles League, formed in 1902, also with 72 teams.

Gauging the total number of players is no easy task however.

In Bristol, for example, instead of each player taking their turn to throw, one after the other (called playing 'down the board'), players take all their turns in pairs or threes (that is, 'across the board'). That way, it is argued, they can build up a rhythm and get their eye in, rather than having to wait a long while before their next turn.

But this system also allows players to complete their contribution in one match, then nip over to another alley and play another match for a different team on the same night.

Similarly, many players register to play for different teams on different nights.

But even taking into account this doubling up of players, the Shoot Out Club estimates that there are at least 50,000 skittlers in the south west and south Wales.

Small fry compared with the number of footballers, rugby players or cricketers in the region, no doubt, but for a traditional pub game, an extraordinary figure.

But lest one gets too excited, there is one major caveat.

Talk to most league secretaries, and although many are relieved to

report that their numbers are for now holding steady, many more are deeply concerned.

In Cardiff, where an estimated 15,000 players were active in the 1970s, numbers have probably halved, a tale that is echoed in Cheltenham. Elsewhere they are dropping only marginally, but secretaries warn that the average age of skittlers is getting older and older. One lamented, 'Young players? It is as if they have simply disappeared from the planet.'

And as interest amongst young people fades, so too the number of alleys drops, especially in pubs.

As reported earlier, one estimate is that the total has dropped from 4,500 to 2,500 in a decade.

That figure may only be a guess, but there is evidence enough at a local level to justify people's fears.

Just a few examples: the Pike and Muscat in Tufley, Gloucestershire, turned its alley into a restaurant in 2007, thereby making ten teams homeless.

Around the same time the Victoria in Taunton and the Three Cups in Wellington closed their alleys too, as did three pubs in Cardiff; the Roath Park, the Albert and the Westgate.

On the other hand, there are some pubs – and clubs where the beer is cheaper – where the alleys attract lucrative business, some of them on several nights a week.

Clearly therefore this a major social phenomenon, and one that, if properly supported, could offer a significant economic driver in a sector crying out for ideas.

Skittles is also a deeply embedded part and parcel of the region's cultural identity, and of its heritage too.

Much, much more than a game, then, and one that it well worth the winning.

▲ There are several listed pubs that happen to contain skittle alleys, and a handful of alleys that form part of or adjoin stately homes (most notably the 16th century Wollaton Hall in Nottingham).

But listed, stand-alone alleys at pubs are few and far between, and this one, at the **Shave Cross Inn**, just north of **Bridport** in **Dorset**, is quite the most intriguing.

Listed Grade II, the alley bears a distinctly medieval appearance. Indeed Shave Cross landlord Roy Warburton firmly believes it to be of Saxon origin. But for their part architectural historians consider the building to be of early 19th century vintage, and surmise that it may have been built as an alley at around the same time that the adjoining late 18th century building (also Grade II) was converted from a farmhouse into what is now the Shave Cross Inn. (An extension bears an 1833 datestone).

But even if the alley is merely 175–200 years old, it is still the oldest purpose built pub alley currently in use in Britain, and certainly the only one with a thatched roof. Some would add that is also the most beautiful, although as skittle alleys go there is not much competition.

Externally the only later additions appear to be brick buttresses.

Internally (*see page 47*) the roughcast walls are plastered and whitewashed, while the 45 foot alley – one of the longest in the region (compared with 24 feet for the shortest) – has a polished wood surface. However, older players in one of the four teams that play at Shave Cross in the Bridport League recall that the alley had a clay floor within living memory.

There is one other listed skittle alley of note in the West Country, albeit not attached to a pub.

It sits in a field in Shirwell, North Devon, and appears to be a basic shed, but is in fact one of the railway carriages that once formed part of Queen Victoria's Diamond Jubilee royal train in 1897.

Retired in 1932 it was bought by a committee of seven villagers and transported to the field in 1933, since when it has performed admirably as Shirwell's skittle alley.

Queen Victoria would no doubt have been most amused.

◄ Despite the fact that skittle balls with finger and thumb holes (as used in ten pin bowling) are known to have existed in Britain as early as the 1830s, for some reason none of the balls used in modern skittles are similarly equipped.

This of course makes them hard to grip and control, especially the larger balls used in some regions.

Partly in response to this and, some might say also as a useful tactic where there is little room in the alley for a run-up, the **Dorset Flop** has recently come to the fore.

As demonstrated on the left by Nick Cavill of the Ashcott 8 skittles team, at the **Royal Oak in Walton, Somerset**, the ball is released two handed as the player springs forward from a crouched position, before he flops onto the alley, hopefully landing with perfect poise on both outstretched palms.

Get it right and the move adds drama to the match. Get it wrong and, well, it truly is a flop that may well be met with merciless jibes.

Some alleys have heel boards fitted onto the floor of the alley, which enable the Dorset Flopper to gain extra impetus as he springs forward. Some players take their own board with them to matches, asking team-mates to add their weight to both ends of the board.

Some players, such as Rachel Bourke, seen in action at the **Kings Arms** in **Taunton, Somerset** (*top right*) manage perfectly well without a backboard at all.

But all its exponents insist that the action offers greater accuracy, which is why it is increasingly used by players at competition level, as seen during the 2008 Blackthorn British Skittles Championships at **Sand Bay,** near **Weston** (*right*), performed by Gary Hounsome of the Gillingham Orchard Lads.

A Dorset lad, of course.

Long alley skittles

Concentrated in the Leicestershire, Nottinghamshire and Derbyshire areas, long alley skittles is the second most popular form of the game in Britain, and is named thus because it is played on alleys measuring in the range of 25–36 feet from the base line to the front pin on the frame.

In fact, although this is longer than the 21 feet once commonly found in London, numerous alleys in the West Country are longer.

But no matter, for the name long alley is in any case long established, while the game itself remains sufficiently distinct from all other types to retain its own identity.

The earliest recorded use of the term long alley has been traced to a book published in 1572 (and cited in a 1903 edition of Strutt).

In *The benefit of the Ancient Bathes of Buckstones*, Dr John Jones not only encouraged his readers to take the waters at Buxton, but to try playing 'trul in madame, wind-ball and shooting at butts, bowling in the allayes, the weather convenient, and the bowles fit to such a game, as eyther in playne or longe allayes, or in such as have crankes with half bowles, whiche is the fyner and gentler exercise'.

The long skittles alley at Wollaton Hall in Nottingham, completed in 1588 and mentioned earlier, might also date from this period.

Beyond this, very little is known about how long alley skittles developed, other than to speculate that it is perhaps closer to pre-modern forms of the game in one important respect.

As we have seen in Western skittles, the most common form of delivery is to bowl the ball along the floor of the alley.

But while this is all very well in a situation where smooth ground or an even floor is available, it simply will not do where the ground is uneven; for example in a fairground or in the rough and ready back yard of a pub.

In those situations the only way to attack a set of nine pins is to throw the ball, as one would at a coconut shy.

The defining feature of the east Midlands game, then, is not the length of the pitch, as the name would suggest, but the fact that the surface of the alley does not have to be exactly smooth or even, and that the missile used is thrown rather than rolled.

Put another way, long alley is to Western skittles what pétanque is to bowls, or what stoolball is to cricket.

Because of this, alleys in the east Midlands can be concrete or tarmac (as they are often simply sited in the middle of car parks). Some are even cobbled, while others have planks laid on the ground immediately in front of the frame, and are then evened up with railway sleepers or slates.

In other words, since the balls are thrown, not rolled, the initial surface of the alley is immaterial.

Long alley enjoys, as a result, a rather rumbustious and primitive feel to it that seems somehow closer to skittles' medieval roots.

It is also a much noisier game.

In Leicestershire, for example, the rules add that the ball must bounce once, but that the bounce can be anywhere along the alley.

But instead of being a spherical ball with a predictable bounce, in Leicestershire they spice things up by using a barrel-shaped ball, as illustrated on the right.

By contrast, in Derbyshire and Nottinghamshire, where spherical balls are the norm, the ball must also bounce, but only after it has cleared a certain point along the length of the alley.

At most alleys this point is not marked by a line, but by a sheet of tin or steel, laid flat on the ground. Any piece of tin will do. An old advertisement sign for example.

But it must not be fixed to the ground, because its purpose is to rattle loudly enough if hit by a ball to let everyone know that a foul throw has taken place.

No need for linesmen or slow-motion replays. The rattle is the giveaway. Ingenious, cheap and virtually infallible.

Inevitably, as in Western skittles, there are sundry other local variations to these rules and to the methods for scoring.

In Ilkeston, Derbyshire – a hotbed not only for skittles but for several other pub games too – several alleys are outdoor and used only in the summer.

Ilkeston skittlers throw at 27 feet from a point in the alley called the 'chuck-hole' or 'chock-hole'.

This is a footprint, either trodden into soft concrete when a new alley is set up, or worn into a sunken hollow by generations of front feet. (In Leicestershire this foothold is called the 'mott'.)

Also in Ilkeston, league rules require that players must hit the front pin first, otherwise the throw does not count, even if it has knocked down all eight of the other skittles.

It is therefore quite possible to throw all three balls and score no points – an occurrence which in one Ilkeston pub during the 1980s was marked by the hapless player being required to walk the length of the alley pulling behind him a plastic duck on wheels, to the assorted jeers of the company. »

▲ Unlike in most forms of Western skittles, in long alley the ball (sometimes called the 'cheese') must bounce once before it hits the pins. But whereas in Derbyshire and Nottinghamshire they play with spherical wooden balls, in Leicestershire their 'balls' are barrel shaped, making them more prone to unpredictable bounces and therefore much harder to master.

This wonderfully bruised and battered ball, part of a set of three at the **Rose and Crown** in **Thurnby** is made from hardwood and weighs 3-4lbs. A well maintained set might last five to ten years, and cost around £150 to replace.

Before each match the sets are laid out for visiting players to see and approve.

▲ At the **Rose and Crown** in **Thurnby**, **Leicestershire**, the sunken area for the front foot is known as the 'mott'.

Captained by George 'Nev' Taylor (seen in action, *right*) the Rose and Crown play in the Tom Bishop Memorial Skittles League, in which 28 teams of eight participate.

As is increasingly the case, their alley – measuring 27 feet from mott to kingpin – has an all-purpose floor so the space can be used as a function room the rest of the week.

The secret in the Leicestershire game is to master the angle of the bounce so that on the second or third throw the barrel-shaped ball can topple pins that in other forms of skittles would appear to be left standing in an impossible broken frame pattern.

Downing all nine in one throw is virtually unknown. Downing them in two is called a 'whack-up'. Missing all nine – easily possible – gains the player a 'monkey face' on the scoreboard.

>> In common with Western skittles there are conflicting reports as to the game's future prospects, some encouraging, some deeply pessimistic.

In Nottingham, for example, once a great stronghold of skittles, league tables are no longer printed in the local newspaper, and a number of pubs have closed their alleys owing to a lack of interest.

The closure or relocation of so many local breweries – the likes of Shipstones, Homes Breweries and Hardys & Hanson – once keen sponsors of Nottingham leagues, has also apparently had a crushing effect on local morale.

Elsewhere, a number of leagues manage to survive, but seem to operate mainly by word of mouth or by personal contact, which may well suit older skittlers but in this digital day and age does little to draw in younger blood.

From what information can be gleaned, it is estimated that as of 2009 there are thirteen long alley leagues still in operation, with a total of around 300 teams in membership, each fielding teams of either six, eight or ten players.

These leagues are based in and around Leicester and Syston in Leicestershire, in the Amber Valley, Clay Cross, Ilkeston and Ripley areas of Derbyshire, in the border area of Derbyshire and Nottinghamshire, and in Nottingham, Sutton-in-Ashfield and Newark.

The problems facing these leagues are exactly the same as those in the West Country. But because the number of players is smaller, there are genuine fears that while in some areas the game has consolidated, in several parts of the east Midlands long alley skittles will almost certainly die out in the next two decades.

▲ In **Morton, Derbyshire,** stands one of several English pubs to bear the name **The Corner Pin**, but one of the few where skittles is actually played. Actually the name was adopted only in the early 1950s. Formerly this was The Station Inn.

From the sign you might think that table skittles or ten pin was on offer inside. But while darts, dominoes and cribbage do get played in this friendly local, the skittle alley is out in the car park.

In fact most alleys in the **Clay Cross & District Skittles League** – formed in the 1980s and recently expanded to 28 teams of 10 in four divisions – are located outdoors, for this is very much a summer game.

Long alley in these parts is played with sycamore balls, called 'woods' (as in bowls), and tall skittles, also in sycamore, with metal bases. The kingpin, held by Corner Pin regular Frank Kendrick (*above right*) is marked with a white stripe and sits at the front of the diamond. For any score to count, this pin must be struck first (a rule also applied in Ilkeston and in several parts of the West Country).

Alleys can be almost any surface, but the diamonds are usually set in concrete, as above at the Corner Pin, with metal bases for the pins.

At the top of the photograph, the furthest square of concrete is the back plate, on which the player's back foot must remain when throwing. From the backplate to the front pin measures 26 feet.

Directly in front of the diamond can be seen the usual tin sheet. This is laid 42 inches from the front pin.

Balls can be thrown at full toss, or bounce once. But they can only bounce after the tin. If they bounce on it, everyone present hears it, and the shot does not count.

No matter if it starts to rain, the skittlers play on, a typical game lasting 30-40 minutes.

▲ 'As big as a frying pan and as thick as a telephone directory.'

That was the verdict of one 1950s newspaper reporter on his first encounter with the legendary **'cheese'** used in Old English, or London skittles.

Despite weighing 8–14 pounds and being made from *lignum vitae*, this is a projectile which requires technique far more than muscle.

Yet once mastered, according to its devotees, it offers skittling at its most satisfying, as testified by the cheese and grin on display at finals night at the **Regency Club, Willesden**, in 1951 (*below right*).

Legend has it that one night when the skittles team was playing away, women members took over the alley for their own activities, and never let the men back.

True or not, scenes like this, from the records of the Amateur Skittles Association, would become all too rare by the 1960s.

Old English, or London skittles

Of all this country's surviving variants of skittles, none has contracted so markedly as the one known equally as Old English, or London skittles, a game characterised by its use of fat pins, heavy, lignum vitae cheeses and its unique scoring system.

Whereas at least 200 venues in and around London are known to have staged the game during the first half of the 20th century, as of May 2009 there was but one pub alley left; the Hampstead Lawn Billiard and Skittle Club, based at the Freemasons Arms in Hampstead, and an alley, used in winter only, at the former National Westminster Sports Club at Norbury (now run by Powerleague).

What makes this catastrophic decline in the game's fortunes all the more surprising is that London skittles is the only British variant ever to have been overseen by a governing body – the Amateur Skittles Association – and that it also enjoyed a good deal of positive press and media exposure.

In particular, the ASA president, writer and reformist MP, Sir AP Herbert, regularly mentioned skittles in newspaper articles and speeches. In his weekly *Punch* column in April 1947, for example, he wrote, 'Forget about the Cup Final, the Ashes and the Guineas: the major sporting event this month is the London skittles championship between FG de B Hart and Lambert'.

Arthur Lambert was the landlord of Herbert's local, the Black Lion in Hammersmith, immortalised by Herbert as the Black Swan in his best selling novel of 1930, *The Water Gipsies*.

Pathé News filmed the game in 1933, featuring 'World Champion' Charles Hillier of Tufnell Park. In 1946, the Kings Arms, Kingston, home to the Lignum Vitae Skittles Club, was featured in a light hearted piece called, predictably, 'Beer and Skittles'.

Both clips can be seen on the British Pathé website.

Meanwhile, at the ASA's annual dinners, held at least until the mid 1950s, hundreds of skittlers from

around London turned out to see the year's honours being awarded. Silverware was in abundance, as was bonhomie. And yet it was not enough.

By the 1960s the ASA was moribund, and worse – for historians at least – those of its records that had survived the Second World War would later be damaged in flooding at The Freemasons, where they had been stored in the pub's basement alley.

So it was that while skittles continued to thrive in the West Country, south Wales and the east Midlands, in London the game simply dwindled away in the space of a few decades.

Not all has been lost however. Thanks to those stalwarts at the Freemasons, in the 1990s at least what remained of the ASA's archives was preserved, while the few remaining ASA shields and trophies have also found a home at the pub.

The London game's history – parts of which can now be found on the Hampstead club's website (*see Links*) – has also been pieced together by Guy Tunnicliffe.

Those who played London skittles at its height, AP Herbert included, often liked to assert that their 'Old English' version was the true one, far superior to the mere nine pins played elsewhere. The heavy, discus-like cheese, wrote Herbert, had a Homeric quality.

But in truth, no historian has yet traced with certainty the roots of this variety of skittles, a variety that differs so markedly even from the type of skittles being promoted in London in the 1780s.

What we do know is that when the ASA was formed in 1900 (exactly where and by whom remains a mystery), an estimated 60 clubs joined up, many of »

First awarded in 1901, the Dewar Challenge Shield was one of the most important in London skittles. Bearing the motto 'Nemo me impune lacessit' (No one attacks me with impunity) the most frequent winners were Chelsea, King's Cross, Barnes, High Cross, the Black Lion, the Regency, and the Freemasons in Hampstead, where the shield is now displayed.

» them based by or near the River Thames in such locations as Brentford, Mortlake, Barnes, Putney, Hammersmith and Ealing.

More clubs were to be found along the River Wey, down to Guildford and Old Woking.

This river connection has led some to surmise that far from being of Old English vintage, London skittles was imported by sea and river barge, either by Dutch seamen, or by their English counterparts who had picked up the game in Holland.

But as Guy Tunnicliffe has pointed out, there were clubs based well away from the river, in Hampstead, Islington, Somers Town, Willesden, Shepherd's Bush, Southgate and Friern Barnet. There was also a Croydon League whose clubs, in common with dozens of others across the capital, chose not to affiliate to the ASA. Many were Working Men's Clubs who referred to themselves as 'timber clubs' equipped with 'skittle saloons'.

Nor was Old English skittles confined to the London area. In addition to the photograph from Kenilworth (*see page 45*), Norwich Museum possesses a single 'badly worm-eaten' skittle whose shape seems not to conform to others found around the country, and which is accompanied by what is patently a London-shaped cheese.

Both objects were sourced from the Eagle Tavern in Newmarket Road, Norwich.

In short, this is a subject which clearly merits further research, and which Played in Britain will revisit in its forthcoming study for 2011, *Played in London*.

Returning to the 20th century, for the ASA the start of its decline was the Second World War, during which several pubs with established alleys and strong teams were destroyed. Among these were the Tufnell Park Hotel (later rebuilt, but without an alley) and the Silver Cup in Cromer Street, King's Cross.

In 1949, J Wentworth-Day (*see Links*) lamented, 'There were thirty skittle clubs or more in London 25 years ago, but practically all have died out.'

Following them into oblivion in the 1960s were clubs at the Duke's Head in Putney, at the Haven Arms, Ealing, and at the Black Lion in Hammersmith (*see right*).

Finally, the dissolution of another club based at the Duke's Head in Putney in the 1980s and the covering up of an alley at the Tooting Constitutional Club left just two alleys in the entire capital, the Hampstead club and the one based at Norbury, south London.

As Guy Tunnicliffe told *The Independent* in April 1996, 'We are like the last mating pair of dodos'.

▲ Reroofed and extended to link up to the back of the pub, this is the former detached outhouse, dating from the Edwardian period, that until the 1960s housed Britain's most celebrated skittle alley, at the **Black Lion** in **Hammersmith**.

Although now used for functions and film shows, internally it is still identifiable as the alley to which a succession of reporters, sightseers and celebrities flocked – Michael Redgrave and Douglas Fairbanks Jnr included – following its depiction in AP Herbert's 1930 novel, *The Water Gipsies*.

The bespectacled Herbert, who loved pubs and who, as an Independent MP campaigned on several issues related to licensing, sport and entertainment, can be seen in the 1946 photograph opposite, standing at the far end, behind the seated woman.

Friday nights were club nights, when the wife of landlord Arthur Lambert – himself a skittles champion – laid on sandwiches for both teams, and when only those in the inner circle could grab the best seats nearest the frame.

The player about to throw was another regular, Cyril Pennington-Richards, an up-and-coming cameraman who was to work on several British film and television classics, such as *The Wooden Horse* and *The Invisible Man*.

A passage from *The Water Gipsies* offers the perfect accompaniment to this photograph.

'Ernest was in good form; he had thrown off his nervousness, the occasion stimulated him, and he rose, as they say, to the occasion.

'He played with grace and fire. In a breathless silence he fondled his twelve pound cheese, and fitted it at last into his hand; he bent low, he crouched, he poised, he swung his arm forwards and back – two steps, left, right – and as his long right leg crossed the line he sped the heavy ball swiftly at the magical angle to the magical spot on the right shoulder of the front pin. Biff! Wallop! A stranger to the game could not have told how it happened, but in less than a second the frame was clear – not one pin standing – a "floorer".'

▲ To achieve a **floorer** (that is, to down all nine pins in one throw) is a rare feat that traditionally gains the player a place on the club's roll of honour. The knack is to glance the right hand shoulder of the front pin so that the chain of events shown here follows (assuming that the thrower is right handed).

As this happens so rarely, over the years skittlers have delighted in giving names to the various 'broken frames' that occur as a result of the first throw. On this page are just a few of the names adopted in London, some of which also crop up in other parts of the country.

In each case the player has to aim precisely to have any chance of downing the remaining pins, though some are fiendishly difficult, if not impossible.

Some of the names are self explanatory, others are pure fun.

The Waterloo is said to be named after a London pub where this configuration was successfully downed for a winning shot.

When the front, middle and back pins are downed, in London it is called Portsmouth Road, denoting a through road, and in Gloucestershire Frampton Green, named after the green in the village of Frampton which is cut in two by a road through the middle.

Crystal Palace Left

Cocked Hat

Novices

London Bridge

Gates of Hell

Open Fender Right

Waterloo Left

Portsmouth Road (or Frampton Green in Gloucestershire)

Tadpole

Brandy and Soda

Arrowhead

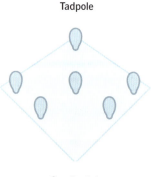

Candlestick

▲ Down in the basement of the **Freemasons Arms, Hampstead**, and unknown to most of the drinkers above, the Tuesday night matches of the **Hampstead Lawn Billiard and Skittle Club** offer a unique glimpse of the once mighty game of London skittles. (As for the once, not quite so mighty game of lawn billiards, *see page 176*.)

Skittles has been played at the pub since at least the 1890s, though the current alley dates from 1936, following the Freemasons' complete reconstruction. Despite its concrete lining, however, the proximity of the River Fleet has led to it being flooded on more occasions than the skittlers would care to remember.

But they are a hardy bunch. As their membership cards state, 'Owing to the robust nature of the game, members are advised that they play at their own risk'.

The throw is, at 21 feet, quite short compared to other games. But the cheese is no plaything, and has to be thrown, full toss, with a precision that can take hours of practise, and no little skill.

At the other end, the 'stickers' (who in former times would be paid in pence and pints) have their work cut out too. It was once calculated that in resetting all the pins during the course of a typical match, a sticker would have to lift the equivalent of two tons of wood.

Scoring is not simple either. Instead of totalling the number of pins downed in three throws, as in other skittle games, you count the number of throws needed to down all nine, up to a maximum of four throws. If any are left standing after that, you score 5. A floorer, explained opposite, scores one.

Thus the lowest score wins.

It gets rather more complicated after that, but that is all the more reason to witness the game in person. That, and the sad fact that the Freemasons is now, for skittles on the London pub scene at least, very much the last chance saloon.

◀ So far we have concentrated on skittle games that employ nine pins. Yet for most non-skittlers **ten pin bowling** is the best known version of this ancient game.

Conventional wisdom has it that the tenth pin was added in the state of Connecticut, USA, during the 1840s, in order to circumvent a ban on nine pin bowling alleys, and that ten pin made its debut in Britain over a century later when the first American-style ten pin bowling alley opened at Stamford Hill in London in January 1960.

But while ten pin is rightly a game we associate with the United States, its introduction to this country came long before 1960.

There is, for example, a double ten pin alley at the Royal Naval College at Greenwich, installed in the 1860s (to which this series will return in our forthcoming study, *Played in London*), while that Jack-the-Lad, the future Edward VII, had a twin alley on 'the American pattern' installed at Sandringham in 1870, apparently after having seen one at the Duke of Sutherland's home at Trentham in the Potteries.

On a more modest scale, the **Manchester Tennis and Racquet Club** installed a ten pin alley at their new premises on Blackfriars Road, opened in 1880 (*top left*). Note the small seat for the 'sticker-upper (or 'pin-setter' as he was known in America).

Birmingham, meanwhile, had several early ten pin alleys.

A double alley dating from 1913, uniquely with one flat and one cambered alley next to each other, survives at the Moorpool Estate in Harborne, as featured in *Played in Birmingham* (*see Links*).

Nearby on Harborne Road, was a similar double alley at the **White Swan** (*left*), seen here in 1953 but taken out of use in around 1983.

▲ Echoing the trend in England, the double ten pin alley at the **Sheep Heid Inn** at **Duddingston, Edinburgh**, was installed in 1882 and is Scotland's only pub alley.

As at Manchester and Moorpool (*see opposite*) the original *lignum vitae* balls are still in use, and being so large and lacking finger holes require two hands for delivery.

The Sheep Heid itself has a fascinating history, traceable to 1360. Skittles, it is claimed, has been played there since James VI was a regular in the 16th century.

But the present alley is most associated with the Trotters Club.

Formed by Edinburgh men of letters as a rambling club, this select group has been meeting at the pub every month since 1882.

But as if to confirm that no club, however august, is immune from harsh economics, in 2008 the Trotters were asked to bring their Saturday evening meeting forward by two hours to make way for more bibulous players. The request came from the pub's owners, Mitchells & Butlers, who coincidentally, also once owned the White Swan, seen opposite.

Placing the 'doll' on its post at The Five Alls in the Cotswold village of Filkins. The pub sign depicts a barrister ('I plead for all'), a vicar who prays for all, a farmer who works for all, a soldier who fights for all, and in the centre, the devil, who smiles and says 'I take all.' Ironically, there can never be a five all result at the pub, as all games of Aunt Sally must end with a winner.

Aunt Sally

Played mainly in Oxfordshire but lapping also into Gloucestershire, Berkshire, Warwickshire and Buckinghamshire, Aunt Sally is similar to the now lost game of loggats (see page 41).

But instead of trying to get near to a jack, the aim is to knock off a 'doll' from its 'iron' or perch.

Aunt Sally may therefore be considered very much a member of the skittles family.

The game's roots lie not so much in kayles or, as has so often been stated, in the English Civil War – those bored Royalist troops again, fresh from inventing darts no doubt – but in a pastime known as 'throwing at cocks'.

Described by Strutt as a 'barbarous and wicked diversion', this involved tying a live cock to a stake, and then charging people to throw sticks at it. Whoever killed the bird took it home for the pot.

The game is well documented and was mainly played by young men and boys on Shrove Tuesday.

A cartoon of the 1820s depicts the then prime minister, the Duke of Wellington, as a cock perched upon a pole, with people throwing sticks at him. The caption reads, 'Shrove Tuesday all the year round – a cock wot every one throws at.'

As in loggats and Aunt Sally there were six sticks in the cartoon.

Strutt offers a key aside on throwing at cocks.

'Upon the abolition of this inhuman custom, the place of living birds was supplied by toys in the form of cocks, with large and heavy stands of lead, at which the boys, on paying some very trifling sum, were permitted to throw as heretofore'.

A game similar to this can be seen in engravings of the Frost Fair on the Thames, in February 1814.

The name Aunt Sally itself derives from a fairground game of the same ilk, imported from the United States in the 1850s, and recorded as being played at the Henley Regatta in 1878.

In its original guise punters were invited to throw balls at the head of a negress, knocking clay pipes from her mouth and ears. But in time it became even simpler, as at a coconut shy, with the aim being simply to dislodge the doll from its perch.

As explained in a 1903 publication, *Lawful Games on Licensed Premises*, 'When an Aunt Sally figure is not readily available, an ordinary block of wood may be made to do some service in her absence. The figure forms a better object to aim at when raised from the ground on some sort of pedestal.'

Farmer and author Fred Archer, further noted that at a village fête in the Cotswolds before the First World War, people had thrown hayrick pegs at coconuts instead of the usual balls.

In short, Aunt Sally is a simple fairground game with an unsavoury past that only achieved respectability in the back gardens and yards of public houses.

The first of the Oxfordshire leagues was formed in 1938, the same year that Sandy Lindsay, the anti-appeasement candidate in the famous Oxford by-election was photographed in *Picture Post*, wielding Aunt Sally sticks in an attempt to cajole local voters.

Lindsay lost his battle, while Aunt Sally grew so fast that by the time Timothy Finn updated his groundbreaking Watneys book on pub games in 1975 (see Links) he was able to reproduce a fixture list showing 169 teams in the Oxford and District League alone.

By 2009 that number had fallen to 120. On the plus side, Oxford has been joined by six further leagues, based around Bampton, Banbury, Bicester, Chipping Norton, Kidlington, Oxford, Wychwood and Yarnton.

Aunt Sally has also been successful in attracting sponsors.

Greene King sponsor the Oxford League, Brakspear sponsor the Bampton League – which, having formed in the early 1970s, now has 77 teams – and Hook Norton sponsor the Banbury League, formed in the late 1960s and now fielding 55 teams.

All told this means that come summer, over 2,500 men and women can be found playing the game, usually on a Thursday night. Many also play it indoors during the winter, while there have even been reports of university teams springing up beyond the game's traditional borders.

Of course this healthy interest in the game can have nothing to do with one of the highlights of an Aunt Sally encounter, the 'beer leg', to which extra spice has been added by the award, in some leagues, of a crate of beer to the winners, courtesy of the sponsors.

Wallops, Irish skittles and corks

We conclude this chapter with three lesser known games that form part of the skittles family.

Played outdoors on August feast days in the Yorkshire Dales villages of Redmire and West Witton, the wonderfully named 'wallops' consists of nine conical skittles (about six inches tall, not unlike those kayles illustrated in Strutt), set out in a square pattern of three lines of three. To topple them, each player has three throws of an 18 inch long wooden stick.

Irish skittles is similar.

Traditionally played at village crossroads, during the 1970s the game was taken off the street and onto concrete pitches.

Newly standardised rules state that five 'standers' (or conical skittles) numbered 1–5, be placed within a five foot diameter circle.

The aim is to knock the standers out of the ring, by hurling wooden batons, or 'throwers', four per turn.

All Ireland skittles championships have been contested every year since 1976, and in 2009 there were at least 35 clubs playing on a regular basis across eight counties.

Finally 'corks' is a miniaturised indoor version of Irish skittles, with five wine bottle corks, again numbered 1–5, within a circle and three corks thrown to dislodge them. It is played mainly in south Wales. For example the Ynysddu Corks League has fourteen pub teams playing from September to May on Sunday afternoons.

▲ The doll gets some stick as the 'caller' and 'sticker-up' watch closely at the **Five Alls** in **Filkins**.

If the stick knocks off the doll, but in doing so first hits any part of the post, or the swan-neck 'swivel' – a small platform on which the doll is perched – the caller shouts out 'Iron!' and the shot is void.

If the doll is toppled cleanly he shouts out 'doll!' and one point is scored. Calling can be a tough job, however, especially as the swivel often rattles, even when the doll has been struck first. And there are no slow motion cameras on hand to settle the issue.

But if Aunt Sally is simple in its rules, it is far from easy to master.

The distance from the wooden strip, known as the hockey or hocking – terms for the front foot line, also once used in darts – to the doll, is 30 feet. To ensure the white doll remains visible against the back screen, a black circle is provided to frame it.

Each player must throw underarm and has six sticks per go. Each stick is 18 inches in length and up to two inches in diameter, varying in weight from 1-2lbs.

The best players treasure their sticks, carrying them in long canvas bags, burnishing them with fine sandpaper and applying talcum powder before throwing.

In most leagues there are eight per team, all of whom throw consecutively, before their opponents step up to do the same. As in Western skittles this sequence is called a leg, or a horse, and each match is the best of three (even if one team wins the first two legs).

As each 'doll' scores one, the maximum score per leg is 48. However, as of 2009 the maximum ever recorded has been 39.

But should anyone fail to down a single doll during their turn they are branded a 'blobber' and must endure stick of rather more verbal nature.

Chapter Four

Table skittles

Peter Lambert of the Spring House table skittles team from Newark swings his ball at the Crown, Bathley, near Newark, in 2008. There has been a table skittles league in the Newark area since 1954, and, as can be seen from Hans Wild's photograph (*right*), one of many taken for *Life* magazine during the Second World War to show how the sturdy Brits were carrying on as normal, the game has barely changed at all.

Numerous games have been transmuted from outdoors to indoors, miniaturised and put onto a table in the process.

Rarely is anyone credited for effecting these transformations. They just seem to happen.

Not only do these games tend to be less strenuous but during the winter, when many skittle alleys are too large and draughty to heat properly, they also offer keen skittlers a warmer alternative.

Three versions of table-top skittles are currently played in English pubs.

Devil among the tailors

This version of table skittles is the most familiar.

A small wooden ball (the devil) is tethered by a light chain or cord to a swivel at the top of a pole. The ball is then thrown away from the player and clockwise around the pole, so that it clatters into a set of nine small pins (the tailors) arranged in the usual diamond formation.

The pins are arranged on a raised platform which stands within a baize or carpet lined tray.

Each turn comprises three throws. If all pins go down in one or two throws, they are re-set, so that the maximum score possible is 27 points. Scores are recorded on a cribbage board, often positioned at the front edge of the table. The usual game is either 101 or 121 up, but the catch is that you have to get out exactly. If you need three, for example, and knock down six pins, you stay exactly where you were.

Such games are fairly common on the Continent. In Finisterre, the Land's End of northwestern France, the game was known in 19th century cafés as le birinic or le birinig, and has been recently rediscovered as part of attempts to revive regional culture in the Brittany area.

Some French writers contend that le birinic is actually a smaller version of an outdoor game of Russian origin. Others think it a direct copy of the English game.

Germany had its own outdoor version, played in public parks and recreation grounds from at least the late 19th century onwards. This was called pendelkegelen.

When miniaturised and taken into beerhalls it became known as tafel-kegelen (that is, table skittles).

Returning to the British game, Timothy Finn (*see Links*) thought that the intricacy of the swivel mechanism, plus the introduction of the cribbage board, point to the late 17th century as a start date.

Finn also claimed that the name devil among the tailors derived from an incident in a London

theatre in 1805, when a play called *The Tailors: A Tragedy for Warm Weather* (a revival of a burlesque first staged in 1783), so annoyed tailors in the capital that they staged a riot inside and outside the theatre. The magistrates called the special constables, the constables called in the cavalry and the Life Guards 'skittled' the rioters.

This encounter certainly happened. It is all there in Alfred Bates' book *The Drama: Its History, Literature and Influence on Civilisation*, published in 1906.

But as Joseph Strutt reported, four years before the theatre incident, there was already a game called devil among the tailors.

Not that he thought much of it.

'There is a childish pastime,' wrote Strutt in 1801 (*see Links*), 'generally known by the ridiculous appellation of the Devil among the Tailors. It consists of nine small pins placed like skittles in the midst of a circular board, surrounded by a ledge with a small recess at one side, in which a peg top is set up by means of a string drawn through a crevice in the recess; the top when loosed spins about among the pins and beats some, or all of them, down before its motion ceases.

'The players at this game spin the top alternately, and he who first beats down the pins to the number of one and thirty is the conqueror.'

Strutt was not impressed.

'This silly game, I am told, is frequently to be seen at low public houses, where many idle people resort and play at it for beer and trifling stakes of money.'

The version of devil among the tailors described by Strutt is unknown in modern Britain.

But in other parts of Europe it has been around for centuries. It is called *table a toupé* in France and *toptafel* in parts of Belgium and Germany.

Essentially, tiny skittles are set up in a open-topped box with different compartments. A spinning top is sent on its way from one end of the table, as Strutt describes, knocking over skittles in a random fashion.

That is, no skill is involved at all, which is why Strutt was right to call it 'childish'.

But if the game did not survive here, its name was apparently too good to let drop and so it was, at some point, applied to the table skittle game we see today, and which is very much a game of skill.

There have been several attempts over the years to encourage pubs to take it up, the first being in the 1930s, when the games manufacturer John Jaques offered different tables for different leagues.

Nowadays Jaques produce just the one 'league table' model.

As can be seen, the skittles themselves are smaller versions of fairly standard West Country skittles, as illustrated in the previous chapter (*see page 47*).

However the way the game is played, with the ball curving away from the player and beyond the skittles, to do damage on its return, is more reminiscent of half-bowl, or roly poly (*page 42*).

Because the game is so compact (at least when not being played) it is not unusual to see sets in pubs in several parts of England.

There is a particularly good set at the Bricklayers Arms in Putney, London, for example.

But for serious table skittles at a competitive level one must go either to Newark (*see opposite*), or to Bedfordshire, where teams, mostly from clubs, compete in and around both Luton and Bedford.

Landlady Jackie Grice sends the devil amongst the tailors at the Crown, this time the Crown in Bedfield, Suffolk.

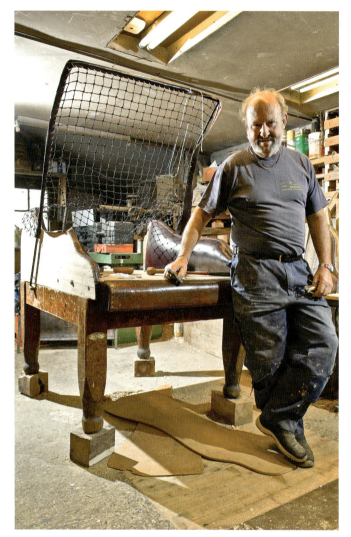

Colin Swinfen, a joiner based in South Kilworth, Leicestershire, has been building and renovating tables, or 'boards' for hood skittles, based on the old Black's pattern, for many years. A new table costs in the region of £1,750, a refurbished one about £1,500. Note the leather upholstery offering a cushion on both the sides and back of the board.

Hood skittles

Hood skittles is a term used to describe two regional games, Northamptonshire skittles and Leicestershire skittles.

But you may well come across the same game in Bedfordshire and Derbyshire, where it is equally (and confusingly) known as plain 'table skittles'.

The table or 'board' used for hood skittles looks like an outsize armchair, with a flat, leather-covered seat for the pins, and leather padding on the arms, back and facing edge.

The attached hood from which the game takes its name, is made of netting on a frame, and is designed to trap any flying skittles or cheeses.

At pubs where tables are set up in more confined rooms, nearby windows and light bulbs tend to be protected also, as the cheeses in a closely fought match can ricochet unpredictably all over the place.

In Northamptonshire most of the tables in use were made by the woodworking firm of WT Black of Church Lane, Northampton.

Although this firm ceased trading many years ago, their 'League Brand' tables can still be seen in pubs all over the region, each with its own number.

Indeed one theory as to the origins of hood skittles is that it was more or less the invention of WT Black's great grandfather. If so, this would date it back to the early 19th century.

But whatever the game's origins, over two hundred Black's tables have been spotted, many of them refurbished in recent years across the border by Leicestershire joiner Colin Swinfen (see left).

The skittles used for the Northamptonshire game are about five inches tall and tubby around the waist, so that they roll and tumble usefully when struck.

Usually they are made from beech, maple, purplewood, lignum vitae or applewood, although nowadays there are plastic pins about as well.

The distinctive Leicestershire pins (see opposite) rise to a point at the top and some sets, as in long alley skittles, feature a kingpin with an extra ball on top.

Leicestershire hood skittles are also set up in a tighter diamond pattern than their Northamptonshire counterparts.

The cheeses for both games are the same, however. Made from laburnum (or plastic), they measure around three inches in diameter and 1½ inches deep, flat on both sides and rounded around the rim so that they fit snugly into the hand.

Just like Dutch cheeses in fact.

The rules for hood skittles are very much in line with other versions of skittles.

For example, each player throws three cheeses per go, and if all nine pins go down after the first or second throw (a 'floorer' or a 'stack', respectively), they are set up again. As in devil among the tailors, therefore, the maximum score is 27.

Perhaps the main difference is that in hood skittles you are allowed to use the padding of the table's arms to bounce off cheeses and therefore achieve extraordinary angles.

Some local rules even allow a 'bounce-back' from the rear of the table, which is otherwise unheard of in other skittle games.

The throw, from a mark, strip of wood or metal, sometimes called the 'mott' (as in long alley skittles) varies. In Northamptonshire and Bedfordshire it measures ten feet from the leading edge of the table, in Leicestershire nine feet.

It is difficult to single out what might be called a 'standard' game of hood skittles, since there are so many minute variations from league to league.

In the Northants Winter League, for example, they play seven singles matches to decide a game, and each player is given five lives, chalked up on the scoreboard as five short vertical lines. Each of these lives is won or lost during a three cheese contest.

If you lose, one of your lives is rubbed out.

In some areas, if both players down the same number of pins, and a life is tied, that life is carried over to the next round, so that two lives are now at stake. In the event of such a tie, the scoring follows what is called the 'on-off', 'first and third', or 'up and down' method to resolve the issue.

The first player throws again and chalks up the sum of his first throw, and his total throw. Thus, if he knocks down six pins with his first cheese and twelve altogether with three throws, he scores 6-12, and his opponent must top both in order to win.

In Leicestershire the Dunton Bassett League, which has 40 teams in four divisions, play eight to a team and all eight players bowl consecutively to set their opponents a target for a leg. Each match is the best of seven legs.

Dunton Bassett do not go in for complicated play-offs. Instead, the end of a tied leg simply counts as a point to each side.

On the other hand in the Welford league, also in Northamptonshire, tied legs are replayed, and as each match is the first to seven legs, the action can go on for several hours.

Hood skittles at the Hollybush in Lutterworth, Leicestershire, one of several pubs to field a ladies team, although there is also a mixed summer league in the county, in which there must be at least four ladies per team of twelve. In Leicestershire the rules require cheeses to be thrown underhand, from the front of the hand, and skimming is not allowed.

Daddlums at the Vigo Inn, Kent, in 1952 (*top*), and (*above*) the replica table that was made after the pub closed, from drawings provided by two enthusiasts. The replica is 5' 6" long and has a set of nine pins only three inches high, and three biscuit-sized cheeses, all seemingly modelled on the much larger pins and cheeses used in Old English skittles (*see page 59.*)

Daddlums

When the Vigo Inn near Fairseat, Kent, closed for repairs in 2007, it appeared to signal the death knell for the old game of daddlums.

The Vigo had been home to the last known surviving daddlums table in Britain (*shown left*).

Daddlums tables, it should be added, were never mass produced or standardised, but appeared in pubs across Kent and Suffolk in the early 20th century, knocked up no doubt by local craftsmen working to a vague brief. No two, it was said, were ever alike.

But whatever happened to all these tables?

Writing in the 1970s, pioneer pub games historian Timothy Finn (*see Links*) recorded the survival of one daddlums table at a pub called the Green Man, at Longfield, a village close to Fairseat. In fact the Green Man and the Vigo Inn used to play each other monthly.

But at some point during the 1970s the Green Man's table disappeared.

Two decades later the Swingate Inn in Guston, on the Dover to Deal road, used to advertise the existence of their daddlums table in the *Good Beer Guide*. For a while it was in such demand that it had to be booked well in advance.

But then a new landlord took over and once again, another daddlums table disappeared.

Daddlums' history has been further complicated by an article discovered in a 1950s edition of the *Morning Advertiser*. This stated that the Gun Inn at Dedham, between Colchester and Ipswich, had a trophy on which was inscribed, 'Ye Olde Dedham Pewter Pot for Daddlums and Darts, 1760'.

Now any item marked as 'olde' in a pub is almost certainly a fake, and this was certainly the case at Dedham. As we learnt in Chapter Two, darts was not played in any pub anywhere in 1760.

On the other hand, how did the fakers on the border between Essex and Suffolk know about daddlums? Could there have been more tables in that area too?

Another possible hunting ground for lost skittles tables might have been Norfolk.

Back in the 1970s, Timothy Finn noted what he called a Norfolk skittles table at the Horseshoes Inn, Alby, near Erpingham. From his description this was virtually the same as a daddlums table, with miniature skittles and cheeses.

But again, although the Horseshoe Inn survives, and still plays host to darts, cribbage, pool, shove-ha'penny and even ringing the bull, no-one there knows what happened to the skittles table.

We conclude this section with one last skittles mystery, also from Norfolk, but via Amarna in Egypt.

When Sir Flinders Petrie was excavating the tomb of a child there around 1892, he turned up nine vase-shaped pieces and four balls. Petrie also found 'three square slips of veined marble', which he thought formed a trilithon, or arch, through which the balls had to be directed.

Howard Carter, the man who went on to unearth the tomb of Tutankhamun in 1922, told Petrie that 'Norfolk skittles are played through a gateway of logs of wood, which must not be upset by the player.' Carter also told Petrie, 'This trilithon game still survives.'

As Carter was brought up in Norfolk his word can surely not be questioned. But if such a skittles game did exist in 1890s Norfolk, again we must ask, plead even, does anything of this obscure regional game survive?

◀ Below an image of old Satchmo himself, Britain's only known **daddlums** table is to be found on occasional nights organised by the local branch of CAMRA, at the **Louis Armstrong** pub in **Dover**.

This is the table modelled on the lost table at the Vigo Inn (which was still closed in mid 2009).

But the skittles and cheeses are much older, having been rescued from another pub in Dover as surplus to requirements. (Suffice it to say that the pub in question no longer had a table of its own.)

In former times cheeses were thrown from 14 feet. Now the distance is nine feet.

Rather than throw the cheese directly at the pins (as in London skittles), the main technique used is to land the cheese onto the front of the table. from where it can slide into the pins.

But then, since no other daddlums tables are known to exist and therefore no matches ever take place against visiting players, players can adopt almost any style or rules they care to.

It is known, however, that the most popular game at the Vigo Inn was called 'nines'. In this, each player has nine consecutive throws, forming one leg. A match is usually the best of five legs. The doubles game is also a best–of–five contest, but with each player throwing only three cheeses per leg.

Chapter Five

Quoits

Coalminers John Murray (*left*) and John Little from the south Lanarkshire pit village of Coalburn pose with their quoits shortly after the First World War. Quoiting is one of great forgotten sub-cultures of 19th century British history. In Scotland in particular there were dozens of purpose built quoiting grounds that drew four figure crowds to high stakes matches.

Mention the name quoits today and most people, if they have heard of it at all, think either of deck quoits played on board cruise ships, or of an indoor or 'parlour' game (as the Victorians would have put it), in which rubber rings are thrown onto hooks.

As detailed in Chapter Six such a game is still played in pubs.

But the mainstream version of quoits is an altogether different phenomenon. A visceral outdoor battle of wits and muscle involving iron and clay, quoiting is one of the few quintessentially British games to have passed from the medieval to the industrial eras and into the 21st century with scarcely a change in its character or equipment.

The same cannot be said for its popularity, however, for despite a mini-revival in recent decades, quoiting today is a mere shadow of its former self.

Indeed from about the 1820s until the First World War quoits was arguably as widespread as bowls or skittles in all corners of England, Wales and Scotland, and was also hugely popular as a spectator sport.

For much of that period, it is true, quoiting was considered by many as a vulgar pastime, rife with gambling and fighting; a source of misery to wives and aggravation to magistrates. And yet like bowls, quoits also enjoyed a loyal, solid middle class following.

For these enthusiasts, no doubt anxious to assert the game's respectability, quoits was often described as being of classical origin, a direct descendant of the discus, one of the five pursuits that formed the Pentathlon at the ancient Olympics.

But as a glance at any one of the representations made of the Greek *discobolus* will confirm, the discus was, as now in modern athletics, a solid object, thrown for distance.

Quoits, a target game played with metallic rings, over a set distance, with pitches, pegs, opposing players and scoring, is patently different.

Another popular theory was that quoits was a Roman introduction. Imperial army officers, it was said, played with bronze quoits while the common soldiery made do with discarded horseshoes.

Putting the quoit before the horse, one might say.

A third suggestion is that the throwing of horseshoes to hook a target arrived a few centuries after the Romans, courtesy of invaders from Jutland and the Low Countries.

But while it is true that latter day Dutch settlers in the United States, Canada and South Africa also took with them games that involved the throwing of horseshoes – forms of which still persist in those countries – there is no evidence to support this, or any other theory.

Nor has anyone ever explained the origins of word 'quoit' itself (although it sounds as if it should be from Old French).

What does seem certain is that its earliest known use dates from 1361. In a diktat issued by Edward III, men were ordered not to 'meddle in hurling of stones, loggats and coits and other games of no value' when they should have been honing their archery skills.

Henry V issued a similar proclamation in 1414 forbidding 'hand-ball, football, coytes, dyces, stone throwing, kailes and other such futile games' on pain of six days imprisonment.

In his 1545 panegyric to archery, *Toxophilus*, dedicated to Henry VIII, Roger Ascham dismissed 'coyting' along with running and leaping, for being 'too vile for scholars, and so not fit by Aristotle his judgement.'

In *Henry IV Part II* Falstaff contends that Prince Henry is friendly towards the roguish Poins because Poins 'plays at quoits well, and eats conger and fennel, and drinks off candles' ends for flap-dragons, and rides the wild-mare with the boys, and jumps upon joined-stools, and swears with a good grace…'

All, reckoned Falstaff, signs of 'a weak mind and an able body'.

In the same play, gesturing to the braggart Pistol, Falstaff urges Bardolph, 'Quoit him down… like a shove-groat shilling.'

We can only guess as to the form that quoits then took, especially as a later description in Francis Willughby's *Book of Games* mentions quoits as 'flat pieces of lead, horseshoes, round pieces of tile, etc' which each player took it in turns to throw at a 'Mistris or a Jack'. The quoits had to fall flat and not land on edge, and the game was five or seven points up.

This appears closer to a French game known as *palets*, whereas Joseph Strutt's description in 1801 fits almost exactly the quoiting we know today. Strutt implied, moreover, that quoits was by then well established, a sentiment echoed in a Scottish source of 1836, describing quoiting as an 'ancient, national game'.

Strutt also noted how 'formerly in the country' when 'rustics' were unable to find a quoit ('a circular plate of iron perforated in the middle') they would play with

horseshoes instead, hence a quoit was sometimes called a 'shoe'.

What Strutt could not know was this 'amusement' was about to become a serious sport, and one that clearly divided opinions.

George Oliver's description of the Yorkshire town of Beverley in 1829 noted haughtily that 'The lower classes of the people have their quoits, their foot-ball, and their cricket, which often lead the way to drunkenness and dissipation.'

Yet Charles Dickens played the game during a 'peaceful and rural retreat' at Twickenham in 1838, while a set of rules was included in the very first edition of what would soon become the cricketers' bible, the *Wisden Cricketer's Almanack*, published in 1864.

Quoits by then was a major focus for gambling. From 1830 onwards there are reports of

games at pubs in Falkirk, Stirling, Newcastle and Plaistow in east London, for stakes as high as £100, between players who were clearly semi-professional.

In 1883, four Liverpool men played four from Manchester at Crown Street, near the Railway Yard, for £20 a side. That equates to around £1,500 today.

To get an inkling of just how significant a social phenomenon quoits became, historian Neil Tranter (*see Links*) has identified several matches in Glasgow which drew crowds of four figures.

One, at Melaugh's Quoits Ground in January 1870, between two of the leading players of their generation, Robert Walkinshaw of Alexandria and George Graham of London, played for £200, drew an astonishing 5,000 spectators.

Crowds of several hundred, meanwhile, were routine. »

A quoits team from Atherstone in Warwickshire pose in c.1910 in their Sunday best. As in most team groups, one member (*back row, far left*) carries the straight-legged compass used to measure the all important distances between rival quoits, while another (*seated, far left*) bears a notebook for scoring. Most teams formed at pubs or in the workplace. In London several Metropolitan Police teams played in the stations' backyards.

THE QUOITING REVIEW.

Official Organ of the English, Scotch and Welsh Associations.

Vol. 1.   No. 2.   APRIL, 1910.   Price 2d.

▲ 'With the advent of beautiful weather,' trilled the second and only known surviving issue of *Quoiting Review* in 1910, 'the musical ring of the quoits can be heard in every town and village.'

Amid the din of London's docklands too. There were new quoiting grounds at Silvertown and at the Tidal Basin Tavern, while at the GER Mechanics Club in Stratford, members were able to play until 10pm on Saturday nights thanks to electric floodlights.

Elsewhere, hopes were high at Peterborough, winners of the All England Cup in 1894. Nearly 300 players had signed up in Shropshire, and the Worcestershire Quoiting Association had a new president, the MP Stanley Baldwin.

» Tranter further identified 52 pubs in 33 Northumberland villages with quoits facilities.

But although the game is rightly identified with mining areas, Kent and south Wales included, farm labourers also took to the game, for example in Somerset, Suffolk, Sussex and Warwickshire, as did mill workers in Lancashire and dock workers in east London.

Tranter also points out that in areas such as Stirling, where there were 45 quoits clubs within a 25 mile radius, most of the players were workers in manufacturing industries or in the building trade.

In other words, this was a game with strong appeal across all sectors of the skilled workforce.

Certainly the *Stirling Observer* approved. As quoted by Neil Tranter, the newspaper noted in 1884, 'No game is more brimful of health and enjoyment. It is inexpensive, can be played anywhere, calls all the muscles into action, steadies the eye, is full of excitement and possesses enough science to make victory over an able opponent honourable. We have never heard of anyone being physically or morally ruined by it as is the case with horse-racing, boating, pedestrianism and many other outdoor amusements.'

The vicar of Neston in Cheshire must have agreed, because he paid for a quoits ground to be laid out on the village green, in an attempt to 'keep the men away from drink', as did the Church of Scotland minister in Dunnottar, Stonehaven, who set up the club there in 1890.

Several local authorities saw fit to include quoits grounds within their newly commissioned public parks. Quoits was also on offer at the Aigburth Cocoa Rooms in Liverpool, opened in 1876 by temperance campaigners.

But quoits was not only for the working classes.

Near Aigburth stood the Childwall Abbey Tavern. This was, and remains, the headquarters of Britain's oldest and most exclusive quoits club, formed possibly as early as 1795 (*see page 80*). Another survivor is the Darlington Quoit Club, formed in 1846 (*page 82*).

Both these, and several other clubs no longer in existence, were solidly middle class in their membership, and at pains to distance themselves from the rowdier goings-on elsewhere.

North of the border this growing respectability resulted in the formation of the Scottish Quoiting Association in 1880.

The following year, at the behest of the Stockton Tradesmens' Quoit Club, The Association of Amateur Quoit Clubs for the North of England was similarly formed, with help from the Darlington club. Clubs of a similar ilk joined from Durham, Guisborough, Middlesborough, West Hartlepool and Whitby.

One of the first measures taken by the new Association was to issue a set of rules, which was then published in *The Field* (a London journal) in June 1881. This in turn drew letters from clubs in Yorkshire, Worcester, Aberdare, Coddenham in Suffolk and Cheltenham, all of which, it became clear, had been playing to quite different rules.

Throwing distances, for example, varied from 11–25 yards between 'hobs' (the iron pin which formed the target), while the weight of quoits varied between 5–15lbs. Scoring systems differed widely too, from club to club.

So it was that the North of England rules set the throwing distance at 11 yards, and the

maximum weight of quoits at 5¼lbs. All hobs, furthermore, were to be set in beds of 'tempered clay', with the pin projecting no more than three inches.

As for scoring, a 'ringer' (that is, a quoit ringing the hob) would count for two points, while the quoit nearest scored one.

But if the north east clubs hoped that their rules would be adopted nationwide they were wrong.

In Scotland they kept faith with heavier quoits and a throwing distance of 21 yards, while in Wales and the rest of England – whose clubs formed their own English Quoiting Association in 1887 – the distance remained at 18 yards.

Thus a distinction arose between the 'short game' of the north east and the 'long game' everywhere else. And because the latter remained prevalent in Scotland and Wales, when the first quoits international was held at Cheltenham in 1896, between England and Wales (16 per side), it was the long game that prevailed.

The Scots, meanwhile – other than when they faced England and Wales in internationals – stuck with 21 yards until finally falling in with their neighbours in 1955.

(This left only one place in Britain where 21 yards was still thrown, and that was the oldest club of all, at Childwall.)

By the 1960s, however, the golden days of quoits were long gone. One factor was the closure of coal mines. Another was the growing popularity of other sports, not least football.

In Scotland, just three clubs cling on. These are the Glenburn Quoiting Club in Prestwick, the Linwood QC in Renfrewshire, and the aforementioned Dunnottar QC in Stonehaven, Aberdeenshire.

In Wales, the Welsh Quoiting Board (*Bwrdd Coetio Cymru*), re-formed in 1979, having faded away 20 years before, has eight clubs. All are in rural locations in West Wales and are proactive.

Indeed it was the Welsh Board that organised the first British championships of the modern era. Held in 2006, at Pumpsaint in Carmarthenshire, 45 players from all three home nations competed.

The Welsh Board also has a wonderful website (*see* Links).

In Wales and Scotland few links between pubs and quoits remain.

As for England, the long game survives only in Suffolk and north Essex, where seven venues survive, four of them at pubs. These are The Emperor in Ipswich, the White Horse in Edwardstone, Sudbury, the Eight Bells at Hadleigh and the Beehive at Little Horkesley.

Quoits is also played on the village greens at Holbrook and Stoke-by-Nayland, and at the Benhall Sports Club.

Two leagues operate: the Hadleigh & District Steel Quoits Sunday League, and the Stoke-by-Nayland Steel Quoits League, which plays on Saturdays.

Suffolk quoiters play by subtly different rules. They still throw to 18 yards, but with lighter quoits and with clay beds raised at an angle towards the thrower.

Also, a 'ringer' is taken off as soon as it is thrown, which results in entirely different tactical battles.

Even so, Suffolk's hardy band of quoiters have adapted well to mainstream rules when facing Welsh and Scottish quoiters in recent British championships.

As for the 'short game', in 1986 its adherents formed the National Quoits Association (which despite the name covers only the north and north east of England).

The NQA leagues are the Danby Invitation League, the North Yorkshire Moors League, the Zetland League and the Swaledale & Arkengarthdale League (all in Yorkshire); the Allen Valley League and the Northumberland League; the Spennymoor League (County Durham), and the Cleveland League (on Teesside).

Inter-league contests are held in May, followed by national singles and pairs competitions in July. But the big event in the NQA is the Wilkinson Sword singles contest in June, of which more later.

Three other leagues play to the same rules, but independently of the NQA. One is based around Berwick upon Tweed. The second, sponsored by Theakston, is in the Lower Dales, and has 20 teams dotted around the town of Masham. There is also a Whitby Indoor League hosted by the Rifle Club during the winter months.

Compared with the glory days of quoits these are slim pickings.

But considering that the game virtually disappeared in the 1970s, today's quoiters have done superbly to keep it alive.

Meanwhile, readers hoping to see a game of horseshoes have fewer options. Although popular in the USA and Ireland, England's last known horseshoe league, in Harlow, has disbanded, and now only occasional friendlies take place in Essex (The Swan, at Little Totham, being a likely venue).

Annual horseshoe competitions are also held at the Queen's Head, Bulwick, in Northamptonshire, on New Year's Day and on Spring Bank Holiday Monday.

Quoiting (or *kite-ing* as it is pronounced in Scotland) at the 1981 Scottish Championships at Birkenshaw, Larkhall, one of many quoiting grounds to have closed in recent years. Note that in the 18 yard 'long game' players need to put considerable muscle into their efforts, especially as in Scotland they prefer to throw with heavier quoits, weighing around 10-11lbs.

▲ Unlike in England, quoiting in Scotland has few links with pubs. This is the public quoiting ground at **East Wemyss** on the Fife coast, captured in the early 20th century.

In the foreground a man prepares to throw on one of two practice 'rinks' (as quoits pitches are called in Scotland, as in curling and bowls). Only if a player could demonstrate an ability to land his quoit on the clay in this area would the greenkeeper allow him to play within the actual enclosure, which, as can be seen, had four rinks.

Quoiting has long since ceased in East Wemyss and the ground, part of an area called The Den, is now a children's playground.

Meanwhile, the old **Quoits Field** at **Claydon, Ipswich** (*right*), is now a housing estate of that name.

▲ One of a series of quoiting images taken by Ian Macdonald in the 1970s, this is **Egton Bridge**, in the **Esk Valley, North Yorkshire**, showing how compact is the 11 yard 'short game' compared with its 18 yard 'long game' counterpart.

Having overhead lights, as shown here, has been common at pub grounds since the early 20th century, for although played in summer, matches can last several hours (one of the reasons landlords are happy to host the game). Now that Egton Bridge has four pitches, however, there is less need for lights as matches can more easily be completed before night falls.

Even for non players there is a sociability about quoits that lends it a seductive appeal. As *Country Life* reported in July 1900, the game 'has the great recommendation of being easy to learn, and also for lookers-on to understand...'

Egton Bridge currently play in the Danby League (on Mondays) and the North Yorkshire League (on Thursdays).

The pub in the background, incidentally, is the Postgate Inn, known to viewers of the television series *Heartbeat* as The Black Dog.

▲ Preparing the clay bed at the **Birch Hall Inn** at **Beck Hole**, North Yorkshire, for the Copper Kettle Open Championships in 2006.

Each quoiting pitch has two beds, facing each other across 11 yards in the short game (as here) or 18 yards in the long game, rather like the wickets on a cricket pitch.

Getting the consistency of the clay right is an important factor.

Too dry or hard and the quoits will not sink enough to stake their position. Too wet and soft and they will sink too far and sit too unsteadily to make their relative positions easily measurable.

Whereas in the short game the hob sticks up to three inches above the clay, in the **long game** custom dictates that the top of the hob is flush with the clay. In order to help the thrower aim more accurately, therefore, the rules allow for a team-mate to act as a **'lighter'**.

The lighter's job is to place a scrap of paper (or in the old days a feather) in the clay at just the position required, as seen at a Scotland v. Wales match held at **Prestwick** in 2006 (*above right*).

Another variation is found in Suffolk, where as seen at the Benhall Club (*right*) the clay beds are angled towards the thrower.

▶ In the **short game**, where the throwing distance is 11 yards – but in practice can be only 9, as players are allowed two steps from the pin – and where the hob is visible to the thrower, greater accuracy can be achieved.

On the other hand, this places a greater emphasis on defensive play.

As demonstrated at the **Birch Hall Inn** at **Beck Hole** in North Yorkshire, here are some of the grips players adopt in order to land the quoit in the desired position.

Note that both the grip and the end position bear the same name, and that the outer sloping ring of the quoit is called the 'hill' while the inner is the 'hole' or 'face'.

(Until recently the traditional means of deciding who threw first was to toss a quoit and call 'hill' or 'hole'. Then someone calculated that quoits land 'hill' up three times out of four, so nowadays a coin is tossed instead.)

The 'ringer' would appear to be the best shot, worth two points. But a skilled opponent can cancel this out by landing his quoit on top.

A skilled player pitching first will invariably therefore try for a defensive shot, such as a gater or a Frenchman, which is difficult for an opponent to nullify.

A quoit that lands 'hole-up' is, however, vulnerable to a follow up throw which hits it on the lip and flips it over and away.

Ringer (or flat ringer)

Push pot

Hill gater

The Frenchman

Face gater (or the Housekeeper)

Side on

◀ As in all of Scotland and Wales the quoits used at the **Dunnottar Quoits Club**, **Stonehaven**, are larger and heavier than those used in the short game (*as above*).

In the short game the maximum diameter is 8½" on the outside and the weight cannot exceed 5¼lbs. In Scotland and Wales the maximum diameter is 9", and most players throw in the range of 6–12lbs, although some go up to 16lbs; that is, three times heavier than the short game quoits, yet thrown over the longer distance of 18 yards. (One Scot was said to have thrown 23lbs in the 1890s, and that was over 21 yards).

Note how the hand holes are shaped for a better grip, and that some have holes into which lead can be added to adjust the weight.

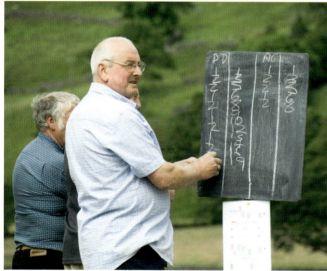

▲ With its four well tended pitches, turfed terraces and elevated viewing areas overlooking Arkle Beck, the 18th century **Charles Bathurst Inn** – better known as the CB Inn – at **Arkengarthdale** in the **Yorkshire Dales**, has on several occasions provided a stunning setting for the NQA's annual pairs championships and for the Wilkinson Sword Invitation Championships.

But although the pub is named after an 18th century landowner whose family set up lead mines in the area, the real hero of the piece is former RAF officer, Charles Cody, who took on the CB Inn in 1996 when it was a derelict hulk.

Often, when a pub gains a makeover and a reputation for its restaurant and rooms, it is at the expense of pub games.

Not so at the CB Inn. After ten years and £750,000 worth of repairs and landscaping, these were the scenes in 2007.

When not rescuing this and another local pub, the Punch Bowl at Low Row (where he has also reintroduced quoits), Cody plays for the CB Inn team in both the Swaledale & Arkengarthdale League and the Zetland League.

▲ Although the hob is visible and 'lighters' are not needed as often as in the long game, the thrower in a competitive short game may well call for help from a 'bibber,' who assists him in aiming his second quoit with points and hand gestures rather than with paper.

There will also be on hand a 'trig man,' whose job it is to look out for foot faults.

Only if there is a real dispute will the referee be called upon, and in the sociable and usually amicable atmosphere of a quoits match that seems rarely to be necessary.

But, more often than not, as here at the **CB Inn**, the tensest moments of all occur when it is time to judge which of the quoits is nearest to the hob, a judgement not always possible with the naked eye, but

one that invariably results in much discussion on bended knees.

If agreement cannot be reached this way, it is the referee's task to bring out his straight-legged compasses and come up with a decisive measurement.

It is a portentous moment, often accompanied either by hushed murmurings or forced laughter.

Every millimetre counts.

Members of the Childwall Quoiting Club, Liverpool, check whose quoit is the winner, in 2007 (*above*) and approximately a century earlier (*right*). The club has played in the grounds of the Grade II listed Childwall Abbey Hotel since 1811, and has had several prominent members. In the hooped beret is one of the Gladstone family.

▶ Henry Pattinson, Secretary of the **Childwall Quoiting Club**, sends his quoit flying through the air in front of the 1837 outhouse which stores the club's equipment.

As well as being one of Britain's oldest sporting clubs – thought to have been formed by members of the Liverpool Light Horse in around 1795 – Childwall is one of the few that sticks doggedly to the eccentric rituals and practices that were once so typical of Georgian and Victorian gentlemen's clubs.

Membership is restricted to twelve men, who meet on six consecutive Monday evenings, either side of Midsummer's Day, starting at 5.30pm with a dinner in the same room at the Childwall Abbey Hotel where they have met since 1811.

The menu has remained constant too. Poached salmon is followed by ribs of boiled beef with vegetables, a shoulder of baked ham and 'black cat pudding' (similar to Yorkshire pudding, but soaked in brown sugar and sweet sherry, and then overcooked, because a chef did this by mistake many moons ago and members decided they preferred it that way).

All this, of course, washed down by generous quantities of wine.

After that comes cheese and biscuits, and two carafes of port to fuel a succession of toasts.

Among the tasks and titles allocated each year are those of 'salmon server', 'ham carver' and 'chairman of the snuff committee'.

But the role of overall chairman is allocated to a different member for each meeting.

Any member caught addressing a fellow member incorrectly, or getting wrong any part of the ritual is seized upon by the chairman, who fines the miscreants in bottles of port (or rather, the cash

▲ Called the 'old pot,' this three handled Doulton loving cup was presented in 1901, to be awarded to the winner of an annual match played against the Liverpool Cricket Club at nearby Aigburth.

This is the only match of the season that the Childwall Quoiting Club plays against outsiders.

The club also has a silver trophy donated in 1911 to commemorate the 100th anniversary of the club's move to the Childwall Abbey Hotel. Having already marked the club's bicentennial in 1995, the 200th anniversary is scheduled for 2011.

And if it survives the ravages of time and local vandals, the club's old outhouse is due for its own bicentennial in 2037.

equivalent of bottles). A mobile phone ringing, for example, cost one member three bottles recently.

The chairman also has first pick for his team for the night. (One former method of dividing up the members was to split 'sparklers' or champagne drinkers from 'stills' who preferred table wine.)

The banter and fines continues out on the quoiting ground, where play commences around 7.00pm.

Considering all that has come before, the exertions that follow are remarkable. For Childwall is the only club left in Britain that still throws to 21 yards. Not only that but their quoits can weigh up to eight, energy sapping pounds each.

To register, a quoit has to 'cut the clay,' the two beds being circular at Childwall, and nicely soft.

Once every player has thrown his pair, the quoit nearest to the 'prob' (as the pin or hob is known at the club) scores a point. An extra point is also awarded to the team with the most quoits nearest to the prob.

The score is then called, chalked up, and once the clay-clagged quoits have been cleaned up with sawdust, a new 'end' commences, throwing towards the opposite bed.

Meanwhile the drinks continue to flow, as does the friendly abuse. For some reason everyone is referred to by their initials. Thus the garden resounds to calls of 'Rubbish JHT!' or 'Stupendous quoit AFT!'

Even elderly members, who are allowed to throw lighter quoits (known as 'wedding rings') at a shorter distance, come in for remorseless heckling.

And so, as the light fades and joints start to ache, the game winds to a close and the members retreat for a light supper and more revelry.

Another meeting of the Childwall Quoiting Club has reached its end.

But that is not quite the end of the affair. Every detail of every meeting, every score, every fine, will later be lovingly recorded by the secretary in perfect copperplate handwriting, in what must surely rank as one of the most beautifully presented minute books of any sporting organisation in Britain.

One entry in June 1909 is particularly enjoyed. On May 18th, it was solemnly noted, Mr FW Rathbone was fined two dozen bottles of port wine. His offence?

To have married without the consent of the club.

▲ Although it is not associated with a pub, no mention of the English quoiting scene is complete without reference to the **Darlington Quoit Club**, whose premises, unbeknown even to many a local, lie behind a maroon door on **Raby Terrace**.

Once through the door – a quoit surrounds its brass handle – the clubhouse reveals a splendid array of artefacts, including a list of the founding fathers in 1846; among them a banker, ironmonger, wine merchant, gardener, coachbuilder and tobacco manufacturer.

One current veteran recalls his mother's horror when, back in the 1970s, he announced he was joining the club. To her, brought up in a mining community, quoits was irrevocably tainted by gambling. But, as he was able to assure her, in the ultra-respectable Darlington club no gambling is permitted.

Nor, by the way, are any women, at least not as members.

▲ Not even the usual 'ring' of quoit on quoit carries beyond the walls enclosing the wonderfully intimate yard of the **Darlington Quoit Club**.

But then this is a club that, despite being the second oldest in Britain and playing a key role in the development of quoits in the late 19th century, has, in one sense, always turned its back on the world by remaining aloof from all leagues.

There is an historical justification for this; competitive quoits having once been seen as disreputable and verging upon the professional.

But in any case, there is little need for Darlington players to travel when so many clubs are happy to play friendlies at Raby Street. The ground has hosted games since the 1880s and is regarded almost with awe by the quoiting community.

Moreso since the club initiated a competition that has grown to become the blue riband of quoits.

It began in the late 1970s when the manufacturers of Wilkinson Sword razor blades offered a limited number of ceremonial swords to organisations who could demonstrate their willingness to promote sport, provided that no cash prizes were offered and that 'the motivation to take part comes from the honour rather than avarice'.

Citing their intention to use a sword 'to further the game of quoits in the region,' the Darlington club applied successfully and ever since has taken on the organisation of the annual North of England Invitation Wilkinson Sword singles competition, in which 64 of the leading players from around the north and north east compete for this coveted trophy.

The event is held each July at various venues, with the winner being entitled to display the magnificent sword in their pub or club, before returning it to Raby Terrace (although they get to keep a replica).

▶ While the Wilkinson Sword is the top singles prize in NQA territory, amongst the membership of the **Darlington Quoit Club**, the **Silver Quoit** is the holy grail, awarded to the winner of a knock-out tournament that has been staged at the club on a Sunday in September ever since 1847.

In the hey-day of British quoits almost every club offered a similar award, making the Darlington Silver Quoit a rare, and rather wonderful survivor of a long tradition.

The winner is honoured in two ways. Firstly, he serves as club captain for the following season, and has his name inscribed on the club's honours board. (The runner up is appointed lieutenant and is similarly commemorated.)

Secondly, his name is etched onto a link that is then added to the chain attached to the Silver Quoit itself.

The only drawback with this tradition is that, over 160 years after it was first awarded, the chain now has three strands and has become so heavy that most winners only manage to wear it around their neck for a few brief moments – just long enough to have the obligatory photograph taken – before handing it back for safe keeping.

The gold Maltese Cross and bloodstone seen in the centre of the Silver Quoit were added to mark Queen Victoria's Golden Jubilee.

Chapter Six

Ring games

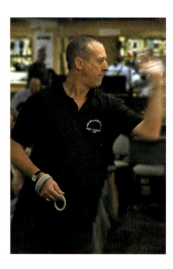

Bobby Towner from Rainham in action at the World Ring-Board Championships, held at the Silver Hall Social Club at Rainham, Essex, in November 2007. It was Irish workers at the Ford factory at Dagenham who first brought the game to Essex in the 1950s. The Irish may also have been responsible for introducing rings to the game's other British stronghold, Ventnor, on the Isle of Wight, in the 1860s.

Landing a rubber ring onto a hook, or a pole, or a board, is one of the simplest forms of target game, played in homes, playgrounds and fairgrounds.

At British pubs and clubs three traditional forms of ring games are still to be found.

They are known as rings, ringing the bull, and indoor quoits. There is also a Suffolk version of the latter, called caves.

Apart from the sheer simplicity of the rules, the equipment required for ring games is cheap, the rings themselves are quite harmless in a crowded bar, and all ages can have a go.

Rings

Before it was superceded by darts in the second half of the 20th century, rings was arguably the most popular game in English and Irish pubs. At some pubs both games co-existed quite peaceably.

One such was Ye Olde White Lion, at Bradninch, Devon, home of Edie Beed (*see Links*), where during World War Two a customer asked a visiting GI whether they played rings or darts in the USA.

'No Ma'am,' replied the soldier, 'we don't throw nothing at the walls.'

Rings may have begun, as did darts, as a parlour and fairground game, but it had certainly caught on in pubs by the Edwardian period, as we learn from Robert Tressell's inspirational novel, *The Ragged Trousered Philanthropists*.

First published in 1914 after the author's death, and a seminal text for generations of socialists and social historians, the novel tells of the struggles of working class painters and decorators in the town of Mugsborough (based on Hastings, where the author himself, real name Robert Noonan, worked as a sign-writer).

Their local is the Cricketers' Arms, 'a pretentious-looking building with plate glass windows and a profusion of gilding. The pilasters were painted in imitation of different marbles and the doors grained to represent costly woods. There were panels containing painted advertisements of wines and spirits and beer, written in gold, and ornamented with gaudy colours.'

In other words, a fairly typical, Edwardian public house.

Hanging on a partition by the pub's polyphone (an early form of penny-in-the-slot juke box), Tressell describes the rings board as measuring about 15 inches square, with a number of small hooks distributed on its surface.

'At the bottom of the board was a net made of fine twine, extended by means of a semi-circular piece of wire. In this net, several India-rubber rings about three inches in diameter were lying.'

Tressell's antagonists in a 50-up game were a 'semi-drunk' who none of the regulars knew, and a 'shabbily dressed, bleary-eyed, degraded, beer-sodden' wretch who spent all day and every day in the Cricketers' and was said to throw 'a splendid ring'.

The 'semi-drunk' went first.

'Holding the six rings in his left hand, the man stood in the middle of the floor at a distance of about three yards from the board, with his right foot advanced.

'Taking one of the rings between the forefinger and thumb of his right hand, and closing his left eye, he carefully "sighted" the centre hook, No. 13; then he slowly extended his arm to its full length in the direction of the board; then bending his elbow, he brought his hand back again until it nearly touched his chin, and slowly extended his arm again.

'He repeated these movements several times, whilst the others watched with bated breath.

'Getting it right at last, he suddenly shot the ring at the board, but it did not go on No. 13; it went over the partition into the private bar.'

Amid great merriment and several pints and pages later, the game ends in a win for the 'Besotted Wretch'.

(Two of the company then go on to have a game of shove ha'penny, using old French pennies retrieved from behind the bar.)

A further reference to rings appears in the equally seminal tome, *The Pub and the People*, published in 1943 by Mass Observation.

Famously, this was an organisation set up in 1937 by Tom Harrisson and others to make a 'scientific observation' or 'anthropological study' of the ordinary. Prior to Mass Observation Harrisson had spent time noting the habits of natives in the Borneo jungle. He now wanted, he said, to study 'the cannibals of England'.

Some fifty researchers were involved in the study, the majority of them middle class Oxford and Cambridge students.

Their focus was the 300 or so pubs in Bolton (called 'Worktown' in the study), where clearly, much of what they saw mystified them.

This included the game they described as quoits, but which is quite clearly rings.

One characteristically patronising entry reads: 'Two young men play quoits with the barmaid, who is, thinks the observer, attractive in a coarse sort of way. She is good at quoits anyway, and wins... This second chap, young, red-faced, blond, healthy-looking, unshaved, cap on side of head, face washed but hands dirty, is apparently on fumbling relations with the barmaid.'

Quoits (or rather rings), the study notes, was played in Bolton with a shield having 12 hooks (although as the norm then was for 13 hooks their observational skills may have let them down).

But in any case by 1939 the boards were seldom played and were being replaced by darts.

One devotee of the old game told the story of how one 'ace local player' could throw five rings into a gill (half-pint) glass, and could stand at one end of the bar and 'ring' all the beer pump handles, finishing off with the small tap on the strong ale barrel.

Though clearly dazzled by this, Mass Observation's researchers (whom many critics branded as 'snoopers') annoyingly left no record of how a game was played, other than to say that each hook had to be ringed consecutively.

Presumably this was a form of rings then popular in Lancashire called 'twice round the board'; that is, hooking the numbers in sequence from one to thirteen.

If you hooked a double, say two rings on the number five hook, your next throw would be at number eleven.

As far as is known, the thirteen hook boards in Lancashire would have been much the same as in Tressell's Hastings. But other rings boards have been recorded.

The Hampshire Hunt Inn at Cheriton, near Winchester, used to have a circular board with thirteen hooks. The players threw four inch diameter rings, six to a turn, in a game that was 121 up, scored on a cribbage board.

The Ferry Boat Inn, Harwich, had a rectangular board, again with thirteen hooks, but the game was 'twice round the pegging board' – again 121 up.

In Kirkhampton, Cumbria, the Rose and Crown had a thirteen hook board, but the game was to score 31 exactly, using five rings.

Today, as we have noted, rings survives in just two main regions, Essex and the Isle of Wight.

The thirteen hook game is concentrated in and around Rainham, having been imported by Irish workers who came to work in the foundry at the Ford plant in Dagenham in the early 1950s.

A generation ago, there were sixteen teams in two leagues, each with eight players.

Today the league is confined to just three clubs, with six teams of six players each betweeen them.

Irish connections continue to keep the game alive. Since the late 1950s Irish and Essex players have enjoyed reciprocal tours. At the All-Ireland Ring Board championships in County Clare, first staged in the early 1980s, there are enough contestants for ten boards to be played simultaneously.

For rings players, this is an event not to be missed.

Meanwhile in 2002, keen to keep the flag flying, a Rainham enthusiast called Joe Norman set up the All-England Ring-Board Federation, culminating in the first World Championships in 2007.

There are also signs of growing interest on the Isle of Wight.

▲ 'Taking one of the rings between the forefinger and thumb of his right hand, and closing his left eye, he carefully "sighted" the centre hook, No. 13...'

Little has changed since Robert Tressell described a game of rings in Edwardian Hastings.

The crucial characteristic of a **Ventnor ring** on the Isle of Wight is the softness and flexibility of the rubber. For that reason, the Ventnor & District League have their rings made to order in Ireland, using their own bespoke mould.

The harder the ring, the more it will bounce off the board. It is also easier to land two rings onto one hook if they are soft. As a result, some players still use rings that are up to 30–40 years old.

▲ A standard **rings** board, such as seen here at the first **World Ring-Board Championships**, held in **Rainham, Essex**, in November 2007, has 13 hooks (compared with 15 on the Isle of Wight, *see opposite*), with the number 13 hook in the centre.

Each player throws six rings per turn, the scoring being between 300–600 up. Unusually, four singles (that is, on the number one hook) are required to finish.

But there are several variations, such as Around the Board, underarm throwing and Polo Rings, in which rings measuring 80mm in diameter are used instead of the standard 100–110mm.

Players in various age groups from under 21 to over 65 compete individually and in teams, the throwing distance of 8' 6" being the same for both men and women.

The Rainham championships and the more established All Ireland Championships have undoubtedly helped re-invigorate interest in rings over the last five years with more pubs and clubs expected to take up the game in Essex as a whole. As they say, once you pick up a ring, you're hooked.

▲ Rings replace arrows for the evening at **The Volunteer Inn**, **Ventnor**, on the **Isle of Wight**, as members of the Volly A and Volly Z teams – having a B team is just too predictable, they quip – prepare for a match in the **Ventnor & District Rings League**, the largest of its kind in Britain.

Local legend has it that, as at Rainham, Irish workers brought the game to the town of Ventnor when the railways and two major tunnels were being built in the area during the 1860s.

Yet no-one can explain why rings is not played in those other parts of the Isle of Wight where Irish navvies also worked.

Also unexplained is why the Ventnor board differs from the Essex and older Lancashire boards by having fifteen rather than thirteen hooks.

As seen below, the shield on which the hooks are mounted is also different from that of Essex, as are the hooks.

Those at Rainham have a curved hook, whereas in the Ventnor League they are L-shaped, which is said to make the game a little easier. It also makes it easier to land more than one ring per hook. (Long serving local champion

Graham Rann was apparently able to land three on one ring with frightening ease.)

On the other hand the throwing distance in Ventnor is marginally longer than in Essex at nine feet.

Teams consist of 6–12 players, playing three pairs and six singles per league match.

For the pairs, each player throws three rings per turn and must finish exactly on the score needed.

For singles matches they play round the board, going from one to fifteen twice round, ending on the number one hook to finish.

Tuesday nights are league nights in Ventnor, with the action running from September to March. And with only a few miles separating the participating venues, it can make for an interesting and, needless to add, convivial way for a visitor to get to know the town.

▲ Pints have been served at the building that is now the **Volunteer** in Ventnor since 1871. But the earliest record of a rings league is a cutting dating back to 1914.

In 2009 the Volunteer was one of eight pubs and clubs in the local league, fielding 12 teams between them. Though down from a total of 20 teams during the post war years – six pubs have closed in the area since then – this is still an improvement on the lowest ebb a few years ago, when only eight teams were left.

Thanks, moreover, to Joe Norman's efforts in Rainham contacts have also been made between rings players in Essex and Ventnor, so that there now exists cautious optimism for the future.

Ye Olde Trip to Jersulam may not be the oldest pub in Britain and certainly does not date back to 1189, as is suggested on the walls. But it does have structures dating back to c.1680. The Ward Room, in which ringing the bull is played (*see also page one*) is one of several cavernous rooms dug out of the sandstone rock under Nottingham Castle.

Ringing the bull

This variety of ring game is one of the simplest, and most exasperating of all pub games.

An upturned hook, often in the form of a bull's horn, is fixed in the wall, at about the same height as the bull on a dartboard.

Six or seven feet from the hook, a length of fine cord is suspended from the ceiling. At the end of this is fastened a ring, usually brass, about two inches in diameter.

A player takes hold of the ring, steps back to a mark on the floor a further six feet or so away from the wall, and tries to swing the ring so that it clunks on to the hook.

For a first timer without exemplary hand and eye co-ordination the task seems all but impossible, until a regular comes along and demonstrates how easy it is (omitting to let on that they have been practising for years).

Certain ringers of the bull can perform spectacular tricks, such as throwing the ring while standing with their back to the hook, or swinging the ring so that it passes tantalisingly over the hook, returns to the sender, then swings round again to land bang on target.

Some experts also claim to have 'ringed' a cigarette that has been impaled on the hook, without disturbing the ash, or of having thrown ten consecutive 'hooks' blindfold.

They may then hand the ring back for you to try again, having surreptitiously twisted the chord, thereby making your task even harder (and making their own prowess even more impressive).

Rules vary from pub to pub, simply because each set up is different, with varying lengths of cord, throwing distances, ring sizes and types of hooks.

For this reason there could never by an inter-pub ringing the bull league, as the advantage would always be too weighted in favour of the home team.

But this still allows pubs to hold competition evenings, for example with each player being given a specific number of throws. Those with the highest number of 'hooks' then go through to a second round, and so on.

No-one knows how the game originated or how old it is, though there are, inevitably, some daft theories abroad.

For example, because the game is played at Ye Olde Trip to Jerusalem in Nottingham – so called because legend has it that Crusaders stopped there in 1189 – it is said that ringing the bull was brought back from the Holy Land. But as Geoff Brandwood and his co-authors of *Licensed to Sell* have noted (*see Links*), local research has found no record of any inn in Nottingham prior to 1483.

Indeed the pub's current name was not adopted until 1799.

Another unfounded theory suggests that the game goes back to the Roman occupation.

The Oxford English Dictionary traces the first reference to 1851, stating, 'It is, or was, common in the ale-houses of Cheshire, and is called ring-the-bull.'

Notice the past tense.

Pub historian Rob Magee has found further evidence of the game in a report of a case put before magistrates in Stalybridge, Cheshire, in 1869, in which boys were caught playing cards at the Globe Inn, Chapel Yard, while men were playing 'Bull-Ringing' for beer money.

What is certain is that whether before the mid 19th century or after, the game spread far beyond

Cheshire, with the northernmost example being found (at least until 2004) at the Badachro Inn in Ross-shire, Scotland.

And, moreover, that the regulars in each pub where it is played consider their own version to be unique, or at least rare.

Certainly it is not identified with specific regions, and in common with several pub games, has come and gone in many a pub purely according to local circumstances.

It was, for example, introduced to the Pineapple Inn, in Shaw, Oldham, in 1976, on the whim of one regular who had seen it played in Newark. At its peak the Pineapple's Boxing Day knockout match drew over 60 players and took several hours to complete.

But then the landlord left, the pub declined, and in around 2001 some youths decided to pull on the ring so hard that they brought the plaster down from the ceiling.

Thus this focus for the game in Lancashire lasted only 25 years.

Outside Britain a version of ringing the bull is manufactured in Cincinnati by a man who first played it while serving with the US military in Europe. In the Bahamas, ringing the bull is called the bimini game and is also manufactured commercially. Its makers dismiss stories that the game was introduced by pirates in the 18th century, preferring to believe that Ernest Hemingway played it first during a fishing trip to the Bahamas in the 1930s. (If so, alas he did not mention it in any of his writings.)

Otherwise, there appears to be no evidence of any similar game being played elsewhere in Europe, which leads us to conclude that ringing the bull could well be that rare phenomenon – a truly home grown British pub game.

▲ A stuffed and mounted bull's head invites hookers to swing the ring at the Grade II listed **Rock,** in **Chiddingstone Hoath, Edenbridge, Kent,** while at the **White Lion** in **Cray, North Yorkshire** (*left*) the game is called the **ringo bull ook**, and has, according to the landlord, been there in one form or another, for over fifty years.

At the **Alby Horseshoes Inn,** at **Erpingham, Norwich** (*right*) a single, almost discreet horn acts as the hook.

Elsewhere, at the Garden City Tavern, in Derby, the target is a carved imitation rhinoceros' horn. There, locals have been known to put a fiver on the bar counter and bet strangers that they cannot 'ring the horn' in five throws. At the Murrell Arms, Barnham, West Sussex (*see page 4*) the hook is a metal coat hook underneath a fine pair of bull's horns.

In the mid 1980s a porcine version of ringing the bull appeared at several pubs. Known as pig snout, this used a life size fibreglass model of a pig's head, and instead of a ring, the cord from the ceiling had a rubber ball on the end. Twopence pieces were balanced carefully on the pig's nose and on each of its ears.

Knocking off the coin from the nose earned two points, and from the ears one point each. The game was 11 points up, but is not believed to have survived.

This handmade indoor quoits scoreboard in the Royal Oak, in Kington, Herefordshire, is typical for the region. Once a team (red or blue) has recorded a score, that total is 'closed' to the opposite team, by covering up the number with a sliding panel.

Indoor quoits

Known also as step quoits, table quoits, Evesham quoits or dobbers, indoor quoits is a ring game confined mainly to the English and Welsh borders.

The earliest known written evidence of its existence can be found in catalogues issued in the 1920s and '30s by Gaskell & Chambers, a well known Birmingham pub supply firm.

Their brand of 'step quoits' cost 17/6d for a table, with quoits at 6d each. But since the catalogues give no impression that indoor quoits was anything new, an educated guess would suggest that it had developed independently, most likely in the Marches region, in the late 19th or early 20th century, before becoming sufficiently popular for manufacturers to start production in the 1920s.

Today, versions of the game are manufactured by John Jaques, who simply state that their design is based on an original design 'over fifty years old'.

The board is 18 inches square, backed by netting, and sits on a table raised 2 foot 6 inches from the floor. Within the board are two concentric scooped out circles, with a central, bolt-headed iron or brass spindle called a 'spike' or a 'peg' (like the hob in outdoor quoits). This peg cants slightly towards the thrower.

Most indoor quoits boards in use today are wooden and painted red and green, as seen here at the Cotterell Arms in Hereford. But some in the Herefordshire and Shropshire area are in plain limestone or even marble.

The quoits themselves are rubber, white on one side, black on the reverse. A quoit which pitches black side up is 'dead' and does not score.

In most versions of the game, a 'ringer' (a shot which encircles the peg) counts as five points. A quoit in the inner circle scores three points, while a quoit in the outer ring is worth just one point.

There are four quoits to a throw, so the maximum from one turn is 20 points. Anyone achieving this ranks highly and is likely to get his or her name in the local paper.

Although the basic equipment is more or less uniform, rules vary from region to region, sometimes from pub to pub. The size and weight of quoits also varies, as does the throwing distance.

In the Forest of Dean League, Gloucestershire, where they play a winter and a summer season, the scoreboard has 'cards', or moveable panels, numbered one to eleven (similar to the Kington version, shown left, which goes up to thirteen). Once a player has cleared a number, by any combination of quoits, that number is closed to their opponent. Whoever scores the most points wins the game.

A league game comprises four singles matches and three doubles.

In the Hereford & District League, which operates only in the summer, the game is run down from 101, rather like a darts match. A league game there has six singles and three doubles.

Overall there are a dozen or so leagues spread across Gloucestershire, Worcestershire, Herefordshire, Shropshire, Powys and Radnorshire. However most have declined in recent years.

In 2009 the Forest of Dean League has just eight teams, down from 25 in the 1980s, while the Kington League, Herefordshire, has six, down from 18, and the Evesham League, extremely popular only a generation ago, has disappeared altogether.

On the other hand, there appear to be plenty of pubs with 'Evesham quoits' tables where casual games are still played.

There is also growing interest in Herefordshire amongst women, where in 2009 there are 22 teams in two divisions, compared with only twelve for men.

Another encouraging development is the introduction of internationals between England and Wales, although these events are held in village halls, since few pubs are large enough to play all the matches on one afternoon.

There also take place occasional late-night virtuoso sessions, often for money, and often featuring a variant called 'spikes up'.

In this, the first player throws as many consecutive spikes as he can, until he misses. The next player has to top this score or drop out.

Another variant is 'cards', in which four players are each dealt a full suit of thirteen cards, face down. Each player is then allowed to discard three cards, sight unseen, leaving ten on the table.

Now, each time a player turns over one of his cards, he must throw the number on that card, using up to four quoits. An ace counts as one, a king as thirteen.

The winner is the first player to dispose of all his cards.

Suffolk quoits and caves
Although it is still possible to come across the occasional board in antique or junk shops in the area, the Suffolk version of indoor quoits appears to have vanished from pubs altogether.

The Suffolk board (*see right*) was wooden, circular, about 18 inches in diameter, painted white and divided into five scoring segments.

The centre circle scored five. The four quarters scored one to four respectively. Battens at the back and underneath meant that the playing surface faced the thrower at a gentle slope.

Four rubber quoits, similar to the ones still used in the Marches, were thrown at the board from a distance of eight feet. The game was 21 up, but a relatively dull business it must have been.

Meanwhile, elsewhere in Suffolk, in 1930 the landlord of the Black Boy, in Bury St Edmunds, patented a game which he called 'caves'.

The patent wording makes clear that he was working on an improved version of the old Suffolk board.

'Instead of having only the numbered ruled partitions on the flat surface of the Quoit board (placed on the ground or on the table) our present invention consists of a Quoit board wherein are made a number of cavities within the ruled partitions.

'By this means a player, instead of throwing a quoit within a numbered ruled partition for the purposes of scoring, will have to throw a quoit within one or other of the cavities for the purpose of scoring'.

The caves board was square and slightly smaller than its Suffolk predecessor. Five rings, or quoits, were thrown and had to settle exactly in a bed to score. A quoit landing in a bed already filled did not count.

Each bed had its own score, numbered from one to five.

Thus a maximum score for one turn would be fifteen.

The game was usually 21 up, although contests of 31 up and even 61 up were apparently played.

Today only one pub in the whole of Suffolk clings stubbornly to the game, and that is the delightful Grade II listed Crown, at Bedfield where a home-made caves board sits at an angle under the dart board.

The only caves board still in play (*above*) is at the Grade II listed Crown, Bedfield, a former farmhouse (*top*). From the same county is this rare surviving Suffolk quoits board (*left*) owned by the author.

Chapter Seven

Cue games

Once a common feature of larger, late Victorian and Edwardian pubs, surviving billiards rooms (or saloons) are now rare. Even rarer is a billiards room that still has a billiards table in it, as is the case with the Grade II listed Lamb Hotel in Eccles, Manchester, opened in 1906 (*above and opposite*). Of the remainder, a few house much smaller pool tables, but the majority have been converted into bars or restaurants.

One of Britain's favourite pub games – almost as ubiquitous as darts – is pool, the latest of a long line of table-top cue games to have caught on in this country since the 16th century.

In fact, since its arrival in the late 1960s, so popular has pool proved that, with only a few exceptions in certain areas, it has eased out all its older counterparts.

Featured in this chapter, those older games are bagatelle, a 19th century game; snooker, an early 20th century craze that of course continues to be popular, but in clubs rather than pubs; and bar billiards, which arrived from France in the 1930s.

But first we must consider the oldest cue game of them all.

Or as Shakespeare's Cleopatra said to Charmian, her lady in waiting, 'Let us to billiards'.

Billiards

Of course the real Cleopatra did not play billiards. But that Shakespeare should have mentioned the game at all in a play he wrote in 1606–07 does at least confirm that it was well known in his lifetime.

Most historians agree that until at least the 15th century, billiards was played outdoors on the ground with hoops, rather like croquet, but using a mace rather than a mallet to strike the ball.

(The maces were similar to putters in modern golf.)

By Shakespeare's time billiards had evolved into a table-top indoor game. For example Mary Queen of Scots was said to have complained bitterly when her *table de billard* was confiscated shortly before her execution in 1587.

Nearly a century later in *The Compleat Gamester* Charles Cotton surmised that billiards derived from Spain (*see below*), but then later in the book wrote that 'The gentile, cleanly and most ingenious game at billiards had its first original from Italy.'

(Other historians have since veered towards France as its likely place of origin, if only because the word *billard* is French.)

In Cotton's time the object of billiards was to propel an ivory or wooden ball from the near end of the table, through a wooden hoop (the 'port' or 'pass') positioned at

the far end of the table, then work it back again to the 'king', which was a free-standing wooden pin.

The final trick was to bring the ball as near as possible to the king without knocking it over.

The table's six pockets were not targets to aim at, but 'hazzards' into which you might knock your opponent's or your own ball.

If a player toppled the king, he had to begin all over again. A player passing through the back of the hoop, rather than the front, was dubbed a 'fornicator' and had to pass 'twice through the forepart' before he could continue.

The game was 'five points by daylight', or 'three points by candlelight'.

Then, as now, the table was covered by green woollen cloth.

Cotton claimed there were 'few towns of note' that did not have 'a publick Billiard-Table'. Nor were they wanting in 'many Noble and private families in the Country, for the recreation of the mind and exercise of the body'.

But Cotton added this warning. 'Where any billiard tables are set up... swarming caterpillars'　　》

Billiards from Spain at first deriv'd its name
Both an ingenious, and a cleanly Game.
One Gamester leads (the Table green as grass)
And each like Warriers strive to gain the Pass.
But in the contest, e're the Pass be won,
Hazzards are many into which they run.
Thus whilst we play on this Terrestrial Stage,
Nothing but Hazzard doth attend each age.

from *The Compleat Gamester*,
by Charles Cotton, 1674

▲ The last of its kind at a British pub – a fully functional Edwardian billiard room, at the Grade II listed **Lamb Hotel, Regent Road, Eccles**, in **Manchester**.

Built by Holt's brewery in 1906 and designed by a Mr Newton of Hartley, Hacking & Co., the pub is a classic red brick and terracotta 'gin palace', replete with mahogany screens, Pilkington tiles, etched glass and Jacobean-style chimney surrounds.

The billiard table, supplied by the London firm of Burroughes and Watts, is surrounded by raised banquettes, fitted with bell-pushes to summon extra drinks, and with cast iron footwarmers underneath.

This set up was not only for spectators. On the far wall is the original scoreboard (made by the Manchester firm Raper & Son), which allows for up to ten players to join in with a once popular game called Life Pool (*see page 97*).

A mile or so to the east is an earlier Holt pub, The Grapes Hotel, on Liverpool Road, also by Newton.

Opened in 1903 this has a similar billiards room, but in its centre, quite lost in the space, is a modern pool table.

(whom today we might call 'hustlers'), whose 'common sustenance' was 'drinking and smoking', would prey on 'ignorant Cullies' (or dupes).

By the time the fifth edition of Cotton's book appeared, in 1734, the port and king on the table had been discarded and a third, red ball introduced, thus bringing billiards closer to the game we know today.

Meanwhile, by the end of the 18th century the cue, with its narrow tip, had all but taken over from the mace, with its flatter head (though mace sets can still be seen on display, for example at Dunham Massey in Cheshire).

But however much the game evolved, clearly its reputation worsened, because in the mid 18th century billiard tables were 'forbidden to be kept in public houses, under the penalty of ten pounds for each offence'.

It was also around this time that a divide opened up between Britain and the rest of Europe.

Here, pockets were retained and became an essential part of the game. In France and Spain pockets were abandoned altogether, and the game evolved into Carrom Billiards, Carambole or Carambola and Three Cushion Billiards.

This divide spread throughout the world. Countries that fell under Britain's influence played with pockets. Those colonised by France or Spain played without.

In 1801 Joseph Strutt (see Links) noted that billiards had 'superseded the game of shovel-board, and is certainly a more elegant species of amusement, admits of more variety, and requires at least an equal degree in the execution'.

Over the ensuing half century the game was to become even more popular, largely thanks to refinements introduced to the design and manufacture of tables.

The individual generally credited for these refinements is John Thurston.

After serving an apprenticeship as a cabinet maker with the firm of Gillow, Thurston set up in London solely as a manufacturer and supplier of billiard room furniture in 1814. Working closely with Edwin (sometimes also known as Jonathan) Kentfield, the first professional billiards champion, Thurston produced the first slate-bed tables in 1827 (which made the balls run more smoothly and evenly), and the first tables with rubber, rather than stuffed, cushions in 1835. Because these rubber cushions tended to crack in the cold, however, Thurston was quick to adopt the newly invented vulcanised rubber, in 1845.

Despite the Parliamentary prohibition on billiards, Thurston appears to have supplied tables to several London pubs. According to his own meticulous records, researched by billiards historian and manufacturer Norman Clare (see Links), these included The Cock and Magpie, Drury Lane in 1818; The Bull and Mouth, St Martins, and the White Hart in 1819; The Grecian Coffee House and Tavern, Temple, in 1820; La Belle Sauvage, on Ludgate Hill and the Angel, Islington, in 1821, and The George and Vulture and the Bull Inn, Whitechapel, in 1829.

But Thurston's most influential customer was Queen Victoria.

While still a princess Victoria had played and even recorded games of billiards in her diary. Shortly after her accession she then took delivery of one table at Windsor, followed by a second at Buckingham Palace in 1839.

Whether her love of the game was a factor or not, the passing of the 1845 Gaming Act repealed the ban on tables in pubs, provided that no play took place on Sundays.

Thurston's business gained another significant boost when its newest table was awarded a Prize Medal at the 1851 Great Exhibition.

Thurston himself had died shortly before this accolade, but his company continued, and in 1892 a Thurston design was chosen by the Billiards Association (itself formed in 1885) as the standard for all competition play. This standard was for a table measuring 12' x 6', dimensions that remain in force today.

Billiards reached a peak in popularity between around 1880 and 1914; a trend that was reflected in the design of public houses.

Indeed the extent to which breweries went to accommodate billiards was extraordinary, unprecedented even, within the history of pub games.

For unlike such games as darts or dominoes that require only the purchase of relatively inexpensive equipment and the clearing of space in a corner of one bar, and compared even with the outlay required to set up a skittle alley or a quoits ground, breweries went to huge effort and expense to accommodate billiards.

Not only were the tables and accessories expensive, but the space needed – at least 20' x 14' per table – was large enough to require in most pubs either a tailor-made room, or, as in several instances, an entire extension.

As Mark Girouard has shown in his seminal study of Victorian pubs (see Links), billiard rooms could occupy up to 40 per cent of a pub's available floor space.

In hindsight this was reckless in the extreme. How could a slow, steady game that only a few people could enjoy at a time, possibly justify such an investment?

In another recommended history, *Licensed to Sell* (see Links), there is a clue, in the form of two advertisements from the *Licensed Victuallers' Gazette* of 1892.

One states, 'Excellent Fully licensed Country Public House – few miles out, Surrey – near railway main line, Surrey – free lease at very low rent, more than cleared by billiards...'   »

Built in 1881, just as the game was entering a new phase of popularity, the Billiards Hotel was one of dozens of pubs lining Liverpool's famous Scottie Road. But as in so many cases, the game has long ceased to be played there and the pub, recently refurbished, is now called the Throstles Nest Hotel.

◀ A modern pool table is dwarfed by the towering magnificence of the former billiard rooom at the Grade II listed **Boleyn Tavern**, **Barking Road, London**.

Opened in 1900 and one of several pubs designed for the Cannon Brewery by WG Shoebridge and HW Rising, the Boleyn (next door to West Ham's Upton Park) illustrates just how much faith breweries must have had in the potential earning power of billiards.

Beautiful though the room's Art Nouveau leaded skylight undoubtedly is, however, this method of illuminating a billiard table hardly accorded with the requirements of the game. Added to which overhead gas lighting, which cast its own shadows, was still required after dark.

But in any case, both skylights and gas pendants were rendered unnecessary once affordable, reliable overhead electric lighting became available c.1913.

Apart from the Boleyn, other surviving examples in London of the shortlived trend for skylights over billiard saloons are at the Old Black Lion (1898), on Kilburn High Road, and the Salisbury Hotel, on Green Lanes, Harringay (1899). Both are listed Grade II* and will feature in our forthcoming study, *Played in London*, even though, sadly, neither still has a table for billiards or pool.

The billiard room at the Pheasant Inn, Attercliffe Common, Sheffield, dates from the pub's reconstruction in 1926, and had the usual raised seating and a fireplace. But unusually it also feaured a basin in the corner, so that steelworkers would not sully the baize with their grime. The pub was renamed The Stumble Inn in 1996, but in 2009 stood closed, its future uncertain.

» The other, on sale for £900, advertised a 'Free suburban public house' on a 'bold corner position' in a 'thoroughly respectable neighbourhood', and stated, 'Rent £100, cleared by billiards and stable, pays £160 per month'.

So it was that the billiards boom led to a flurry of construction at pubs during the period 1895–1914.

We have already mentioned the nation's single most intact billiard room from the Edwardian era, at the Lamb in Eccles (b.1906).

Other billiard rooms of a lesser quality but still with full-sized tables are at The Sportsman, in Hyde, Cheshire, where 'a capital billiard table' is reported to have been in place in 1857 (though the pub has been rebuilt since); the Commercial Hotel in Wheelock, Cheshire; the Malt Shovel in Spondon, Derby; the Stumble Inn, Sheffield (*see left*), and from 1930, the Douglas Arms, Bethesda in Gwynedd, Wales.

One can also have a game in the billiard room of the Grade II listed Alexander Hotel in Edgeley, Stockport, which retains its original timber roof with painted glass skylights, and has windows etched with the word billiards. But here, as in the Boleyn Tavern in London (*see previous page*), the table is for pool rather than billiards.

As mentioned, the Boleyn boasts one of the finest skylights of any Edwardian billiard room.

From the same period, but now without tables, mention must also be made of two Liverpool pubs: the Grade II* listed Philharmonic, in Hope Street (1900), where there were two tables in what is now called the Grande Lounge, and its sister building, The Vines, in Lime Street (1907), where a single table once stood under the pub's beautiful glazed dome.

One further billiards haven from this period was The Crown, on Aberdeen Place in St John's Wood, London, opened in 1898.

Unlike its contemporaries, the Crown's billiard room had no skylight but instead featured overhanging lights suspended from an ornate, Jacobean-style plaster ceiling, with a huge baronial fireplace and two, richly carved tables surrounded by seating for some 30–40 spectators.

Sadly, this wonderful room, like the rest of the Grade II* listed Crown (which was crassly renamed Crocker's Folly in 1987), has lain empty since 2004 and has since been placed on the *Heritage at Risk Register*.

But such problems are hardly new. As reported by pub historians Mark Girouard and Peter Haydon (*see Links*), the crippling costs of these grandiose 'gin palaces' led to some spectacular bankruptcies amongst breweries in 1899.

Billiards, it eventually sank in, was simply not worth the outlay.

Indeed more tables and rooms would have been lost sooner had it not been for one unexpected development.

At a meeting held in December 1900, the Billiards Association decided to add another game to its approved list. Called at the time Snooker's Pool, snooker had been invented by army officer Neville Chamberlain (not the later prime minister) in Jubbelpore, India, during the monsoon in 1875.

Played on a standard billiards table, snooker was an amalgam of Pyramids, Black Pool and Life Pool, all games ideal for gambling.

The name itself was adopted when a subaltern described one rookie player as 'a regular snooker', that being a term used at Woolwich for an inexperienced cadet.

Snooker differed from billiards in two key respects. Firstly, it used 22 balls compared with three. Secondly, it was infinitely more fun both to play and watch.

In the early 1920s it was still regarded as a novelty, an end-of-evening crowd pleaser put on by professional billiards players.

By the 1940s it had virtually killed off billiards altogether.

But that was of little consolation to pub landlords.

For although full sized tables, whether for billiards or snooker, were still being provided at pubs here and there between the wars, the initial popularity of billiards, followed by that of snooker in the 1930s, in any case resulted in the opening of so many billiard and snooker halls that pubs, with their one or two tables, could hardly compete.

Pub tables became even less viable once opening hours were restricted from 1914 onwards.

Used less, earning less, by the 1950s billiard tables became space-consuming liabilities. Those that survived were then threatened further by the arrival of pool.

Nor could the resurrection of snooker during the 1980s, thanks to the popularity of televised coverage, save the day.

The new breed of players went to clubs, not to pubs, where they could emulate their heroes – the likes of Steve Davis and Alex Higgins – by playing all day on the best equipment and in tailor-made surroundings.

Hence so few full-sized tables survive in pubs, and where they do, you can be certain of one thing.

Whatever game is being played on them, it will not be billiards.

▲ Multi-functional scoreboards such as this fine Edwardian example, at the **Wallasey Yacht Club, Merseyside**, were standard issue at pubs with billiard tables.

Top and bottom are numbers on rollers, to record scores for billiards or snooker, while the colour coded tabs in between are for Life Pool, a once popular game that allowed, in this instance, up to ten players to join in, usually on payment of a stake (despite the Gaming Act).

Each player was allocated one coloured ball. If that ball was then pocketed, the player would lose a life. To record this the appropriate tab was slid sideways to reveal one gold circle. Players had three lives, but could redeem the first two on payment of a further stake, in which case a star rather than a circle was displayed. The last player to survive won the pot.

BIRMINGHAM
ENGLAND

BAGATELLE TABLES
SUPERIOR QUALITY AND WORKMANSHIP.

Correct League Pattern, Latest Improved.

10ft. *League Pattern, Circular Ended Bagatelle Table,* superior quality and finish, massive *Bolted Mahogany Frame* on 4 Turned Legs, thick Slate Bed, best India-rubber Cushions, superfine West of England Cloth, 9 Cups, complete with 9 Balls (Bonzoline or Crystalate), Mahogany Marking Board, 2 Cues, Framed Rules, Chalks, etc. ... ... **38 guineas.**

9ft. *Ditto* ... ... **30 guineas.**

Be sure your Table bears a PADMORE **Name Plate.**
Thomas Padmore & Sons were the Original Makers of these Tables for the League 50 years ago, and have been appointed Sole Manufacturers to the League. They guarantee them correct to League Templates and Specification.

Strong Cord Net and Brass Fittings to go round cup end of Table **£2 10 0**

WOOD COVERS.

Hinged Wood Cover, covered with American Cloth, for 10ft. Tables **£4 10 0**

For 9ft. Tables **£4 0 0**

Waterproof Covers, for 10ft. Tables **30/-** ; for 9ft. Tables **28/-**

59

Thomas Padmore & Sons of Birmingham started making tables for billiards and bagatelle in the mid 19th century. This page is from their 1930s brochure, by which time Padmore was one of Britain's leading manufacturers. The table seen here is unusual in being curved at both ends, but at 10 foot long with two pockets is of a type used commonly in Coventry.

Bagatelle

There are two related games that go under the name of bagatelle.

One is an early version of pinball and is featured on page 172.

The other, popular in pubs since the early 19th century, is played with a cue and nine balls, on a small, baize-covered table. This table has at least one semi-circular end, and nine wooden pockets, called 'cups', sunk into the cloth, arranged in a circle of eight, with the ninth in the centre (*see opposite*).

Bagatelle appears to have evolved from a number of similar cue games using small tables.

One was Mississippi, a popular gambling game in 18th century Britain, in which players tried to cannon balls off the side cushions, through one of nine arches forming a bridge across the table, and into a cup beyond. If a player shot through the same arch twice the second shot would not score.

Many pubs are described as having a dedicated Mississippi room, as a result of which the game was specifically named, and banned, in the 1757 Gaming Act (which also prohibited gaming with cards, dice or billiards).

Trou Madame – called Trol-my-Dames by Shakespeare in *A Winter's Tale* (written in 1610–11) – followed much the same rules, except that balls could be shot through the arches without having to ricochet off a cushion. Trou Madame was also referred to as 'Small Trunks' in Robert Burton's *Anatomy of Melancholy,* published in 1621, and was the forerunner of another pub game, the splendidly named bumble puppy (*see page 175*).

Another version of bagatelle played in 17th century France was with pins, or small skittles set up on the table. Some accounts go on to explain that in order to avoid the time consuming business of resetting these pins after each go, sunken pockets were used as targets instead.

Another story has it that a similar game was first unveiled at a party thrown in 1777 by Louis XVI's brother, the Comte d'Artois, at his newly built hunting lodge in the Bois de Boulogne, the Château de Bagatelle (hence the name).

Yet there exist drawings from the Lancaster and London furniture makers Gillow & Taylor, dated 1771, of a table that appears almost identical to a standard bagatelle table of later years.

Certainly by the time Gillow's former apprentice John Thurston went into business on his own account in 1814, the game was sufficiently popular for Thurston to describe himself as a maker of both billiards and bagatelle tables and equipment.

In fact, the first items in a Thurston's order book from January 1818 are three bagatelle tables, measuring six foot (sold for £4), seven foot (for £4 14s 6d) and eight foot (for £5 10s, plus an extra cue for 1s 6d). Thurston also sold tables to the French, describing bagatelle in one catalogue as 'billard anglais', which has led some to speculate that the game might have originated on this side of the Channel after all, and not, despite its name, in France.

Bagatelle crops up in various Old Bailey trials of the time.

In 1820 one William Spink had his pocket picked while playing bagatelle at the Black Boy in Long Acre. Two years later a defendant was accused of making his living 'by swindling and playing bagatelle'. In 1823, John Williams was transported for seven years for stealing '18 bagatelle balls, value 16 shillings'.

In *Pickwick Papers*, published in 1836–37, Charles Dickens relates how Messrs Tupman and Snodgrass 'beguiled their time chiefly to such amusements as the Peacock afforded, which were limited to a bagatelle board on the first floor and a sequestered skittle ground in the back yard.'

Along with billiards, bagatelle was freed from most restrictions by the Gaming Act of 1845, though tables still had to be covered up on Sundays, Good Friday and Christmas Day.

Otherwise, bagatelle grew to become one of the most popular and ubiquitous pub games of the next hundred years or so, at least until the arrival of bar billiards in the 1930s (*see overleaf*).

Nowadays, and for reasons that no-one can fully explain, the game clings on for life in just two places, the cathedral cities of Chester and Coventry (although as recently as the 1990s it was also spotted in Bristol, North Wales, St Helens and Walsall).

In Coventry there used to be at least 40 venues, mostly members of the Working Mens' Club and Institute Union (CIU), with 10 foot long tables, each with pockets at the sides. But only one pub still has such a table, and that is the Humber Hotel on Humber Road.

Different tables and different rules are to be found in Chester, where there are now just ten teams left in the Chester & District Bagatelle League. As the league's informative website admits, this is well down on the 48 teams that once played in the 1950s.

Whereas in Coventry the game is played up to 121 points, with two red and seven white balls, in Chester there are four white and four reds, one black ball, and shorter tables with no pockets.

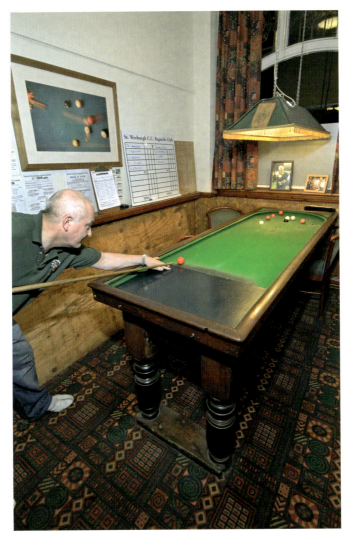

◀ One advantage of bagatelle is that its tables are played from one end only, so that, as at the **St Werburgh's Club**, on **Brook Street, Chester** (built originally as Ye Olde Bowling Green Hotel in 1914), they can be tucked into a corner.

Pubs with tables in the vicinity are **The Railway Inn** (*above*), The Stanley Arms, the Union Vaults and the Cross Foxes. The latter boasts the newest table in town, and such are the variations in age, size and feel of each table that visitors are given 15 minutes to practice first.

They go further in Coventry by insisting that once a table has been approved it cannot be repaired or even repositioned during a season without a further inspection.

Each player (in a team of eight) has two rounds or 'sticks', the aim being to score as many points as possible, to a maximum of 54 points per stick.

To achieve this, the black, which scores double, should be potted into the nine cup, preferably as early on as possible, as the rules state that the black ball must be hit before any other, until it is potted.

It is thus possible to score no points, by hitting the black each time but still failing to pot.

This is known in Chester as 'a green field', or a 'Tom Jones' (after the singer's hit called *The Green Green Grass of Home*).

There are of course many other subtleties to the scoring, but in general a decent player will average 40 or so points per stick.

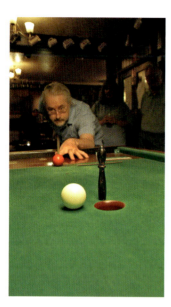

Bar billiards

Compared to bagatelle and billiards, bar billiards is a relative newcomer to the British pub scene, although versions of it were common in Europe long before its arrival here.

The individual generally credited with its introduction to England is a businessman, David Gill, who had come across the game while on a walking holiday along the French and Belgian border during the early 1930s.

The tables Gill saw were Belgian, but crucially they were fitted with a recently perfected French timer mechanism, which made them much more of a paying proposition for bar owners.

Clearly impressed, Gill made detailed drawings then, once back in England approached the firm of William Jelkes, billiard table manufacturer on London's Holloway Road.

Judging by the tables that survive from this period Jelkes did a fine job, turning out slate-bedded tables in mahogany and beech that were said to have been far superior to Continental versions.

But what to call the game?

In France and Belgium it was known as *billard russe*, or Russian Billiards. (In fact various cue games since the 18th century have borne this cognomen, including Russian Carambole, Russian

Pool and Russian Bagatelle, each of which share rules relating to penalties incurred for potting the wrong ball in the wrong hole or pocket.) However Gill felt that anti-Soviet sentiment in 1930s Britain called for a different name to be adopted, and came up instead with 'bar billiards'.

It was an apt choice, for not only was the game designed to be played in bars, but one of its key characteristics was a clockwork operated baffle bar which dropped down inside the table to prevent more balls emerging after a pre-determined time.

The first known Jelkes table to be installed at an English pub was at The Rose and Crown, at Elham, Kent, in December 1933, where, at a time when a pint cost just 4d, the cost of a game was set at 6d.

Meanwhile, also in 1933, George Jeune, landlord of The Caesarea in Jersey, ordered four tables, on behalf of himself and the local Licensed Victuallers Association. Ever since Jersey has remained a hotbed of the game.

Bar billiards took off rapidly, in the south of England at least. Like bagatelle it did not require much space, yet at 3d or 6d for a game lasting barely 20 minutes it was also a good earner, prompting rival companies such as Sams Atlas of Hoddesden and Jeffrey Bros of London to follow in Jelkes'

footsteps. Each maker's table sizes varied, as did the distribution of holes, and the design of the pins or skittles (*as seen left*).

Some were marketed under different names, such as 'skittle billiards' and 'Snookerette'.

Bar billiards' peak years came in the 1960s.

In Oxford, for example, where the first recorded league formed in 1936, it was said that by 1970 there were 120 tables within a five mile radius of the Oxford Clock Tower.

High Wycombe had 80 teams in five divisions, while in Jersey there were 50 tables and two leagues.

Since then numbers have reduced considerably. At the last count Oxford had just 21 teams, Jersey had thirteen, and Reading's league had shrunk from 42 teams to 12 in barely a decade.

Similar contraction has taken place in leagues based in Witney (Oxfordshire), Lewes, Brighton and Worthing (Sussex), and Tunbridge Wells, Dover and Deal (Kent).

The main reason cited for this decline is the introduction of pool in the late 1960s (*see page 102*), a claim that is made in relation to several pub games, but is particularly relevant to bagatelle and bar billiards, whose tables are of a similar size.

But pool was not the sole factor. As one bar billiards player in Jersey

At the Black Horse, Lewes (*top left*) the hazards are pegs, at the Case is Altered in Five Ways, Warwickshire (*left*), mushrooms, both designed so as not to fall down the hole and block the mechanism. At The Case is Altered the mechanism has never been altered, hence old sixpences are kept behind the bar for intending players. Seen right are the numbered ball compartments.

reported ruefully, 'The landlord told us he could make far more money from a dining table than he could from us, at a pound for 15 minutes, so our table went.'

A familiar story.

Yet bar billiards is by no means the critically endangered species that one journalist has recently suggested.

Although the number of players and tables has diminished, those who do play on are exceptionally committed, and well organised too, under the auspices of the All England Bar Billiards Association (formed in 1970), which presides over 18 counties, mostly, but not all, in the south of England.

The game is subject to an agreed set of rules, and has sufficient support to maintain a busy calendar of annual tournaments.

These include the Bournemouth Pairs, the National Pairs in Reading and the Sussex Singles in Brighton. There is a Singles Grand Prix, which takes in Didcot in February, Portsmouth at Easter, Worthing in June, Tunbridge Wells in July, High Wycombe in August, Reading in September and St Helier in Jersey in November.

Since 1981 Jersey has also run the British Masters Singles tournament, which in 1998 was renamed the World Bar Billiards Championships, a title that the organisers also copyrighted.

Not everyone welcomed this move, but the event, held each November around Armistice Day, is undeniably a spectacle.

Sixteen fine Burroughes and Watts tables are set up especially for the occasion. The organisers used to borrow tables from local pubs, but there were so many complaints that the tables did not 'play right' when they were returned that Nigel Ryall, a local

bar billiards fanatic, joiner and cabinet maker, started buying up tables and keeping them just for the World Championships and for such showpiece matches as Jersey v. Guernsey, and the Channel Islands v. England.

In the days before each tournament commences each table is lovingly assembled, polished, tested with a spirit level and its green baize ironed and then 'blocked', or brushed, to raise the nap.

Each table has its own referee plus a marker, or 'shouter'.

The timers are set at 16 minutes, which means that it is possible to predict when each round finishes.

And so the event, like the tables themselves, runs like clockwork.

The standard of play is pretty awesome too.

▲ Match night at the **Black Horse**, one of nine venues in the **Lewes and District Bar Billliards League**.

As seen here, an approved table has nine holes with scores ranging from 10–200. White pins stand either side of the 100 hole. A black (or red) pin guards the 200 hole.

On payment of £1, the timer releases one red and seven white balls and offers around 17 minutes of play, which is fairly typical.

Play starts as seen here, with the red spotted directly in front of the black pin. Knock over a white pin and you lose all points scored in that go. Topple the black and your entire score goes back to zero.

Every bar billiards table has its own feel, but also its own distinct sound. For as each ball is potted it drops down into a channel hidden within the frame and rumbles back

towards a numbered compartment at the baulk end of the table.

These balls can then be brought back into play, so that in theory a skilled player can 'run down the clock', potting one ball after another, without his opponent ever getting a single shot.

As a result, total scores reaching 12,000 are not unusual, although the world record, chalked up in Oxford in 1999 by Mark Sawyer, is 29,000.

When the clock does eventually run down and the baffle bar descends, potted balls stop reappearing, and play continues until one ball remains. This is then placed on the baulk line and must be aimed, off a cushion, at the 200 hole. But since that is guarded by the black pin, matches are often won or lost on the very last shot.

Pool

According to the American billiards historian Mike Shamos no fewer than 85 different games have borne the name 'pool' since it was first mentioned in an 1819 edition of *Hoyle's Games*.

The word pool itself is derived from the French *poule*, meaning a collective stake, or kitty (as is also its meaning in relation to the football pools). In other words, all cue games that bear the name pool have their origins in gambling.

Life Pool was the most common of these in early 19th century England (*see page 97*), and it is worth repeating that, in its original late 19th century form, snooker was known as Snooker's Pool.

In the United States, other early versions of the game were called Pyramid Pool, Fifteen Ball Pool and Continuous Pool.

As Shamos explains, a 'pool room' in America was not a billiard hall. It was a room in a betting establishment, laid on by the proprietor to keep gamblers occupied as they waited for the horse racing results to arrive.

Tainted by this association – WC Fields made a film in 1917 called *Pool Sharks* – the game had fallen into the doldrums by the 1950s, until another film transformed its prospects entirely.

Based on a 1959 novel by Walter Tevis, and starring Paul Newman as 'Fast Eddie', Robert Rossen's 1961 classic, *The Hustler*, for all its brooding despair, struck a chord on both sides of the Atlantic.

When *The Hustler* was released there was not a single pool table in Britain. By the time its sequel appeared in 1986 – *The Color of Money*, directed by Martin Scorsese

and starring Tom Cruise and again Paul Newman – there were an estimated 45,000 tables.

Pool's colonisation of Britain's pubs and clubs may thus be compared in scale, and in its swamping effect on other pub games, as no less transformative than the spread of the London trebles dart board had been from the 1920s onwards.

Yet ironically, this invasion did not emanate from America at all.

Three individuals may claim to have introduced pool to Britain.

First there is the former British billiards and snooker professional, Rex Williams, who in the late 1960s saw the potential of pool's compact, coin-operated tables whilst on tour in Australia.

But the tables he imported were actually French, made by the Paris firm of René Pierre (also famous for table football). These tables were initially trialled in Midlands pubs by Ansells Brewery, and were soon taken up also by their rivals, Mitchells and Butlers.

René Pierre tables at that time were 6′ long with sunken pockets, as in bar billiards. The cue ball was $1\frac{7}{8}''$ in diameter, while the object balls measured $2\frac{1}{10}''$. (In a coin operated game the cue ball has to be smaller so that if potted it alone returns to the players via the channels under the table.)

Around the same time, in 1969, the Australian bowler and former Australian rules footballer, Neil Hawke – in England to play for Nelson in the Lancashire League – became involved in the import of what were called Poolomatic tables from Australia.

These tables were also 6′ long but with ordinary pockets, and slightly different sized purple and orange object balls.

Britain's third pool pioneer was

Ron Hulme, operations manager for a large leisure group. His first tables, imported from Italy, were first installed in Scotland during the early 1970s.

All these versions of pool differed from American pool.

Firstly, US tables were larger, at 9′ x 4′ 6″. Secondly, the form of pool which caught on here, known as Eight Ball Pool would not even have been recognised in the USA.

Nevertheless, pool was seen as the latest big thing from America, and was even featured on Yorkshire Television's legendary pub game series, *The Indoor League*, first transmitted in 1973. For such a new and seemingly foreign game to have been shown alongside all the other old favourites proved a massive coup.

Organisation of the game followed soon after. In 1975 the British Association of Pool Table operators (BAPTO) was formed. Four years later a group of players formed the English Pool Association. Between these two bodies agreed the competition standards which pertain till now.

Tables were to measure 7′ x 4′, cue balls $1\frac{7}{8}''$ in diameter, and object balls 2″.

(Nevertheless differently sized tables and balls can still be seen, plus even a few maverick hexagonal, octagonal and even circular-shaped tables.)

Thus the world of pool found itself split between two camps: Britain, France, Spain and Australia playing on smaller tables, and the USA, Germany and Sweden preferring the larger size.

In Britain, Eight Ball Pool still reigns supreme. In this version, fifteen balls are racked up (*as seen left*) with the number eight ball (usually coloured black) tucked in the middle.

Most early versions of Eight Ball Pool played in Britain were played with multi-coloured balls called spots (numbered 1–7) and stripes (numbered 9–15), with the vital black number 8 (tucked into the centre of the rack, as here), being the last to be potted. More recently plain red and yellow balls have become the norm. But purists still prefer their old spots and stripes.

Whichever ball a player pots first (red or yellow, spot or stripe) that is the category he must continue to pot, before going for the black to finish and win. Otherwise, no scoring being necessary, the game could hardly be simpler (though of course at competition level there exists a whole raft of rules).

Oddly, in France they call this game *Billard Anglais*.

American versions of pool tend to be much harder, for example requiring each player to nominate which ball he intends to hit, and which pocket he is aiming for. Or in Nine Ball Pool each ball must be potted in numerical order.

The contest with the oldest pedigree in Britain is the National Team Trophy, first staged in 1977 and won by a seven man team from the Jolly Carter, Manchester. Since then it has grown to attract over 600 players to a three day event, held at Pontins in Blackpool.

Quite a spectacle it is too, with 32 Sam 'Atlantic' tables being played upon simultaneously.

There are other tournaments for professionals, but at Blackpool it is strictly pub teams only.

'Fast Eddie' need not apply.

Pool in the Docklands – a game of Eight Ball at the Watermans Arms on the Isle of Dogs, London. BAPTO claims that pool is now played regularly by two million people in Britain, and by a further three million on a casual basis. At the Watermans, needless to add, the billiard room is now a dining area. But one tradition survives. Note, the London Fives dartboard.

Chapter Eight

Bowling games

Some 300 miles north of Plymouth Hoe, a pub sign in Charnock Richard, Lancashire, reprises Francis Drake's game of bowls, played supposedly as the Spanish Armada sailed towards the English fleet in 1588. When this tale first emerged in a 1624 pamphlet it stated merely that various 'commanders and captaines' had been playing. Only in the 1730s was Drake's name then inserted. Just as elusive is the bowling green at this pub. The name was adopted in 1972, but there has never been a green on the site.

The word 'bowling' must surely be one of the loosest terms used in sport, as we have already touched upon in Chapter Three.

There is bowling in cricket, and bowling in alleys, in which the object is to knock things down, be they wickets, skittles or ten pins.

Then there is the true family of bowling games, in which one set of balls or bowls is bowled, rolled, hurled or chucked against another, in order to score points.

When it comes to pubs, games that involve 'bowling' can take place on gravel, on a road or stretch of moor, on a circle of concrete or even on a billiard table.

But of course the best known form is played on a green, and is essentially a contest to see which player can land his bowls the closest to another, smaller bowl, known as a jack.

Simple enough, and inevitably therefore, an enterprise of the utmost complexity and seriousness.

Bowling greens at pubs

According to figures compiled in 2001, bowling on outdoor greens (and now increasingly on indoor mats) is Britain's fifth favourite participation sport, with nearly 600,000 players and around 5,500 clubs in England alone.

Bowling is also, arguably, Britain's longest established sport, having been played, if certain claims are to be believed, on greens that date back to the 13th century. The Chesterfield Bowling Club, for example, claim that their green existed as early as 1294, while the Southampton Old Green Bowling Club believe theirs has been in use since 1299.

The origins of three other greens have been traced to the 15th century, followed by a further ten from the 16th century.

As to whether any of these bold claims can be substantiated or not – and if they can, the greens in question will be deemed the oldest surviving places of sport in this country, by some margin – Hugh Hornby will report further for *Played in Britain* in his study, *Bowled Over*, scheduled for 2012.

In the context of pubs, however, we must take a narrower view. For despite the chocolate box image of the country pub with its pristine green and pipe smoking players on a summer's evening, the truth is that, since the late 19th century pub greens have been greatly outnumbered by public and private club greens.

There are obvious reasons for this. Above all, pub greens can survive only if they have backing from sympathetic breweries and landlords, being expensive to maintain and used only seasonally.

In many areas they compete against public and private greens that are available all day long, outside of licensing hours.

In addition, needing a steady hand and a good eye, bowlers are hardly renowned for drinking. (Hence in the 19th century some pubs insisted that bowlers spend a minimum of 6d on drinks.)

Given these hurdles, and the undeniable drop in the number of people playing the game since the 1960s, literally hundreds of greens have been turned either into car parks or beer gardens or, more often, sold off for development.

Hence pubs bearing such names as The Bowling Green Inn or The

Bowler are common enough, just as there are countless roads named Bowling Green Lane, Bowling Street or similar. But the greens themselves have long gone.

That is not to say that bowling is now in terminal decline.

Away from pubs, the overall number of clubs, greens and bowlers has rallied, and is now thought to be holding reasonably steady. 'Old mens' marbles,' as bowling has often been dubbed, is fighting back, as it has often done over the centuries.

But bowling on pub greens is undoubtedly endangered.

Until the codification of bowling started in the 1840s there were few distinctions between different forms of the game.

Today there are three.

In southern, eastern and north eastern England, in south Wales and Scotland, the dominant form is known as 'flat green'.

In this the greens are absolutely level and are divided into rinks, or alleys, with games proceeding up and down alongside each other.

Also, the players dress mainly in white, according to a strict code.

Flat greens at pubs are now exceedingly rare.

In the Midlands, Yorkshire, the north west and north Wales, the dominant code is 'crown green'.

In this the green rises to a crown in the centre, but may undulate elsewhere. Dress codes are more informal. Betting on matches is common or at least tolerated, and games can be played simultaneously in any part of the green and in any direction.

To a flat green player this *laissez faire* approach is tantamount to anarchy. For their part, crown green players revel in their freedom and in the challenge of each uneven surface.

The vast majority of greens at pubs, you may not be surprised to learn, are crown greens.

Thirdly there are a dozen or so clubs who play a game akin to crown green, but closer to how bowls was probably played before the 19th century.

Loosely termed Old English bowls, this form survives at the aforementioned Chesterfield green, at Lewes (where bowls has been played on the castle's former tilting yard since at least 1658), and by eight clubs in the Portsmouth area, forming the Old English Bowling Association.

Only one pub is known to host bowls of this ancient lineage, and that is the Sun Inn at Barnes, in London (*see right*).

Before this division of bowls into different codes there were »

▲ Claiming to have formed in 1725, the **Barnes Bowling Club** in south west London is based at the Grade II listed **Sun Inn**, where the charming, walled green is neither flat nor crowned, but uniquely slopes up at the edges and is played only from corner to corner.

Another highly unusual aspect of Barnes is that their 'woods', or bowls (*below*) have far more 'bias'

than the modern norm. In crown and flat green bowling the typical bias is labelled 2–3. At Barnes the bias is 12–13, meaning that when released the woods run in almost a semi-circular trajectory.

Bias is achieved by adjusting the shape of the bowl from spherical to oblate, although early bowls had lead or iron inserted or 'clapped on' to achieve the same result.

As we note on page 42, biased bowls have existed since at least the 13th century (for rolly polly).

There is an oft repeated yarn nevertheless that bias on the green originated in Goole, in 1522, when the Duke of Suffolk, his own bowl having split, sawed off a not-quite-spherical ornamental ball from his host's staircase and used that instead. He then went on to win, of course, by a clear margin.

» really only two rules that counted. One was for the rich, the other was, well... for everyone else.

In common with most other games enjoyed by the general populace, bowls was subject to repeated prohibitions from Edward III onwards.

But surely none was quite as draconian or as mean spirited as the statute handed down in 1541, during the reign of Henry VIII.

As noted in Chapter One, although a keen bowler himself, Henry used the plight of the nation's bowyers, fletchers, stringers and arrowhead makers – all clearly feeling the pinch since Englishmen had ceased to practise archery on a regular basis – as an excuse to crack down on bowling for all but the richest members of society. Anyone running an alley or a place of bowling was to be fined 20s for every day on which the law was broken, and anyone caught bowling, 6s 8d for each offence.

To make doubly sure, the 1541 Act then added a list of all those workers and their apprentices and servants who would be further fined 20s if caught bowling not in alleys but in open places, gardens or orchards on any day other than Christmas Day (see Chapter One).

Only noblemen and men worth £100 or more per year were, under licence, exempt from the ban.

Had law enforcement at this time been more efficient, the 1541 Act alone might have killed off bowling for good amongst the lower orders. But even though Court Leet records do show instances of fines being applied, there were enough 'subtil inventative and crafty persons' around (as referred to in the Act) to make sure that the game survived.

After all, Francis Drake appears not to have been fined or censured for his seemingly illegal act of bowling on Plymouth Hoe.

Moreover, while both Charles I and II shared Henry VIII's passion for the game, and bowling greens became de rigueur in the gardens of 16th and 17th century country houses, lower down the social scale, greens start to appear openly on town maps from the 17th century.

Wrote John Locke in 1679, 'The sports of England are becoming horse-racing, hunting, hawking and bowling. At Marebone and Putney we see persons of quality bowling two or three times a week.'

Among these persons of quality were John Evelyn, Samuel Pepys, and even John Calvin and John Knox, said to have enjoyed playing on Sunday afternoons, no less.

But were any of them bowling at public houses?

Certainly the majority of greens named on maps appear to have been owned by private individuals, who may well have been worth more than £100 a year, or able to buy the necessary licence. Typically these greens were at tea gardens or pleasure grounds.

But as the 18th century wears on we start to find greens positively linked to public houses. In London, the Yorkshire Stingo at Marylebone, offers bowling by the 1770s. In Birmingham there are greens recorded at the Hen and Chickens, New Street, in 1791 and at the Union Tavern, Cherry Street, a year later.

Around the same time, in Manchester the physician John Dalton was said to have played regularly at the Dog and Partridge, then a country inn on Chester Road, Old Trafford.

Given that it is inconceivable that the landlords of these and many other inns and taverns over the ensuing decades operated their greens without the knowledge of local magistrates, we can only assume that bowls was now popular enough to justify not only the licence fee (which may well have remained at £100), but also the considerable expense of laying out and then maintaining the green.

In 1845, those costs did at least reduce, when the 1541 Act was finally repealed as part of a general reform under a new Gaming Act.

But whether the growing number of greens can be truly attributed to this repeal is hard to say, especially as so many other factors were at play during the same period.

For example, as the urban population expanded rapidly, so too did the number of inns and taverns, all of them competing for new business. The appeal of a bowling green – a precious oasis of open space – was obvious.

Hence in 1848 the Gun Inn, in Deal, Kent, changed its name to the Bowling Green. (The pub is still extant, if not the green.) Similarly, the Rifleman in Northwich, Cheshire, turned into the Bowling Green in the 1850s.

Bowling, in other words, was just the latest fad in the publican's battle to pay his way.

Other likely factors included the drawing up of codified rules by a Glasgow solicitor in 1848 – rules that would become the basis of flat green bowling – and at the most grass roots level, the invention of the lawnmower in 1830, which made green keeping all the easier and more affordable.

Before long inter-pub matches started to draw not only players but spectators, and as in Tudor times, gamblers too.

Bowling thus came full circle;

returning to its roots as a game of the people. On one hand there were the sober, white clad gentlemen who, in 1903, rallied under the banner of the English Bowling Association (of which the cricketer WG Grace was a leading light). On the other were the industrial workers and white collar workers of the Midlands and the north, who formed the British Crown Green Bowling Association in 1907, and staged most of their showcase events at pubs, most notably The Talbot Handicap and the Waterloo Handicap, both in Blackpool (see right).

Typical of the sort of encounters promoted was this, one of many advertised in the Sporting Chronicle.

'A match will take place today between two Blackpool gentlemen, for £40. Neither bowler to send a wood before they start'.

And so the late 19th and early 20th century witnessed an astonishing revival. Thousands of clubs formed, and continued to form even into the post war period, so that a 1957 handbook estimated that four million players were active. (Even if this estimate is halved, the numbers are still extraordinary.)

Yet rather as happened with billiards and billiard halls, so popular and successful did the game become that pub greens became outnumbered by club greens and by those laid down by local authorities in public parks.

There was a last upsurge in the number of pub greens during the 1930s. But since the 1950s the numbers have been falling steadily.

As one report in 1961 warned, between 1945–56, a total of 665 new flat green bowling clubs were formed, an increase of 50 per cent since 1930. But during the same »

◀ Described as the 'Wembley of Bowls', but with superior repartee, cheaper beer and more scope for betting, the **Waterloo Hotel, Blackpool** is the crown jewels of the crown green community.

The pub itself, opened in 1901, is frankly of no great note. But tucked behind it is Britain's most developed bowls arena, with stands and terraces which, until recent safety cuts, held 4,500 spectators.

The best and most raucous time to sample this extraordinary mini-stadium is on the finals day of the **Waterloo Handicap**. Held annually since 1907, 64 finalists (whittled down from 512 entrants) compete over four days in mid-September.

For years there have been fears that the Waterloo might share the fate of another great bowls venue in Blackpool, the Talbot Hotel, now the site of a supermarket, especially since the pub's owners, London and Edinburgh Inns Ltd., went into administration in 2006.

Since then, new owners and landlords, together with the British Crown Green Bowling Association and the Waterloo's dedicated bowls manager, Jim Parker, have pledged to keep this unique plot of sacred turf open for bowls.

But with crowds down, only lukewarm interest from television and a constant need for investment, winning this latest battle for the Waterloo will be no easy task.

▶ Opened in 1933, the **Magpie Inn** in **Botcherby, Carlisle**, was one of several inter-war pubs built with bowling greens by the **Carlisle and District State Management Scheme** under architect Harry Redfern.

The scheme, initially set up to control excessive drinking by munition workers during the First World War, evolved during the 1920s into a successful state-run enterprise in which games, food sales and specially brewed low-alcohol beer were encouraged.

Tables were decked with white cloths and flowers, while prints and lithographs lined the walls.

One Fleet Street cynic dismissed these pubs as 'Sunday schools with a licence'. Another critic called them 'about as cold and uncomfortable as a third class waiting room at a country railway station.'

Yet they gained many friends and, since being privatised in 1973, have continued to stand out for their architectural qualities.

Two survive with their greens: the Magpie, and the Grade II listed Redfern (opened in 1940 and named after the architect). The green at the recently closed Horse & Farrier can also still be seen, albeit now an overgrown wilderness.

Elsewhere, in Birmingham, where the 'fewer and better' pub scheme pursued similar goals, the Black Horse, Northfield (1929) and the Three Magpies, Hall Green (1935), both Grade II, still have their greens, while in Scotland the Gothenburg movement (set up to promote co-operative pubs) spawned, in 1910, the Fallin Public House Society, in Fallin, Stirlingshire, one of only four pubs in Scotland whose bowling green survives.

period the number of crown green clubs fell, as did the number of greens of either code at pubs.

Today, of 2,983 crown green clubs, around 350, or 12 per cent of the total, are still based on greens attached to pubs (although many of the clubs in question are run independently).

By comparison, in flat green bowls today's total is below 20, with some counties having no pub greens at all. For example, only one pub green survives in Cornwall (The Pickwick Inn, St Issey) and only four in Scotland. Similarly, the aforementioned Sun Inn at Barnes may well be the last functioning pub green in the whole of London.

As more greens are sold off, and as more pubs close, one therefore wonders, how long before the link between pubs and bowls is severed for ever?

Meanwhile, for one other form of bowling, it is already too late.

Distance and road bowling

During the 1920s the police in Colne, Lancashire, finally stamped out the old sport of stone bowling.

In this, fist sized balls, chiselled from local quarries, were bowled along roads between two points; both points, as one report put it, 'being drinking places'.

The player who covered the distance in the least number of throws was the winner.

As reported in the *Colne Times*, at its peak in the latter half of the 19th century, 'every fine Sunday morning, men would leave the district to play bowls on quiet country roads, well out of the reach of the arm of the law. Wagers were as high as £50 a side'.

A similar form of bowling, popular amongst miners in the north east at least until the First World War, was 'potshare bowls', so-called because players put equal sums of money into a pot.

The bowls were made from a vitreous substance used to line the furnaces of local glassworks, and were designed to carry as far as possible along open ground, often in matches organised and promoted by publicans.

Such were the crowds drawn to Newcastle's Town Moor that in 1880 the council tried to ban the game, only to back down after protests from local tradesmen.

Today, road or distance bowling survives in Ireland, where, under the auspices of the All Ireland Bowling Association, set up in 1954, solid iron balls, or 'bullets', about 2½ inches in diameter, are thrown underarm along roads for distances of between 2-5 miles.

Table bowls

Played on billiard tables, table bowls was once common in pubs. Between the wars there were leagues in London and Blackpool, and it was also taken up by pubs in Carlisle's State Management System (*see left*).

Today, Carlisle appears to be its last bastion, confined to just a few clubs and one pub, the Currock.

As in the outdoor game the bowls are biased, but are only 2–3 inches in diameter, and instead of being bowled by hand towards the jack, they are rolled onto the table down a small wooden chute.

As it is still possible to buy sets, table bowls might easily be revived, were it not for the fact that, in common with bowling greens, most pubs have got rid of their billiard tables.

And just as pool tables have, since the 1960s, taken their place, in outdoor bowls another foreign import has staked its claim... »

'Bowling green and good stabling' reads the raised lettering on the side of the **Red Lion, Westhoughton**, just outside Bolton.

Not surprisingly, no trace of the stabling remains, but nor is the bowling green obvious either, at least, that is, until one crosses Wigan Road and there it is, hidden away behind walls and housing – the headquarters of a venerable sporting institution, **The Panel**.

Formed as the Lancashire Professional Bowling Association in October 1908, the Panel is nowadays a select group of around 24 crown green bowlers who play each other at the Red Lion green every weekday afternoon of the year, whatever the weather.

If it snows, they brush a swathe across the green. If it is foggy, the referee holds a lamp above the jack and the players bowl towards the lamp. If it is sunny, they sweat. If it rains heavily, they throw, rather than roll, their bowls through the puddles (known in local parlance as 'a cobbin' match').

Added to this, the players must endure constant barracking from the sidelines.

One might imagine therefore that players on the Panel were highly paid professionals.

In the early days, the best of them were. When it was formed, certain Panel bowlers could claim to be the highest paid professional sportsmen in Britain, averaging some £750 per year.

They made their money by taking a percentage of the gate – and four figure crowds were not unknown – plus any prize money and winnings from side bets.

By the 1930s, there were some 50 pub and club bowling greens along the Wigan–Bolton axis hosting matches in the Panel, and by the 1950s some 600 paying members. Many were miners, as were the spectators, their early shift having finished after midday.

Of course the main attraction was not so much the bowling – although Panel players were amongst the elite of the crown green world – but the gambling.

To an outsider, this is conducted in a baffling fashion, by men wielding notebooks into which they scribble constantly, taking bets and laying them off too, always on credit (that is, no money changes hands until after the event).

Everyone bets, even the players, even the referees, and in the middle of a match too!

'Eight and a half to five,' goes up a cry from the sidelines.

'Three to one', or 'three fives, I'll lay', comes the reply.

Inevitably there are tales aplenty of skulduggery. Because the distance between the jack and the nearest bowl is sometimes measured casually with players' feet, one yarn has it that a player wore a size eight on one foot and a nine on the other, using each one as circumstances required.

In the 1970s an evening match was raided by Customs and Excise. Half a dozen spectators and players were charged with acting as bookmakers, only for the presiding judge to dismiss the case and accuse the Customs and Excise of wasting everyone's time.

'Of course, t'judge were from Bolton, so 'ee understood,' said one of the players afterwards.

And so after a century of managing to stay on the right side of the law, but these days earning its players only pin money, the plucky Panel plays on.

Not only that but in 2005, the Panel bought the green from the pub, making it a safe bet they will be there for years to come.

▲ La Belle France? Pas du tout. It is the walled garden of a Lancashire pub, **The Baum** in **Rochdale**, a town usually associated with the Co-op and Gracie Fields, but now boasting eight teams in the Rochdale & District Pétanque League.

Lancashire pubs with 'terrains' may also be found in Blackpool, Cleveleys, Croston, Great Eccleston and Westhoughton, while similar concentrations of pub-based pétanque teams are in Hampshire, Kent, Rutland and the Isle of Wight.

Pétanque

Despite the fact that we British have been happily importing and adapting games from Europe on a regular basis since the Roman era – as this book, nay the entire *Played in Britain* series, has amply demonstrated – Britain's rapidly growing community of pétanque enthusiasts still face accusations that theirs is an alien introduction to the hallowed grounds of our traditional pubs.

To which one need only quote from Francis Willugby's *Book of Games*, compiled in the 1660s.

In this Willughby described a game that was played either on 'greenes, which must be kept very smooth… or upon very smooth allies of gravel'. Such a game, he went on, 'is counted the most gentile play and is more generally used than any other in England.'

Willughby called this game 'boules'.

Today's British *boules* players go further by suggesting that the game played by Francis Drake and his contemporaries in the late 16th century might well have been closer to *boules* than to the crown or flat green bowls we know today.

What cannot be doubted is that French *boules* and British bowls are close cousins. Or that one form of *boules*, pétanque, is now firmly entrenched on this side of the English Channel.

On the opposite side there exists a diverse array of regional variations, such as *La Bourle* in the north of France, *Boule de Fort* along the lower Loire, and *Boule Lyonnaise* in the south east.

For its part, pétanque originated a century ago from a much older game, *Jeu Provençal*, played in the Midi region of southern France.

Still played today, *Jeu Provençal* is one of the most physically demanding and spectacular of all the various forms of *boules*, involving as it does players taking a three step run up to hurl nail-studded wooden balls at a wooden jack, some 15–20 metres away.

The story goes that around the turn of 20th century one of this game's finest exponents, Jules Hugues (known as Le Noir, because of his black beard) was struck down so severely by arthritis (or was it rheumatism?) that he could only sit in a wheelchair and watch others play his beloved game at the Béraud Club, up above the harbour of La Ciotat, a town just east of Marseille.

That is until, in 1907, one of the club's owners, Ernest Pitiot, took pity on his old friend and together they contrived a different game.

For this new game they drew a circle around Le Noir's wheelchair, to form a throwing area, and reduced the throwing distance to six or seven metres.

Some onlookers scoffed at this game for invalids and called it *ped tanca*, Provençal slang for 'feet tied together' (in French *pieds tanqués*).

But Le Noir and Pitiot had the last laugh. Pétanque, as their game became known for short, held its first official competition at La Ciotat in 1910, and spread sufficiently widely for Pitiot to form the Fédération Française de Pétanque et Jeu Provençal (FFPJP) in 1945, an organisation that still runs the game today.

Britain's first *terrains de pétanque* were laid in private gardens during the 1930s. But the first to be laid at a pub is thought to have been in Braintree, Essex, in the early 1960s. A club in Chingford, Essex, then became the first from Britain to be affiliated to the FFPJP in 1966.

This was followed in 1974 by the formation of the British Pétanque Association (BPA), by a group of friends who, having returned from a holiday in France, wanted to play the game nearer to home.

Led by a Francophile academic and writer, Maurice Abney Hastings, they laid out a terrain at Sam's Hotel (since renamed Samuel's Rest), in the village of Shedfield, Hampshire, and a year later hosted the first BPA National Championships.

In the same year, the first British team was dispatched to the World Championships, in Quebec, Canada, while four years later the BPA showed just how far the game had advanced by staging the World Championships on home soil, at Southampton.

Since then pétanque has grown and grown, so that the current governing body, the British Pétanque Federation (formed in the 1980s) now has some 250 affiliated clubs and around 3,000 players spread across England, Scotland and Wales.

But what of their links with pubs?

As it has transpired, the more organised British pétanque has become, seemingly the less the governing bodies are happy for their sport to be considered a pub game, even though maybe a third to a half of their affiliated clubs still use terrains laid out at pubs.

Instead, in order to foster youth development and pétanque's image as Britain's 'fastest growing family sport', new terrains are increasingly to be found at sports centres, private clubs, recreation grounds or in public parks.

Meanwhile some landlords, having initially embraced pétanque, have since decided that the players do not drink enough to justify the space and upkeep of a terrain. (There is, for example, only one pub in the London area, with a team affiliated to the BPF, the Alexandra in Kingston.)

Nevertheless, the links between pubs and pétanque remain sufficiently close for it still to be considered a pub game, particularly in areas such as Lancashire and Hampshire.

Other counties with a handful of pub terrains include Berkshire, Warwickshire and West Sussex.

Moreover, there are potentially a hundred or more pubs, such as those in Rochdale, whose pétanque teams have elected to remain independent of the Federation, content to enjoy a more casual approach.

But whether played seriously or for fun, there are certain rules generally adhered to.

Before releasing his *boule*, a player must stand with both feet inside a circle scratched onto the surface of the terrain, measuring 35–50 cms in diameter.

The aim, as in bowls, is to land one of their *boules* as close as possible to the jack, which has been thrown 6-10m from the circle. (Boulists have a glorious array of names for this jack, including *la blique*, *le cochonnet*, *le coche*, *le gari*, *le but*, *le kiki*, *le pitchout* and *le petit ministre*.)

There are of course obvious differences with bowls.

The throwing sequence and the rules for scoring differ.

The boules (three per player in singles and doubles, two for triplettes) can be rolled or thrown, even in a high trajectory (known as un *carreau*, or mortar), and the boules themselves have no bias. They are also smaller, being 70.5–80 mm in diameter, metallic, and must be stamped with the manufacturer's name and the weight (between 650–800 gm).

▲ There is a plane tree in the way, plus a downward slope and garden walls to contend with, and there are no barriers to prevent stray *boules* from getting tangled up among the marigolds and petunias.

In other words, not the sort of terrain of which the British Pétanque Federation would approve, but then again, not that far removed from the average terrain to be found outside the average village café or bar in rural France, where the imperfections, lumps and bumps form part of the challenge.

This is one of two *pistes* (or lanes, as in the rinks on a flat green bowling green) at **The Baum** in **Rochdale**. Both were laid in 1983, shortly after two of the pub's regulars, one a former rugby player in France, started playing casual games in the garden.

Terrains for pétanque are generally surfaced in some form of gravel, such as limestone grit, pea shingle, granite dust or chippings, and if intended for competition should measure at least 12m x 3m, with plenty of room around the edges. Many club terrains also have floodlighting.

But at pub level *boulistes* take whatever piste is on offer and say 'vive la différence!'

Marbles

'Marbles,' wrote Joseph Strutt in 1801, 'seem to have been used by the boys as substitutes for bowls...'

But try telling the hundreds of players, young and old, who gather at various pubs and sites in Sussex every year that theirs is a children's game, and be prepared either for a long lecture or a dazzling display of skills that will have you hunting through your cupboards for any old oilies, steelies or swirls left over from your childhood.

Marbles – originally made from wood, clay, stone or simply in the form of nuts or cherry pits – have been toyed with since the days of antiquity, and may well have been brought to Britain by the Romans.

In the early 18th century Daniel Defoe described marbles as 'alabaster globes'. But it was in the 19th century that marbles started to be mass produced, mainly in Germany, first in agate, then, by the 1890s, in glass. Millions were imported to Britain in the form of ballast on cargo ships.

Of course the majority found their way into the pockets of schoolboys. But a good number also ended up in the backyards of pubs, and for reasons unknown, pubs mainly in Sussex.

In West Sussex, inter-pub contests form part of the Arundel Fringe Festival each August, while in September there is an annual

tournament at the Red Lion in Turners Hill. In East Sussex, Good Friday marbles matches are held at the Lewes Arms in Lewes and on the Abbey Green at Battle.

But the real epicentre – the Wembley of the marbles world, as it were – is in West Sussex, at the Greyhound Inn, Tinsley Green.

The first championships were staged there on Good Friday 1932, shortly after the current pub building opened. But this may well have been a revival of earlier contests, for as was stated in the journal *Notes and Queries* in 1879, in some parts of Sussex Good Friday was also known as Marble Day.

(Other sources state that the marble season traditionally ended on Good Friday, having started at the beginning of Lent, on Ash Wednesday.)

Further evidence of the event's possible vintage came on the day of the 1932 contest from one of the competitors, 71 year old cowman Sam Spooner. He claimed to have been reigning marbles champion 50 years earlier, which would date the event back to at least the 1880s.

But if this claim rings true, what are we to make of a further claim, made in 1938, that the Tinsley Green event dates back even further to 1587, having started as a

contest between rival suitors for a local fair maiden?

To put it bluntly, not a lot, for that is just the sort of 'fakelore' that after a beer or two many a wily local might feed to a gullible reporter down from London.

Or a cameraman. For the claim was aired on Pathé News, in one of several newsreel features filmed at Tinsley Green between 1936 and 1962 (now available to view on the British Pathé website, *see Links*).

Tudor myths aside, footage of the 1936 event is particularly instructive, showing a team representing London Transport, all dressed in their uniforms, hats

Eighty year old Pop Maynard of the Copthorne Spitfires, also known as a folk singer, and his 51 year old son Arthur, compete in the British Marbles Championships at The Greyhound Inn, Tinsley Green, West Sussex, in April 1952. The circle used today is on almost exactly the same spot.

included, beating a rival team from the Southern Railway.

Two years later Pathé were back to film bus crews from Crawley playing in the final.

Subsequent Pathé clips, and also numerous press photographs – from the off, the event has been lapped up by the media – also show a succession of servicemen playing, including soldiers from Canada in 1941.

In other words, not all marbles players were from Sussex.

But nor were they all adults.

For example, according to the splendidly named British Marbles Board of Control, the longest established team competing in the annual championships are the Handcross Rebels, from a village a few miles south of Tinsley Green.

Formed amongst boy scouts in the 1950s, four members of the original Rebels were still turning out at the 2009 contest.

Other local teams from the early days, now defunct, were the Copthorne Spitfires, the Toucan Terribles (winners of 20 consecutive team titles in the immediate post war years), and the Greyhound's home team, the Tinsley Tigers.

Today's entrants still come predominantly from Sussex, but with a few honourable exceptions.

In 1975 the trophy went to a Gulf Oil team from Pittsburgh, and in 2004 a German team, Saxonia, beat a fellow German team in the final, to complete an impressive hat-trick of wins.

But the Brits have since fought back, and in 2008 and 2009 the winning team, the Yorkshire Meds, hailed from Leeds.

So seriously did one of their number view Marble Day in West Sussex that he flew in especially from Algeria.

▶ Where once turf and ropes surrounded the six foot ring at the **Greyhound Inn, Tinsley Green**, now there is a tarmac car park and white plastic chairs. And where once London bus drivers and Sussex farmhands did battle, as seen here in March 2008 the Beavers from Australia are pitted against a German team, 1st MC Erzgebirge II.

But one aspect of Marble Day at Tinsley Green has not changed at all, and that is the game itself.

Called **ring taw**, it is played between two teams of six players and starts with 49 marbles in a tight pack in the centre of the ring. Provided by the organisers, these marbles measure approximately half an inch in diameter.

From the edge of the ring the first player then shoots his own 'tolley' (a slightly larger marble), the aim being to scatter as many of the 49 marbles out of the ring as possible, at one point per marble.

If he succeeds with this first shot, he plays on, and if skilled and lucky can start to build a break, just as in snooker. Apparently the Tinsley Green record, notched up by an American in the 1990s, is

43 points on the trot. But breaks of 15–30 are more common.

If no marbles are knocked out of the ring, or if the tolley itself leaves the ring, the next player from the opposing team steps up.

Should a tolley be left in the ring after an unsuccessful shot, as is common, but is then knocked out by another player, that tolley's owner is 'killed' and plays no further part in the game.

The first team to 25 points wins.

There are also contests for the best individual player (male or

female), the best female (since women now form 10–15 per cent of the total), and a shield for the least successful player of the day.

Since 2002 there has also been a Golden Oldie competition for players aged 50 or over, in which contestants play a game adapted from an American marbles game, starting with thirteen marbles laid out in the form of a cross. Whoever reaches seven points wins.

Golden oldies they may be, but they have clearly not lost their marbles.

Dave Atkin from the Handcross 49ers delivers his white tolley at the 2008 championships according to the prescribed 'knuckle down' method, using only his thumb to propel the marble. Note how the concrete ring is brushed with an even layer of sand, to prevent the marbles skitting about too lightly.

Chapter Nine

Bat and trap

One of the best known portrayals of bat and trap is an 1809 painting by Henry Thomson, which the Bat & Ball in Brighton has since adapted as its sign. The game itself is played opposite the pub, each Good Friday, on open ground called The Level. But turn the corner and there is a second Bat & Ball sign, depicting a cartoon cricketer. This is to commemorate the fact that from 1791–1823 The Level served as a cricket ground for the Prince of Wales, whose Royal Pavilion lies a short distance away.

Bat and trap, originally known as trap ball, is the last survivor of a whole family of games that involve the launching of a ball up into the air before it can be struck.

When played by 'boys and the common herd of rustics' (as Joseph Strutt put it in 1801), the usual method was simply to place the ball inside a hollow at one end of a piece of wood or bone that was itself balancing either on a peg, or on the edge of a small hole in the ground. Striking the other end smartly would then launch the ball upwards.

Other games in this family, which goes back to at least the 14th century (see below), but may date back even earlier to the Vikings, include the northern variants knur and spell, nipsy, billets and peggy, all of which feature in our chapter on lost games, on page 172.

In those games, the aim was to hit a ball or piece of wood as far as possible, whereas in trap ball, as in cricket (which it predates), the aim was to score runs and avoid being caught out by fielders.

There was a similar game involving fielders known as tip cat, in which players would attempt to flip up and then hit the 'cat' (a six inch piece of wood) out of a circle, or, rounders-style, run after hitting the cat between a series of holes, or stations, marked out in a circle.

Famously, tip cat, or simply 'cat', was the game that in the 17th century, the writer John Bunyan was playing in a village square one Sunday when he heard a voice in his head.

As Bunyan later recalled in his autobiographical work, *Grace Abounding to the Chief of Sinners*, published in 1666, '… as I was in the midst of a game of cat and having struck it one blow from the hole, just as I was about to strike it a second time, a voice did suddenly dart from heaven into my soul, "Wilt thou leave thy sins and go to heaven, or have thy sins and go to hell?"'

Clearly cat and god were not to be reconciled.

As for trap ball, this got its name from a simple wooden device created to launch the ball – the 'trap' – which appears in at least three portraits of young boys during the late 18th and early 19th century when, perhaps owing to the Prince of Wales' patronage, trap ball appears to have been briefly in vogue (as seen left).

Certainly Strutt, who saw trap ball played by 'rustics' in Essex, called it 'a childish pastime… when compared with cricket'.

Yet, as seen opposite, adults played it too, at least in Newington, London in the 1780s, while in 1837, Donald Walker included the rules of trap ball in his book of *Manly Exercises*, from which he pointedly omitted any sports or games that he considered 'frivolous or dangerous'.

In the 1890s, Alice Gomme would add further sightings of trap ball, or of variants of it, played by young men on Shrove Tuesday in Shropshire (where it was called trib and knurr), and on Shrove Tuesday, Easter Monday and at Whitsuntide festivals at Bury St Edmonds in Suffolk, by 'twelve old women' who played 'with the greatest spirit and vigour until sunset'. Apparently the women of Chester were also keen.

In September 1900, *Country Life* reported on a lively match

As reproduced by Joseph Strutt in 1801 (see *Links*), this depiction of trap ball appeared in a 14th century illuminated book of prayers, now held by the Bodleian Library. Note that the tailor-made 'trap' is hinged on a stump of wood at thigh height, whereas in all known later versions of the game the trap has been placed at ground level.

26. TRAP-BALL.—XIV. CENTURY.

of what it now called 'bat and trap', at a village flower show in Hertfordshire.

But however widespread bat and trap might once have been, apart from the annual game noted opposite in Brighton, at a competitive level today it is confined entirely to the county of Kent, and, more importantly in the present context, is played almost exclusively in the gardens or grounds of pubs.

The story of how this came about starts between the wars, a period when so many pub games were codified and organised.

In this case the credit must go to a Canterbury man, Bill Humphries (of whom little else in known), who in 1921 decided that bat and trap would make an ideal summer game for local pubs.

Within a year, Humphries had not only drawn up a list of rules based on existing sources, but had also persuaded six publicans to set up pitches on their premises.

Starting in May 1922, the founding members of the Canterbury and District Bat and Trap League were Ye Olde Beverlie Inn, the Brewers Delight, the Rising Sun, the Two Brothers and the Royal Artillery, all in Canterbury, and the Golden Lion at nearby Broad Oak.

Within six years the league had expanded to two divisions, and had sufficient confidence when it reconvened after the Second World War to make it a condition of membership that, from 1951 onwards, every venue had to be equipped with floodlights.

This, it should be noted, was in the same year that Southampton became the first League football club to stage a competitive match under lights (albeit only a reserve match), and even then, the football

authorities withheld permission for first team matches until 1955.

To bat and trap must therefore go the honour of being the first game in Britain to give their official sanction to floodlights, and to make them compulsory.

According to the league's historian, Brin Tyndall, to whom we are indebted, the reason for this ruling was that because most of the players were agricultural workers who had to work later in the summer months, a start time of 8 o'clock rather than 7 o'clock was more convenient all round.

In addition, so many matches were already carrying on after sundown that a backlog of unfinished matches was clogging up the fixture list. »

▲ One of the best known and most often reproduced sporting scenes we have of Georgian London is this print of **trap ball** being played, it is thought, on the grounds of the **Black Prince** pub, on Walworth Road, which backed onto **Newington Butts** (close to the modern day Elephant and Castle).

The butts, of course, were formerly used for archery training.

Published by the well established printmaker, Carington Bowles of St Paul's Church Yard, on September 22 1788, the print was one of a set of six London sporting scenes (which *Played in Britain* hopes to reproduce in *Played in London*).

To modern day players of bat and trap, the game seen in this print is immediately recognisable.

At the batter's feet is the trap itself. Note the shape of his bat, like a shortened cricket bat.

Behind him two scorers are seated. (In modern bat and trap each team still has its own scorer).

On the right, standing behind a line between two upright posts, can be seen the opposition's fielders about to make a catch. In the rules of trap ball published by Donald Walker in 1837, the distance between trap and posts was set at 21 yards – a distance that remains in force still – though clearly in this image it appears less, whereas the posts are much further apart than the modern limit of 13 feet 6 inches. These discrepancies, however, may simply be the result of artistic licence.

▶ A warm, early summer evening
at the **Market Inn, Faversham** in
Kent, in June 2009, as the home
team entertains its opponents from
the Golden Lion at Broad Oak, one
of the six founding members of the
**Canterbury and District Bat and
Trap League**.

Note the stance of the batter,
staying low and to the side of the
trap as he waits to strike the ball on
the rise. Another method (*below*)
is to stand directly behind the trap
and almost scoop the ball forward.

Bat and trap is a wonderfully
sociable, and relatively benign,
game which, at the last count,
some 60 pubs in Kent now host
– although not all have space
for two pitches side by side, as
both here and at the **Red Lion**, in
Dunkirk, shown in the two lower
images opposite.

» The effect of the lights and growing interest in bat and trap led to another three decades of expansion for the Canterbury and District League. In 1952 a ladies division was formed, and proved so popular that it quickly grew to three divisions. The men's league, meanwhile, expanded by 1982 to reach an astonishing peak of 80 teams in eight divisions.

It could have grown even further, such was the demand from teams hoping to join, but the league's administrators felt that they could not cope with more.

This impasse resulted in a stormy annual general meeting in 1986, at the end of which, appropriately enough at the behest of players from the Way Out Inn, at Westmarsh, near Sandwich, a breakaway league was formed.

Pointedly, the rebels called this the East Kent Friendly League.

Today, the league has 19 mixed teams, playing at fifteen venues, thirteen of which are pubs.

Another league, serving Sevenoaks and District, also has 19 mixed teams, while the original Canterbury and District League has 39 teams in four divisions for the men, plus a separate division for the ladies.

Other leagues, in the Medway towns, in Tunbridge Wells and Tonbridge, and in Margate, Ramsgate and Broadstairs have also popped up in recent years.

All in all then, a remarkable phenomenon, and one which, although now reduced from its peak in the 1980s, when as many as 4,000 players would be involved from May to September, does Kent and Kentish pubs proud.

The only mystery is, why are other counties not taking up the bat? There may be a trap involved, but where is the catch?

◀ The **trap** is 20–24 inches long, with a narrow piece of wood called a 'striker' pivoted in its centre. A metallic plate protects the striking end. At the other end is a small hollow in which to position the ball.

Having launched the ball, the batter's aim is to strike it between the two posts at the far end of the pitch. If he misses the ball, or if he hits it wide of the sidelines, or if it goes between the posts at a height greater than seven feet, or if he is caught by one of the opposing fielders, he is out, and the next man on his team steps up to bat.

But if the ball does get through to the other end without any of this happening, he steps aside for a moment and waits while one of the fielders returns the ball, underarm, back down the pitch.

The fielder's aim is to strike the wicket. Given that this is a five inch square, hinged flap at the front of the trap (with a black circle in the centre) and that the pitch is 21 yards, hitting it is no easy task.

If the fielder fails, the batsman is credited with one 'run' – though this being an undemanding sort of game, he does not actually have to run – and he can then take another strike. If the fielder does hit the wicket, the batter is out.

Once all six or eight members of each team (depending on the league) have batted, the runs are added up and a winner of that leg is declared. A league match is decided by the best of three legs, although if time is running out or if it is a cup match, the result can also be decided by a 'bowl out', in which each player has one attempt at bowling at the wicket.

With the floodlights on and last orders being called, hitting that black circle from afar can seem like an absurdly impossible task.

And usually, it is.

Chapter Ten

Pushing and shoving

'Coridon and I have had not an unpleasant day, and yet I have caught but five trouts: for indeed we went to a good honest ale-house, and there we played at shovel-board half the day.' So wrote Izaak Walton in *The Compleat Angler*, first published in 1653 and later expanded by Walton's great friend, Charles Cotton (author of *The Compleat Gamester*). This pen and watercolour depiction of the scene, by celebrated illustrator Arthur Rackham, featured in an 1931 Harrap edition of Walton's classic.

Remember that sequence, once so popular with Hollywood film directors, showing a bottle of hooch or a tall glass of frothing beer being slid, inch perfect, down the length of a polished bar, to the waiting hand of a thirsty cowboy, gunslinger or morose private eye?

In this section we look at games that work on the same basic principle – that of an object, usually either a coin, weight or wooden counter – being pushed or shoved along a polished surface.

In Britain variants of these games have been called shovel board, shuffleboard (a quite different game from the former), or, when involving coins in a pub setting, variously shove penny, shove groat, shove ha'penny or push penny.

The Scots have their own variant, a form of table-top curling known as summer ice.

Shovel board
Although Izaak Walton came across shovel board in 'a good honest ale-house' in the mid 17th century (*see left*), for a good hundred years prior to that the game was very much the preserve of the aristocracy, if only because the tables required were so large and expensive.

Henry VIII's Privy Purse expenses for 1542 reveal that in January of that year, one Lord William won £9 from the King at 'Shovilla Bourd' while 'my Lord of Rocheforde won of the King £45'.

In his *Book of Games*, published in the 1660s, Francis Willughby noted that 'shillings, halfecrownes or round brasse or silver pieces made of purpose' were used for shovel board, 'very smooth on one side'.

In other words, not the sort of coinage that ordinary working men would have chosen to play with. But in any case, in common with so many games associated with gambling and ale houses, shovel board was one of many games prohibited to the lower orders until after the Restoration in 1660.

Samuel Pepys recorded in his diary that he played the game at the White Hart, Woolwich, in July 1662, while two pubs were actually called The Shovelboard. One, in Portsea, was mentioned in 1715,

the other, in nearby Old Common, the year after.

Perhaps typical was the fate of the shovel board at Oxnead Hall, Norfolk. When its owner, William Paston, the second Earl of Yarmouth, went spectacularly bankrupt in 1732, laden with gambling debts, his table ended up at the Black Lion Inn at Buxton, a few miles away, no doubt cut down to size but presumably a real catch for the landlord all the same. (Today the Black Lion, rebuilt since 1732, still offers a range of games, though alas no trace of the table survives.)

A further reference to the game appears in a report from the Old Bailey in 1773. Mary Clews stole 'eighteen pieces of brass, which were shuffleboard pieces' from the Half Moon, Islington, then sold them for 16d.

For this poor Mary was transported for life.

That shovel board had gone down market by this time was confirmed by Joseph Strutt in 1801 (*see Links*). He described a table measuring 39' 2" x 3' as being the longest in London. »

▲ 'In former times,' wrote Joseph Strutt in 1801, 'the residences of the nobility or the mansions of the opulent, were not thought to be complete without a shovelboard table; and this fashionable piece of furniture was usually stationed in the great hall.'

Today, Britain's best preserved Tudor **shovel board** is in the Long Gallery at **Astley House**, near Chorley in Lancashire.

Dating from c.1570, it measures 23' 6" x 3', and is supported by ten pairs of sturdy, turned legs.

Although the table top is made up of numerous pieces of wood, each measuring 12" x 3" and laid like a herringbone parquet floor, the surface is as smooth as glass

(if not perhaps as level as it once was). This, despite the fact that when it was moved into the newly completed Long Gallery some time around 1666, it had to be sawn up and reassembled.

Displayed next to the table in a glass case are two flat brass weights (*centre right*), while the end of the table (*top right*) retains a 'swallowing dish' to catch any weights that had been over hit.

The table top of a slightly later but even longer shovel board survives at **Tredegar House, Newport**, south Wales (*lower right*).

Made in c.1640 for **Cefn Mabli House**, which stood five miles away, and measuring 42' feet in length, it is all the more

extraordinary for being made from a single plank of oak, which may well make it the longest single planked oak table top in the world.

And yet according to Thomas Dineley, who visited in 1684, the plank from which it was made was originally 20' longer.

When Cefn Mabli was sold in 1924 the shovel board was moved to the stables at Tredegar House, where, during the Second World War its legs and frame were reportedly chopped up and used for firewood by American troops billeted at the house.

In 1951 the surviving top was then moved to the basement of Newport Civic Centre and all but forgotten until uncovered during

rebuilding work in 1987. Finally its significance was recognised, and after being restored and fitted with a new set of legs, it was returned to Tredegar House, where it can be seen today, in the Orangery.

As described by Strutt, the rules of shovel board were as follows.

There were two lines drawn across the width of the table; one about 3–4" from the end, the other at 4' nearer to the players' end.

Each player had four weights. Shoving a weight between the lines was worth one point, beyond the second line scored two, or three if the weight teetered on the far edge. If it dropped into the trough, no points were recorded. The first to eleven points was the winner.

A cross between shovel board and billiards, *jeu de fer* (literally 'game of iron') remains popular in Belgium, where every September the annual championships attract over two hundred players to the magnificent 17th century Halle-aux-Draps (or Cloth Hall) in Tournai. As can be seen, a cue is used to propel a puck-like brass disc, known as a *palet*, from one end of the 9' long table, towards copper pins at the far end, negotiating additional pins and a bridge *en route*, as they say. Just like early billiards in fact.

» Yet despite its presumed aristocratic pedigree, it was housed 'at a low public house in Benjamin Street, near Clerkenwell Green'.

No one plays shovel board in Britain today, not in pubs and certainly not on either of the tables that survive (*see previous page*).

Just across the water, however, near Abbeville in northern France, they play a game called *jeu d'assiette*, which is clearly a cut down version of the old game.

Having been played in that region from the 17th century until the 1960s, *jeu d'assiette* was revived so successfully during the 1980s that no village fête these days is complete without it.

The tables are around nine feet long, and each player has seven large wooden discs. Otherwise the rules are more or less the same as those of shovel board.

Another table-top game which blends elements of shovel board with those of early forms of billiards is *jeu de fer* (also known as *jeu de plomb* or *billard de fer*), tables for which can be found in cafés across Belgium, but particularly in Tournai, as shown on the left.

Shuffleboard

Confusingly there are three quite different games which go under the name of shuffleboard.

The first and perhaps best known was invented in the 19th century as a means of amusing passengers on board ocean liners.

One source credits this innovation to the recreation directors of the Peninsular and Oriental Line. However newsreel from 1902 shows passengers enjoying a similar game on board the SS Deutschland, owned by P&O's German rival, the Hamburg America Line.

Certainly the game varied from one shipping line to another, until in 1913 the rules were formalised on the dry land of Daytona Beach, Florida. At one point the St Petersburg Shuffleboard Club in Florida had 5,000 members and 110 courts. The national Shuffleboard Association was formed there in 1929.

This form of shuffleboard is played on a long court of either polished wood, concrete, or latterly, a synthetic track. Wooden discs are shoved, using a cue with a crutch-like end, into a numbered area. Each player has four discs, one set black, the other yellow. The game is usually 75 points up.

There have been recent attempts to import this game to Britain, using 'roll-out' courts of plastic or vinyl. But, as the organisers admit, any game that requires 40 feet of track is unlikely to catch on in pubs.

The second version of the game, seen recently in wine bars more than in pubs, is table shuffleboard.

Similar to the old shovel board, this form developed on the eastern seaboard of the USA and Canada in the late 19th century. Some hotels had five or six tables until Prohibition halted its progress.

It was then revived during the 1930s, and was later spread around north America by US troops who had learnt to play it in east coast bars while waiting to be shipped out to Europe during the Second World War.

The standard American or Canadian table shuffleboard used to be 32' long. Now it is 22', with three boxes at the end (rather than the four seen in British versions).

Texas is the hotspot, and apparently there is even a table on board a nuclear submarine, the USS Theodore Roosevelt.

The third form of shuffleboard, and the one most likely to be encountered in a British pub is also table-based, though strictly speaking, as shown opposite, it is really the Dutch game of *sjoelbak*, or *sjoeloen* (known in Germany as *Jakkolo* and in France as *billard Hollandais*).

Shove penny or ha'penny

While Henry VIII was losing money on shovel board, a miniaturised version, using coins on a small board, appears to have taken hold at the Inner Temple, where in 1521 trainee lawyers were castigated for spending more time on 'slype-groat' or 'shove-groat' than on their studies.

Those caught playing were fined a massive 6s 8d, and for anyone, let alone a student, that was a lot of groats (20 to be precise).

The game they were playing was the precursor of what we know today as either shove ha'penny or push penny.

Other names for it have included 'slide thrift' and, at the time of Joseph Strutt around 1801, for reasons unknown, 'Justice Jervis', or 'Jarvis'.

This game, sneered Strutt, was 'confined to common pot houses and only practised by such as frequent the taprooms'.

Strutt went on to describe a board of 3–4 feet long and 12–14 inches wide, divided latitudinally into nine equal partitions, or beds.

This, however, was not quite the same game that we would come to know in the 20th century.

'Each of the players provides himself with a smooth halfpenny, which he places on the edge of the table, and striking it with the palm of the hand, drives it towards the marks; and according to the value of the figure affixed to the partition wherein the halfpenny rests, his game is reckoned; which is generally stated at thirty one, and must be made precisely; if it be exceeded, the player goes again for nine, which also must be brought exactly, or the turn is forfeited".

Even more of a challenge was an ingenious adaptation of cribbage, played on a board with ten numbered beds.

They play this, wrote Strutt, 'with four halfpence, which are considered as equivalent to so many cards at cribbage; and the game is counted in a similar manner, by the 15s, sequences, pairs and pairials, according to the numbers appertaining to the partitions occupied by the halfpence.'

Nearly a century later, one James John Hissey came upon another game, clearly from the same family, in the course of a seemingly interminable ramble through the pubs of the eastern counties, which he described in 1917 in *The Road and the Inn* (*see Links*).

Though he failed to name the pub, Hissey at least described the game in detail.

It consisted of 'a long smooth board placed flat on a table, the board being marked on horizontal lines, some two inches apart, with figures at their ends.

'Each player, in turn, placed a penny at the foot of the board, which he struck with the palm of his hand, so that it slid towards the top, and the score was calculated from the figure at the end of the line where the coin stopped, he whose penny stopped by the highest figure being the winner.

'Two or more men played the game, and there was always the chance that later players might, as at bowls, for better or for worse, disturb the position of the pennies already on the board, or even »

▲ This form of table **shuffleboard,** seen at the **Louis Armstrong** pub in **Dover, Kent**, is more accurately the Dutch game of **sjoelbak**.

It is claimed that the game was played by Dutch fishermen as long ago as the 1660s, although it seems more likely to have evolved in the early 20th century.

Each player slides 30 wooden counters up the board, under a bar, towards a line of four slots, each of which (*right*) is marked by studs showing its points value of one, two, three or four. (In this respect sjoelbak resembles the lost games of trou madame, nine hole stones and bumble puppy, as featured on page 175).

Landing at least one counter into each of the four slots doubles the final score.

Since the first attempts to popularise the game in Britain began in the 1960s, finding tables of this sort is a fairly random business. But it is often seen played at beer festivals.

drive them off it, so that they did not score.

'I noticed that the game was in request for most of the evening. If there were only two players, then each player played six pennies each – one penny at a time in turns.'

Apart from the fact that Strutt's game was played with halfpennies and Hissey's with pennies, they are obviously similar, although still slightly different from what we know today as shove ha'penny or push penny.

The version we know today is essentially the product of the 1920s, when in common with darts and several other pub games, manufacturers took an interest (that is, saw the potential profits), and started producing standardised tables (*see opposite*).

One of the best sources for seeing how shove ha'penny is played is a four minute film clip recorded in the 1960s.

Available to view on the BBC's *Nation on Film* website (in the Wearside and County Durham section), the film shows men in an unidentified pub in Durham, playing what they called locally push ha'penny, and explaining the rules along the way.

For those who have never seen the game played, the clip is much recommended.

The basic procedure for this 20th century game is to propel the coins up the board with the heel of the hand. Each player has five coins and for every coin which ends up exactly in a bed, a chalk mark is made in the appropriate square. If the coin ends up touching a line, even by a whisker, it does not count.

Once a player has three coins in one bed – called a 'sergeant' in some areas – this is marked, and his opponent cannot trespass into that bed. The game is won by the player who wins the majority of the nine beds on his side of the board.

That said, local rules do vary. In Guernsey, for example, they insist on five coins in a bed – known as a 'sergeant major' or 'gold watch' – instead of three, in order for it to be marked.

In some pubs, if you fill a bed which is already yours, the point goes to your opponent.

In the 1970s, pub games historian Timothy Finn (*see Links*) noted a rather more sophisticated version of shove ha'penny, called 'progressive', played in Oxford.

In this version coins that scored were chalked, then retrieved and played again, so that it was possible to build up a break of most, if not all, of the 27 chalks needed for a game in one break.

Regrettably, since that game was recorded shove ha'penny has suffered an almost catastrophic decline in popularity, even if it is still touted here and there as a pubby tourist attraction in sentimental guide books.

In Oxford, for example, where in 1973 there were reportedly 28 teams playing in 25 pubs and clubs, the league appears to have disappeared.

In the spring of 2009, just as this book was going to press, news arrived that one other once-mighty league had given up the ghost, in Louth, Lincolnshire.

Formed in the 1930s, at its height in the 1950s this league had had two divisions. As one veteran player recalled, on Saturday nights you had to put your name down to get a game, whereas now none of the younger generation are interested.

Similarly in the city of Durham, once a hotbed of shove ha'penny with leagues and even its own 'world' championships, the game has ebbed away, although rumours persist that one or two landlords keep a board behind the bar for old times' sake.

Yet time was in Durham that if anyone so much as opened a door in mid-match or created a draught, thereby disturbing atmospheric conditions, they could expect a right earful.

And much worse besides if anyone dared touch the board with a finger made greasy from eating crisps, or spill beer on it, or »

▶ Pictured at the **Coors Museum of Brewing** at **Burton** (sadly now closed), this slate **shove ha'penny** board was made by a firm called Goddard & Sons, it is thought some time between the wars, and was designed to be screwed down to an ordinary table top.

As can be seen, its design was authorised by the Shove Ha'penny Control Association, an organisation of which nothing is known, but which may well have been set up by Goddards or a group of board manufacturers in order to regularise and popularise the game.

The board is divided, as are all boards, into nine beds, each measuring $1\frac{1}{4}$ inches deep, just enough to accommodate one half-penny (or a modern two pence piece, as shown here).

On either side of each bed is a space for marking the score, in chalk. The semi-circular ridge surrounding the beds is to stop coins from sliding off.

Experienced shove ha'penny players often debate the relative merits of different board surfaces, whether they be mahogany, teak, slate, or even marble or glass.

Equally, rival claims are made for various cleaning and polishing agents, such as petrol, paraffin, French chalk, black lead, powdered arrowroot and even beer.

But whatever the surface or method of cleaning, the rubbing down of the board seen repeatedly between shots is an important and time consuming part of the shove ha'penny ritual, with rival teams watching each other closely for any possible hint of chicanery.

Any slight mark or blemish may lead to an argument, which is also why some landlords keep their boards and old half-pennies under lock and key, only bringing them out for serious players.

▲ Three shove ha'penny boards whose varying designs show how hard it can be for visiting players to beat their hosts.

Above, at **The Cockpit** in **Blackfriars, London** is a hinged table that folds down against the wall when not in use and features metal strips between the beds. This is so that in the event of a dispute as to whether or not a ha'penny is on the line, the matter can be settled by lifting the strip via a handle at the side.

Another foldaway, but this time with a slate board in a wooden frame, is at **The Star**, in **Bath**, while **The Crown** at **Bedfield** in Suffolk (right) has a typical modern board that can sit on any table.

» perhaps 'accidentally' dampen the underside of a rival's coin. These were serious infractions that might easily lead to fights.

But if the game has all but disappeared in Durham, there are other pockets of England and Wales where shove ha'penny leagues still operate. These include Ryde, on the Isle of Wight, Barnstaple in Devon, Blandford in Dorset, Bath, Radstock, Chew Valley and Shepton Mallet in Somerset, and Newport in Gwent.

Between them, some of these leagues organise annual world championships; most recently at the Borough Arms, Barnstaple, in 2006, at the Bryanston Estate Club, Blandford, in 2007 (sponsored by the brewery Hall & Woodhouse), and at the Railway Hotel, Blandford, in 2008.

Push penny

This is an identical game to shove ha'penny, apart from the obvious fact that old pennies are used and therefore the beds are deeper.

Rarely, if ever, would you expect to find shove ha'penny and push penny in the same pub, although there is an intriguing old two-sided table at the Woolpack Inn at Brookland in Kent.

Nowadays, push penny is largely associated with Stamford in Lincolnshire, where, when last reported, the town's sole surviving winter league, which had 18 teams in two divisions as recently as the 1990s, had shrunk to seven teams from five pubs.

Each September the Stamford players also contest yet another 'world' championship, in which contestants from as far afield as Hastings and Margate (where there is said to be another small league in operation), have been known to compete.

Because no manufacturers have ever bothered with push penny, the tables used in Stamford are all made by local craftsmen, using whatever wood they can source. Discarded shop and bar counters in mahogany or oak are apparently ideal, as long as they are free of any cracks, joints or knots.

As a result, boards vary so much that teams playing away consider a draw to be a major achievement.

Some boards, for example, are slow and need a heavy hand to get the pennies into the far beds, while others only need the lightest touch. Hence solo matches and the world championships are played on neutral boards.

The care of each board is vital. Most are wrapped in felt covers, stored in a cool room and brought out only an hour before a match.

There is variation too in the pennies, but this is deliberate.

Three coins are used, usually classed as heavy, middling and light, so that, for example, a light one may be bounced back from a heavy one, while the heavy one can go 'through' a light one and push it further up the board.

Incidentally, although old pennies and halfpennies ceased to be legal tender in 1969 and 1971 respectively, they can still be bought, albeit at rather more than their original value. Those that might once have been used in pub games have little value, however, because their tails' sides will have been milled to provide a smooth surface. Why only the tails?

Because it has long been rumoured in pubs that to mill the heads' side, and therefore deface the monarch's likeness, would amount to a capital offence.

Suffice it to say that no such cases have ever been brought to court and no-one, as yet, executed.

▶ There is much about the **Isle of Purbeck**, once a remote part of Dorset cut off by tidal inlets, that makes it unique, and one of them is its shove ha'penny, or rather shove halfpenny, as known locally.

Regulars will tell you that the game was invented in the late 19th or early 20th century, by workers belonging to Purbeck's famous Company of Marblers and Stonecutters; formidable drinkers, it seems, who would happily spend their annual week's holiday in pubs, playing and betting on the game.

Purbeck boards are longer than usual, as here at the **Red Lion** in **Swanage**, at around 4' 6", and are marked not with beds but a target area. Table sizes vary, but this target area is always the same.

The four squares score from 1–4 (no need to mark which, the regulars know the values by heart). The centre circle scores five, the semi-circle nearest the player is worth 10 and the other 20.

The main game is 101 up, played over three legs and using wafer thin halfpennies from England, Ireland, Guernsey and Jersey, some dating from 1906 (a clue to the game's vintage perhaps). But be warned, if you allow one of these precious coins to get damaged, to make up for it you will be requested to put in a few hours of penitential coin rubbing on a piece of slate the next day.

In the 1970s some 15 pubs played the game. Now it is only a handful, their season running from October to March. But do not expect to see a table other than on Thursday match nights. The rest of the time they are kept out of sight, their polished surfaces lovingly preserved, until just before play, in time honoured fashion they are squirted with a soda siphon and rubbed down with a paper towel.

Chapter Eleven

Pitching and tossing

Part of the furniture – 'penny seats' or 'pitch penny' corners were once an integral part of the pub games repertoire in East Anglia. Today only one such seat is known to survive in the area, at the Grade II listed Cock Inn, in Brent Eleigh, Suffolk. Note how not only the lead surrounding the hole has taken a battering but so too has the woodwork and the paintwork behind.

Much of what we know about the gambling game of pitch and toss (or pitch and hustle, 'a game played in the fields by the lowest classes of people,' as Strutt called it), derives from reports of players being hauled up before the local magistrates.

Writing in July 1873 about the 'prevailing vice' of Dudley, a Northumbrian pit village, the *Newcastle Weekly Chronicle* set the tone. Pitch and toss, it noted, though hardly peculiar to Dudley, held such a grip on the locals that 'all attempts to dislodge it seem in vain'. Even on Sundays 'coins may be seen spinning aloft among the hedgerows to the accompaniment of "heads a croon", or "tails a shillin"...'

'To bet on the spinning of two pennies seems so ridiculously absurd that, making all due allowances for the passion of Englishmen to back their opinion, we cannot help wondering at the folly of men who are content to form an opinion and hazard money on the whirl of a coin.

'If the Northumberland pitman who gambles in this fashion has the money to spare and superfluous energy to work off, let him, in God's name, throw away this senseless amusement, and turn his energy into other channels. Let him play at ball, and at quoits, or cricket; let him row, or dance, or swim, or even back his opinion in these matters in his hours of leisure; but as a first step to nobler sports, let him abjure the stupid game of pitch and toss'.

Champion knur and spell player Selwyn Schofield remembered seeing his first game of pitch and toss in the backyard of a pub in the Calder Valley, West Yorkshire, during his childhood in the 1930s.

Wriggling his way between the legs of a circle of cloth-capped men, to his amazement he saw the floor covered in silver coins.

'All the money in the world was scattered on the ground,' he later told his mother breathlessly.

The school of pitch and toss that young Selwyn had come across was played with two coins, tossed simultaneously in the air from a small, flat piece of wood called a 'stick' or 'paddle'. If two tails came up, the banker lost. If two heads were up, or a head and a tail, the banker won.

But as ever, rules varied from region to region and from school to school.

Durham miners called the game the 'hoy', while the individual who ran the game was the 'hoyer' or 'chucker'. Scouts were posted to watch out for the police, who were known to stand by in plain clothes in order to nab participants.

Those caught were fined on a sliding scale, but after four or five court appearances miscreants could expect a 28 day jail sentence.

The Durham game was two heads for a win for the chucker. Two tails and the chucker lost. If a head and a tail, no-one won and the stake money stayed put.

Pretty much the same game was played by Australian troops during both World Wars, only the banker was called a 'boxer', and he used a 'kip' to flick up two or three coins.

In fact 'two-up' is still played in Australia, especially on Anzac Day, when the authorities turn a blind eye.

Back in Britain, in another variation of pitch and toss, a knife

If you can make one heap of all your winnings
And risk it on one turn of pitch-and-toss
And lose, and start again at your beginnings
And never breathe a word about your loss...

from *If*, by Rudyard Kipling (1865–1936)

or sliver of wood referred to as the 'mot' was stuck upright into a circle of clay. Each player pitched a penny from a distance of about ten yards, with the one whose coin landed closest to the mot being the winner.

He then gathered all the coins, lined them up on his forearm and tossed them into the air.

Any that landed heads up he kept. The remainder went to the player whose original pitch was second closest to the mot.

In some schools, the coins were tossed one at a time, with the thrower calling heads or tails.

In Hulme, Manchester, where the game was called 'Nudger', five coins were tossed from the dealer's forearm. (Nudger, incidentally, was the nickname also of the Golden Eagle, near Hulme, where prostitutes made their presence felt by nudging prospective clients.)

More often than not pitch and toss was played for stakes much higher than pennies, for the coins themselves were used merely like dice, with every toss being subject to bets and side bets. According to games historian RC Bell, who observed Scottish colliery workers playing in the 1950s, 'the fivers floated round like toilet paper'.

But not any more. Observers noted that the game petered out during the 1960s, almost certainly as a result of the legalisation of betting shops.

Instead, the forms of pitch and toss that survive in pubs today are games of skill rather than chance, and are not at all associated with gambling.

As detailed in this chapter they go under a variety of names, but each have in common the aim of landing a coin or similar object into a hole or target.

▲ Names such as pitch penny, the penny game, penny slot, tossing the penny and penny in the hole – all once common in East Anglia, Essex, Sussex and Kent – are pretty much self-explanatory.

But in the snug at the **Jackson Stops, Stretton**, in **Rutland** they call the same game **gnurdling**.

Why so? Possibly because it is one of those catch-all, ribald words that seems to fit a variety of 'traditional' games. The comic actor Kenneth Williams, for example, always described dwile flonking (*see page 166*) as 'nurdling', while in Dorset it applies to a game involving dustbin lids and poles.

That said, gnurdling in Stretton is clearly pitch penny in all but name.

The target is a 2¼ inch diameter hole cut into a settle with a drawer to catch the coins. As can be seen, the back of the settle is lined with lead, initially there to protect the furniture but in time offering players

a useful bouncing board to add an extra dimension to their game.

Rules state that each player has to pitch thirteen 'gnurdles', the number thrown in each subsequent round to be reduced by the number of gnurdles previously holed.

A similar set up can be seen in the tap room of the Morning Star, in Shaw, Lancashire, where the game was known as **leathers** because, instead of coins, the discs tossed were cut from redundant leather drive belts used in cotton mills.

Alas since regulars stopped playing the leathers have had to be hidden away to avoid theft.

Meanwhile no trace remains of a Yorkshire version of leathers. Known as **pitchin' in t'pot**, and briefly revived in the Huddersfield area during the 1990s, the target was a section of four inch diameter drainpipe, placed on a bench (*see opposite*) Apart from Brent Eleigh (*see opposite*) one of the last outposts

of East Anglian **pitch penny** was the Lifeboat Inn, Thornham, on the Norfolk coast. Known briefly as 'the Penny House' while the game last flourished there during the 1960s, it is now a gastro-pub.

Each player threw thirteen discs from a standing position with 'one foot in the fireplace'. Anyone managing to land all thirteen in the hole won a gallon of Scotch (a feat last recorded in the early 1950s).

Another former stronghold was The Fox, in Great Bradley, Suffolk (closed in 1986), where, according to the *Morning Advertiser,* landlord Nat Gooch was famed for once throwing three consecutive rounds of twelve – that is, 36 pennies pitched in the hole.

If true, the feat would have been remarkable enough. But Gooch was blind, having been injured by an exploding ginger beer bottle while on military duty in Ireland during the 1920s.

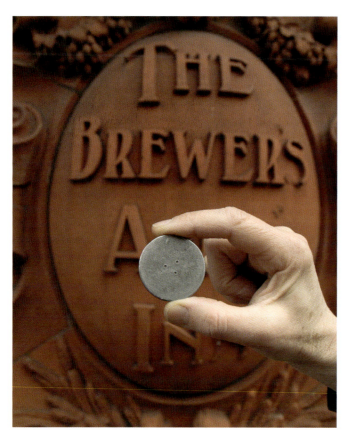

▲ Nowadays the **'toads'** used for toad in the hole are brass or steel discs, such as this one from the **Brewer's Arms** in **Lewes, East Sussex**. For obvious reasons these modern toads are virtually worthless. But their size and weight closely echo their predecessors, which in many pubs until the mid 20th century were genuine coins of the realm.

Mary Hufnet, whose family kept the Ram Inn at Firle, near Lewes (where toad in the hole is still played), from 1908 until the 1980s, recalled that the toads thrown there used to be William IV pennies, which may well offer a clue as to the game's origins.

Known as 'cartwheels', these and earlier issue pennies from the period 1797–1839 lost their value when the coinage was reformed in the early years of Victoria's reign.

Being both heavier and slightly larger than later Victorian pennies, cartwheels thus became highly prized for pub games, and their sheer ubiquity may even have been a catalyst for the spread of such games as toad in the hole.

Then, as the old pennies themselves became more collectable, pubs had to adopt substitutes. At the Ram Inn, as in many pubs, this meant using lead tokens, then brass, before the modern discs we see today.

Toad in the hole

The charming East Sussex town of Lewes is known for many attractions: its annual bonfire, its ancient castle and bowling green, its secondhand bookshops and, since 2008, its own currency (the Lewes pound).

Harveys, the distinguished local brewery, established in 1790, might also be known to readers.

But Lewes is also a veritable hotbed of pub games, of which, with respect to dwile flonking and pea throwing (*see page 132*), toad in the hole – a distinct East Sussex form of pitch penny – is by far the most popular.

As recently as the 1990s the game had all but died out, at least at a competitive level, although plenty of distinctive toad in the hole tables survived in local pubs, gathering dust under dartboards and in forgotten corners. (One pub turned theirs into a condiment table for the restaurant.)

But then came a remarkable revival. Initially this was due to the efforts of the Lewes Lions Club, who in 1983 were asked by the local Town Twinning Association to organise a toad in the hole evening for guests arriving from Blois in France and Waldshut-Tiengen in Germany.

Though a success (using tables borrowed from local pubs) the event was not followed up, until in 1995 the Lions were once again asked to organise a competition as part of the Lewes Spring Festival.

Repeated in 1996 and now grandly re-titled the World Toad-in-the-Hole Championships, the event was so successful that it has been an annual fixture (usually held every April) ever since.

Staged in the Corn Exchange at Lewes Town Hall, with a limit now set at 48 teams, each with four players, a taste of the event can be sampled on YouTube.

But toad in the hole is no mere once a year event.

Inspired by the Lions, and by another annual competition organised by the Lewes Arms (four times winners of the International Championships), the game is now regularly played in an estimated 35 pubs within a 15 mile radius of Lewes town centre.

In 2009 there were 18 teams in two divisions of the local league.

There is now also a European Masters event held at Christmas, with splendid toad trophies for gentlemen and ladies.

Meanwhile Lewes-based comedy writer and performer Ben Ward has created a toad in the hole website (*see Links*), where members of the public can order their very own newly built tables and find a list of pubs in East Sussex and Kent where functioning tables can be found.

▲ As seen here at the **Lewes Arms**, in 2002, the best spot for a **toad in the hole** table is under the dartboard. That way players can throw from the oche, roughly seven feet from the table, and use the blackboard for scoring (although cribbage boards are also used).

A game consists either of two single players, or of two teams of four, with each player throwing four toads (or discs) per turn.

Under Sussex rules, a toad in the hole scores two points. A toad that lands on the lead surface of the table scores one, provided it remains on the table after four toads have been thrown. Any toad that strikes the backboard cannot score, although it can influence play by knocking another toad either into the hole or off the table.

In some pubs, house rules used to dictate that a player getting four toads in the hole in one turn would win outright, but this is now rare.

Otherwise the game is 31 up and, as in darts, there are rules for finishing on the exact score.

Each game is the best of three.

At league level home advantage is all important, as each table is different. The one at the Lewes Arms, for example (*right*), had, in early 2009, distinct curls in the corners and a rise towards the hole, like a shallow volcano.

This is because after years of being peppered by toads, the lead slab distorts, becoming more brittle with each hit. For this reason the lead has to be melted down and remoulded every five years or so to restore its original, slightly cambered profile.

◄ When the International **Toad in the Hole** Championships in Lewes became established in the late 1990s one of the organisers' main priorities was to have made a set of standard tables so as to provide, almost literally, a level playing field for all entrants.

For as seen here, older pub tables vary considerably in terms of their height, angle and the undulations of the lead.

The main method for ensuring uniformity at the Championships is for the table tops to be formed by a block of wood, encased in lead sheeting, rather than the traditional method of using a solid lead block, which is more prone to warping and disintegration around the hole.

The Lewes Championships have therefore helped spark a revival in the manufacture of toad in the hole tables, with new models costing from around £160 each.

But for all the advantages of new tables, regular players still relish the idiosyncrasies of each pub table, at least until the lead distorts or breaks so much that scoring becomes too easy.

Seen here are tables from the **Brewer's Arms, Lewes** (*above left*) and **Red Lion, Snargate**, in Kent (*left*). The former tilts towards the thrower, the latter is cambered towards the centre, like a cushion.

Seen far right is a table formerly at the White Lion, Seaford, now in use at the **Black Horse, Lewes**. As its stamp shows, it is one of a dozen or so made in the late 1970s by Evan Williams and Andrew Bannister from nearby Barcombe.

Meanwhile, waiting to be melted down and remoulded is the Black Horse's former table top, held up by John Cooper (*above right*). As can be seen, in addition to the undulations, the actual hole has been worn away from years of use.

▶ Wildlife experts would argue that one should never mistake a toad for a frog. Similarly in the field of pub games, toads and frogs really are quite distinctive.

This splendid contraption, displayed in the **Brighton Museum and Art Gallery** is most definitely not a toad but a frog, and what is more, it is almost certainly of French origin.

In France such games are known either as *La Grenouille* (literally 'The Frog', though it can also be interpreted as 'the money box'), or *Le Tonneau* (meaning 'the cask').

Other 'frog' games around the world are known as *La Rana* in Spain (or *La Rada* in Catalan regions), and *Tonspel* in Belgium.

The latter is still played in Antwerp's oldest pub, the Quinten Matsijs, where the table is said to be at least 250 years old.

In each case, the tables have five holes or more, the centre one being covered by a brass frog (or toad in Portugal) with a gaping mouth pointing towards the player.

Many tables have in addition a festoon of obstacles, including flippers, deflectors and mill wheels, all of which make scoring more a matter of luck than judgement.

As each coin or disc is holed, it trundles down into an open, numbered compartment, rather like the end of a bar billiards table.

The score is then totted up on a chalkboard next to the table.

Apparently versions of *La Grenouille* were extremely popular in the bars and dance halls of Paris during the mid 19th century, when the frog in the centre was often replaced by a caricature of an unpopular politician's head – with gaping mouth, of course.

But examples may still be found in *estaminets* (or bars) on either side of the French/Flemish border,

so it is not at all surprising that one or two examples appear to have strayed across the Channel.

For example, Horsham Museum in Sussex has a frog game (albeit not currently on display) that is almost identical to the one at Brighton and is believed by the museum to have been played in the nearby village of Southwater.

Indeed this could well have been the very table that farmer and historian Aubrey Charman mentions in his history of Southwater (*see Links*), in which he recalled seeing what he described as a 'complicated' game with a table of five holes being played in Alfriston, east Sussex, in the 1920s.

Charman called it toad in the hole, but it sounds much more like *Tonspel*.

The British Travel and Holidays Association made a similar mistake in the 1950s when they produced a short film depicting traditional British games, such as lawn billiards (*see page 176*), Old English skittles (*page 54*) and what the commentator called toad in the hole, being played at the Bull Inn, West Clandon, in Surrey.

But again, the game shown in the film was most definitely a frog and not a toad.

Finally, returning to Brighton, the Booth Museum of Natural History has a famous exhibit that might well explain how the British game of toad in the hole came to get its name in the first place.

There, visible within a piece of flint discovered in 1898, is the fossilised head of a toad.

Whether a genuine fossil or not, it was a celebrated find at the time, and one which may well have led someone in East Sussex to re-evaluate the game of pitch penny he was playing, and as it were, to coin a phrase.

Chapter Twelve

Throwing and cobbing

World Championship pea throwing at the Lewes Arms in Lewes, East Sussex, in October 2007 – a competition started in 1999, like so many, following an argument in the pub. There are categories for men, women and under-14s, and contestants must throw only peas provided by the pub (after allegations of foul play involving nail varnish). As of 2008, the men's record stood at 38.7m.

One of mankind's oldest and most basic forms of sporting contest is the throwing of an object for distance.

The ancient Greeks threw the discus and the javelin. Londoners from at least the 12th century threw bars of wood and iron, an amusement also much favoured by Henry VIII. In the 18th century competing strong men threw stones and cricket balls at country fairs. Highland Scots took to tossing the caber, while of course modern athletes putt the shot.

But there is in Britain a fine tradition of throwing victuals and household items.

In the early 20th century dockers and market traders in Manchester competed by throwing potatoes over the Ship Canal. There are also claims, unverified, that the modern international sport of 'wellie-wanging' originated not in Australia but amongst Yorkshire farmers in the 1960s. Apparently a Dunlop size eight Challenger wellington boot is the preferred projectile of today's wellie wangers, the best of whom come not from Britain but from Finland. (To which it is also worth noting that the winner of the first ever mobile phone throwing world championships, held in 2008, was also Finnish, and, further, that he claimed to have honed his skills also by potato throwing.)

One recent tradition whose origins can be verified is the annual Stroud Brick and Rolling Pin Throwing contest. This began in 1960 and is held simultaneously in four towns called Stroud, in Gloucestershire, Oklahoma, Ontario and New South Wales. The men throws bricks, the women (since 1962) throw rolling pins, and the results in each town are then compared before the annual winners are announced.

Clog cobbing

Britain's oldest extant pub-based throwing competition would appear to be clog-cobbing, which has been staged in Rossendale, Lancashire since the 1960s.

The game was invented by the landlord of the Hargreaves Arms, Lumb, and originally involved throwing, or 'cobbing' in local dialect, a steel-capped, brass-studded monster of a clog, weighing over 2lbs, through one's legs, backwards.

No easy task, and one which made spectating a hazardous business.

Nowadays the clog is still thrown backwards, but over the shoulder, and the event has been

switched to the Roebuck Inn, Waterfoot. Held every Easter Monday, the current men's record stands at 93 feet, and there are contests also for women, boys and girls.

Black pudding throwing
Described in loftier academic circles as a symbolic re-enactment of the War of the Roses, black pudding throwing was dreamt up in the mid 1980s by the landlord of the Corner Pin, a pub in the hamlet of Stubbins, Lancashire, just outside Ramsbottom.

The original event took place in the Corner Pin's car park, where, high up on the wall of the pub, reached by a fire escape, a pile of Yorkshire puddings was set up on a platform as the target.

With one foot on a drain cover, each contestant had three Lancashire black puddings to throw, the aim being to dislodge as many of the Yorkshire puddings as possible.

Much to the chagrin of locals, in 2001 the Corner Pin was turned into a private home.

But the contest would not die, and now, on every second Sunday in September a 'golden grid' (in truth a drain cover painted yellow) is borne with immense pomp and ceremony (recently with a miliary escort), via an East Lancashire Railway steam train to the competition's new home at the Royal Oak in Ramsbottom.

Entrants pay £1 for three black puddings, each a comfortable handful weighing 6oz and supplied by Chadwicks, a firm that has run a black pudding stall on Bury Market for over 70 years.

To prevent seepage on impact with the road below, or on the heads of photographers – always a treasured moment – each pudding

is wrapped in mesh taken from ladies' tights. Typically, a winning shot will dislodge maybe three or four Yorkshire puddings at most.

Some local black pudding manufacturers remain critical of the event, considering it to be demeaning to black puddings and a waste of good food.

For their part the organisers point to the large sums of

money raised for charity, to the annual boost brought to the local economy, and also to the worldwide television coverage that the contest now regularly attracts.

It might also be added that very few visitors to the event can resist trying some black pudding for themselves. Best accompanied by mustard, ask for 'puddings with fat' if tempted yourself.

Lancashire faces Yorkshire at the Black Pudding Throwing Championships on Bridge Street, Ramsbottom, in September 2008. As seen opposite, the Yorkshire puddings are placed on two platforms, the lower one being for women and children. Note also that each contestant must have one foot placed on the 'golden grid'.

Chapter Thirteen

Twisting and spinning

Thought to date from the early 20th century, this painted wheel is held by the Gressenhall Farm and Workhouse museum of rural life in Dereham, Norfolk. Retrieved from the former Red Lion, Banham, it is one of a type known variously as a twizzler, twister, or Norfolk wheel. Further north on the coast and still in situ with its central spinner intact, is the 'village roulette' wheel at the Three Horseshoes, Warham (*below right*), claimed to date from c.1830. There are also twisters at the aptly named Wheel of Fortune, Alpington and The Feathers, Aylsham, both in Norfolk, and at the Sorrel Horse Inn, Shottisham in Suffolk.

Not everyone has the bottle or the nous to stake money on, say, a round of cribbage or a game of poker dice.

Whereas, rather like entering a sweepstake, anyone with a fancy for a flutter can place bets on the twist of a wheel or the spin of a top.

According to James Masters' excellent website on traditional games (*see Links*), the most popular of all spinning games, *roulette* (or 'little wheel'), emerged in France in the early 18th century and arrived in Britain soon afterwards, where it seems to have become known as roly poly (not to be confused with the skittles variety, rolly-polly, *see page 42*).

At least that would seem to be the inference of an Act of Parliament of 1744–45, which banned the setting up of gambling dens for the playing of, not only cards and dice but also 'a certain pernicious game, called Roulet, or Roly-Poly...'

But while roulette (and another early form of it called Even-Odd) caught on in gentlemen's clubs and in the homes of the rich, in pubs a simpler form emerged.

Twister
Cheap to make, from wood and iron, and simple to understand, twister can be played for high stakes or low stakes, for a round of beer or simply for points.

To which we must add that, strictly speaking, it has long been illegal to bet on games of chance in a pub, which perhaps explains why twister appears to have survived only in rural backwaters.

On the other hand, pub games historian Timothy Finn (*see Links*), stated that twister was once common in pubs on busy turnpikes and in country towns, where the spin of its pointer offered the chance for a simple wager at the end of a busy day at the market.

From Norfolk there are tales of farmers gambling away sacks of potatoes, even cattle, as well as money, and of one inebriated carter who lost first his horse, then his cart and finally his load before making a sorrowful retreat.

It is also said that when the fishing fleet came in to Lowestoft, all the play in nearby pubs was for fish filched from the docks.

Finn believed that, as well as East Anglia, twisters had been known in Essex, Hertfordshire and Buckinghamshire, but did not name specific locations.

To this list we can add a sighting at The Woolpack Inn, at Brookland, on Romney Marsh in Kent, where the twister is called a 'spinning jenny'. Locals reckon that smugglers, having dodged the excise men, used to spin the wheel in order to determine how they would divide up their spoils.

In 2005, a ten segmented twister was also identified at the Selsey Arms, Coolham, in West Sussex.

Folk memory in the village having apparently faded, neither the Selsey's landlord nor older customers knew the purpose of the wheel, until, through the columns of the Pub History Society's newsletter, games historian Patrick Chaplin was able to solve the mystery, and beg the pub to keep its twister turning.

Which suggests that there may be many more twisters out there, unidentified and puzzled over.

The Norfolk twisters shown on this page, it will be noted,

have twelve numbered segments, whereas the one illustrated below at the Alby Horseshoes Inn, Erpingham, has 20.

Ten of these are numbered. The other ten are marked with a club, diamond, heart and spade, a glass of wine, a pint of beer, a barrel, a horseshoe and, mysteriously (at least as far as the current landlady and her regulars are concerned), a box of matches and a pipe.

Apparently a similar design was produced commercially in the 1970s, and in a pub where one of these is still in use – a pub that understandably prefers to remain anonymous – the game is as follows.

Every player puts a sum into a kitty. If ten people are playing, the game is 51 up. If five, it is 101 up.

Each player in turn scores whichever number the pointer points to after it has been spun.

If it lands on a playing card symbol this means missing a go.

One of the drinks symbols means that that drink, paid for out of the kitty, must be drunk before the player's next go if he wishes to stay in the game.

The winner takes whatever is left in the jar.

Spinning games

Apart from a spinning wheel, or for that matter a coin or a set of dice, one of the simplest and most ancient devices used in gambling games is the spinning top, in which a four or six sided piece of card or wood is twirled with a forefinger and thumb on a central spindle.

In 18th century Britain such tops were known as a totum, a T-totum, or Teetotum. A typical version would have four sides; one marked respectively with a P for 'put down' (which required the player to put down the equivalent of his original stake), T for 'take all' (allowing the player to take the entire pot), H for 'half' (take half the pot), and N for 'nothing (meaning that you put in nothing but win nothing).

In the *Oxford History of Board Games* historian David Parlett refers also to versions with different initials, such as J for *jocque* (the equivalent of the English 'put down'), either P for *piller* or F for *fors* (the equivalent of 'take all') and either R for *rien* of N for *nada* (both meaning nothing).

In his *Book of Games*, written in the 1660s, Francis Willughby

describes a similar game called Long Laurence. This was 'a long parrallelopipedon,' or length of square wood with a different mark on each of its four faces.

'Everie one of the plaiers stakes one at first and then they throw the Long Laurence by turnes as a die.'

The face with one scratch meant that the player picked up one (that is, his original stake). Two scratches meant the player picked up two. The third side was marked 'soope all', meaning take all, and the fourth was blank, meaning 'neither take up nor lay downe'.

Put and take

Supposedly based on a prototype made from a spent cartridge case by a First World War soldier, put and take is a modern version of Long Laurence.

The six sides are marked Put One, Put Two, All Put, Take One, Take Two and Take All.

In the 1920s commercially produced pieces sold in huge numbers. In the USA it was briefly second to poker in popularity, while according to Robert Graves' social history of the inter-war years, *The Long Weekend*, put and take became all the rage in fashionable London in 1922, spreading to pubs and clubs all over Britain.

And because it was easy to slip the piece into a pocket at a moment's notice (the 1930s one shown above measures a mere 30mm in length), it was a hard game for the police to detect.

Put and take pieces are still made today, and still played with, discreetly in pubs. Vintage pieces are highly collectable too.

To avoid accusations of foul play and to allow all players to follow the game, twisters are usually attached to a ceiling, as at the Alby Horseshoes Inn, Erpingham, Norfolk (*left*). By contrast, one reason why the game of 'put and take' fell out of favour is that the pieces were easier to tamper with. Seen above is a six-sided brass put and take from the 1920s.

Chapter Fourteen

Table football

Britain's oldest table football game still in public use is this 1955 Sokaball model, at the Peveril of the Peak, Manchester. When the spread of pool forced the Salford-based Sokaball to shut in 1975, ex-employee Bill Rush promised the Peveril's landlady, Nancy Swanick, that if she kept the table he would service it. Which he has done ever since. Of 116 Sokaball tables built, just three survive; this one, another in a private house in France, and one recently restored by Bill for use in a Stockport club.

As played on occasionally by Eric Cantona during his spell at Old Trafford – 'babyfoot' being a Gallic speciality – the Sokaball table at the Peveril of the Peak is open topped, with a red dial to keep the score. The choice of red and blue for the teams has nothing to do with Manchester but is a convention that most table footballs follow, old and new.

The British have invented so many sports and games that it was no surprise when, in the 1990s, table football enthusiast Tim Baber discovered that the first patent for his favourite game appeared to have originated also in this country.

Another first for the Brits!

In fact Baber found several patents for table-based football games dated prior to 1914, including one for blow football in 1890. But the earliest that was clearly for bar, or table football as we know it today, dated from 1922.

And who was the inventor of this magical new game that would ultimately sweep Europe and North America? A young surveyor called Harold Thornton, from Crouch End in London.

In 2002, another table football enthusiast, international player and, by chance, a Crouch End resident himself, Dave Ziemann, received a letter from Thornton's nephew, Denis, recalling how the game had been invented.

An avid Spurs fan, Thornton had apparently been on his way back from White Hart Lane one cold Saturday afternoon in 1920 when he turned to his brother (Denis's father), and said that there really ought to be a realistic indoor football game that could be played in any ordinary home.

Harold, wrote Denis, 'pondered the idea for a while then, when taking a box of matches to light a cigarette, he suddenly had a brain wave. By placing the matches across the open box and then attaching the men to the sticks he had the basic idea.'

Two years later Harold's uncle, Louis Thornton, took out a similar patent in the USA, where he lived, his only refinements being that the bars were inserted through holes in the sides of the table (rather than being fixed to the top of the table surrounds), and the players lined up 1–2–5–3, rather than the 1–2–3–5 formation favoured by Harold (and by British soccer teams generally at this time).

But, if either Harold or Louis did ever manage to get their tables into production, none has ever been found. Meanwhile, in the USA and Europe other entrepreneurs launched their own designs, so that when Tim Baber started his research, he came across rival claims from the French, Germans, Italians and Spanish that they, and not the British, had invented table football.

The French, for example, attributed its invention to a well known automobile engineer, Lucien Rosengart in the 1920s.

Then in 2000 a new piece of evidence came to light.

On display at an exhibition in Oberhausen, Germany, there appeared a five-a-side table-top game, with three rotating bars per player. Belonging to the Deutsches Spielemuseum in Chemnitz, the game was made by a French firm, Breve Simon, and dated not from the 1920s but from 1903.

Since that exhibition, an American table football player Kathy Brainard, who has written extensively on the history of the game (see Links) has confirmed her belief that the Breve Simon table is the oldest in the world, predating Thornton's patent by 20 years.

So, not a British invention at all.

Not only that but none of the British firms that did eventually go into production after the Second World War – making the coin-operated tables that would become familiar fixtures at pubs, clubs and student unions from the 1950s onwards – have survived.

Britain's first brand name table, called Sokit, was made by PIP Ltd of Llandudno in the 1940s and '50s. The National Football Museum in Preston has a fine one, alas not on public display.

PIP's rivals were Lilliput of Northampton, who started production in 1947, and Sokaball of Salford (see opposite), formed a few years later.

But although their tables lived on, none of these makers survived beyond the 1970s.

Instead, companies such as Bonzini, from France, Garlando (Italy), Kicker (Switzerland) and Tornado (USA), came to dominate the world market.

And it is the American name for table football, 'foosball' (from the German fussball) that is now used most widely.

As for the game in Britain, apart from a thriving pub league in the Manchester area during the 1950s and 1960s, a British Table Soccer Association was formed in 1972, but disbanded a decade later.

In contrast, on the Continent the French and Belgians were the first to organise leagues in the 1950s, and in the USA, where there are now nearly two million players, big prize money has raised the game to a professional standing.

According to the International Table Soccer Federation, formed in France in 2002, the top three ranking nations in 2009 are Germany, the USA and the Czech Republic, while in the open singles championships, a Belgian, Frédéric Collignon, has dominated since around 2003.

Under the auspices of the British Foosball Association (see Links) Britain's foosballers have fought back, however. And although it is true that on the pub scene, table football has drifted in and out of fashion, Bristolian Joe Hamilton, who won the world doubles title in France in 2009, still plays at the Crown in Keynsham and the Bush in Totterdown, while his partner Robert Atha, ranked four in the world, is based at the Rainbow Snooker Club in Manchester.

Other leading players have graduated from clubs at Warwick, Oxford and Cambridge universities; the college sector being stronger than ever.

So we may not have invented the game, and we may no longer make the tables. But like darts and pool, table football is still a game that you can pick up in your local, and then go on to conquer the world.

▲ A typical glass-topped, coin-operated **Garlando** table, in play at the **Crown and Sceptre** in London's **Shepherd's Bush** (top), and (below), open topped, free play Garlandos set up for a tournament at the **Holywell Inn, Hinckley**, in June 2008.

To committed foosballers, the make of the table is crucial, each having its own characteristics.

Italian-made Garlandos have a fast, smooth playing surface. French Bonzinis (best sampled at Bar Kick in Shoreditch, London, where there are ten) have a linoleum surface which offers more grip, while the US Tornados have players with wedged feet in a 3–2–5–3 line-up.

Every individual has his or her favourite, but to succeed, a top player must master them all.

Chapter Fifteen

Rifle shooting

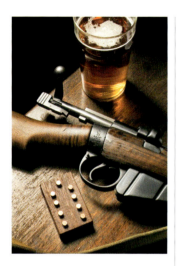

Beer and bullets – a 1918 vintage BSA small bore rifle and a 'block' of .22 cartridges lie primed for action at the Grade II listed Lamb Inn, Devizes, one of three pubs hosting teams in the Devizes and District Miniature Rifle League, Wiltshire. Formed in 1906 by a staff sergeant in the Royal Army Medical Corps, the league was one of many set up in response to the poor marksmanship of British troops during the Boer War.

Martin Parry takes aim with his German .177 Weihrauch air rifle, at the Live and Let Live in Whitbourne, Worcestershire. The pub's team is one of ten in membership of the Lord Ednam Air Rifle League, also set up after the Boer War.

The very idea seems outlandish, does it not? You wander into a pub for a quiet pint one evening and there in the bar, bold as brass, stands a chap with a rifle. And, what is more, it is loaded.

Yet no-one is running for cover or calling the police, and the bar staff seem quite happy to serve the shooter and his mates, several of whom also have rifles at the ready.

Rifle shooting as a sport started in the 1860s under the auspices of the National Rifle Association – established in response to the threat of a French invasion – then gained further support during the 1870s from volunteer regiments formed to counter the perceived threat of Prussian militarism.

But it was the inadequacies of British riflemen in the Boer War that led to it becoming a working men's sport, with Birmingham as its epicentre, for one simple reason. By the 1870s there were over 300 gun makers in the city, the largest of which, the Birmingham Small Arms Company, was, despite the Boer War, suffering from a downturn in orders (hence it successfully branched out into making bicycles and motorcycles).

So when various military leaders, supported by the likes of Robert Baden-Powell (founder of the Boy Scout movement) started to agitate for more shooting practice among civilians, BSA was only too happy to offer support by manufacturing cheap, small-bore air rifles for general sale.

Within a few years over 4,000 clubs had formed, 1,600 of them in Birmingham and, much to the alarm of the local authorities, many of them were based in pubs.

In 1905, therefore, Birmingham magistrates decided to withhold licences from any participating pubs, claiming, without a shred of evidence, that such events led to drunkenness and gambling.

What happened next was unprecedented in the history of pub games. Virtually half the adult male population of the city, 47,000 people, signed a petition, while an estimated 10,000 sober and scrubbed-up air-gunners protested outside the Town Hall.

They won their case too, so that shooting continued to flourish in Birmingham, and in leagues all over England and Wales.

Black Country enthusiast Frank Spittle (*see Links*) has written perhaps the fullest account of this unlikely pub activity.

'Space would be limited, so in order to accommodate as many people as possible, the shooter would in many instances shoot over the heads of several tables of spectators in front of him.

'The beer would be quietly passed from the bar counter along the tables and benches lining the walls, as movement could put the shooter off his aim. This was not only frowned on by the visiting team, but by the home side also.

'Anyone with a persistent cough could be asked to leave or move to another part of the premises...'

Pub riflemen had to contend with quite different conditions to those of an ordinary range.

'By now, of course, the room would have a fug in it that would kill a dog. There was the warmth of the fire and close proximity of bodies that had laboured all day without the benefit of showers, anti-perspirants and toiletries...

'Then there was the most evil of all, "twist", a dark round ring of compressed tobacco that was hand rubbed to feed those many personal furnaces of meerschaum and clay pipes...

'Smoke poured forth.'

But at least everyone knew when a bull had been scored, for the targets were fitted with a bell, which sounded out whenever a pellet entered a tiny hole in the centre. The remaining target area, meanwhile, was coated in white, non-drying paint, so that each shot could be scored according to how close it came to the bull. After each player's six shots had been totted up, a new coat of paint was applied, ready for the next man.

Today several miniature rifle leagues with pub teams survive, in Swindon and Devizes (*see right*), in Newport, south Wales, in Hinckley and Nuneaton, and in Worcestershire, where the ten team league was set up by Lord Ednam of Witley Court, who was not only a friend of Baden Powell but also a shareholder in BSA.

The Ednam league still has bell targets, and uses a special non-drying mix of oil-based undercoat and engine oil to repaint the target's surface after each round.

Pubs where matches take place, from October to March, are the Live and Let Live in Whitbourne, the Rose and Crown at Shrawley, the Fox at Monkwood Green, and the Cross Keys at Menith Wood.

▲ Whereas in other leagues shooting takes place in open bar areas, or occasionally skittle alleys, in the **Devizes and District Miniature Rifle League** the custom is to shoot down specially made tubes, such as here at the Grade II listed **Lamb Inn**, in **Devizes**.

Accessed from a hole in the wall and running 37 feet down the length of the building, the steel-lined tube was installed in 1939. Alas an intricate pulley system in which a brush with non-drying white paint was activated from the bar in order to coat the target in between rounds no longer works, and paper targets are used instead.

There are ten teams in the league (including the George and Dragon at Potterne and the King's Arms at All Cannings), each having their own arsenal of assorted guns. The New Inn team, for example, use an 1888 .22 Lee-Metford while the Conservative Club has an 1874 .22 Martini-Henry (both made in Enfield). Most modern rifles are German or Chinese.

Miniature rifles acquired for use on ranges do not need licences, but nevertheless all guns and club members are tightly regulated.

Chapter Sixteen

Racing

Why are these lads hauling a beer barrel a mile and a half up a Northumberland hill on Easter Monday in 2008? Because in 1970 a regular at The Feathers in Hedley-on-the-Hill thought it would be a good idea. Only three people took up the challenge, but numbers have grown to over 60 since, and the race now forms part of an annual beer and food festival. Another reason these lads might have been tempted is that though their barrel is empty, the victors win one that is full.

As readers will now be well aware, pub games answer a number of basic human needs, of which the instinct for 'play' forms only one small part.

In the chapters that follow we look at pub games that exercise the mind. But in this chapter we look at games, or rather events, which, to borrow a phrase from that long running Heineken advertising campaign of the late 20th century, refresh the parts that other pub games fail to reach.

These are games that exercise the body, and above all, the imagination.

Most originated in that most fertile of forums, the saloon bar.

A group of sages, suitably fortified, gathers around a table, one thing leads to another, and before anyone quite realises the full implications, a challenge has been issued. A gauntlet has been thrown down.

Such has been the genesis of a legion of pub games and activities over the years; signed and sealed over a pint, before the absurdity of the notion can reveal itself in the dregs at the bottom of the glass.

No doubt that for every challenge issued and accepted, only a fraction ever come to fruition. But for those that do, and for those that attract enough willing victims, it takes only a decade or so before a madcap idea has matured into a 'tradition', and before much longer, a 'tradition' whose origins have been miraculously traced back hundreds of years to some long forgotten local custom.

Such invention is of course nothing new. Pub games have been sustained by flights of historical fancy for generations.

Which is why, however modern most of the events in this chapter may be, they are in truth part of a seamless continuum; the British tradition for tradition, as it were, bound by characteristics that have changed little over the last century.

Firstly, they invariably start and end either at, or near a pub.

Secondly, they are necessarily arduous, if not actually bordering upon the sadistic.

Thirdly, it appears to be incumbent upon a large number of participants to turn out in fancy

dress. Men dress as women, or increasingly, as babies in nappies (a propensity we will leave others to analyse). Women dress as nurses, or tarts (ditto). Urbanites transform themselves into rustic simpletons, and farmers don the costumes of superheroes.

Thousands of pounds will be raised for charities. Organisers will pray for sunshine, but fully expect rain.

And all will require participants to hump some heavy local commodity in a barrel or a sack, or push some object – a wheelbarrow, a pram or a wheelie bin – across a fearsome terrain or up a thigh-sapping hill – for the simple reason that someone slumped in a pub one evening thought that such a challenge might be fun.

Naturally only a few of the participants will even think of victory, or of breaking records.

For races that were conceived in pubs do not call out to athletes.

Instead, they call out to the brave, and to all those for whom it is not the winning that counts, but the pint of beer that awaits at the finishing line.

▶ Racing with **beer barrels** has been an international sport since the 1990s, with events taking place amongst bourbon distillers in Kentucky and brewers in Czechoslovakia.

In Britain the tradition goes back to 1933, when teams from various breweries in Burton-upon-Trent first competed, two per team, rolling a 36 gallon barrel through the town with the aid of sticks.

As the race evolved, non-brewery entrants and women were invited to join in. Teams grew to six a side, and before the race petered out in the 1990s the record over a mile stood at 8 minutes 7.2 seconds.

Compared with the **Great Kinder Beer Barrel Challenge**, across Kinder Scout in Derbyshire, however, the Burton event was a mere stroll in the park.

The challenge originated, it is said, one day in January 1998, when the **Old Nag's Head** in **Edale** ran out of shepherd Geoff Townsend's favourite brew. Half jokingly Townsend offered to nip out and fetch a barrel from the **Snake Pass Inn**, a pub 17½ miles away by road but a mere 4½ miles as the crow flies, albeit across some of the most rugged moorland in the High Peak district.

Half jokingly in return, the landlord told Townsend that if he could manage that then he was welcome to drink the entire contents of the nine gallon barrel.

The rest you can guess. Using a stretcher borrowed from the local mountain rescue team and with the help of a dozen mates, Townsend brought home the beer. The landlord kept his word, let the barrel bearers drink its contents on the house, and this fearsome challenge has since been issued by the Old Nag's Head every September since.

Teams are restricted to eight members, and can choose any cross country route they fancy from the Snake Pass Inn.

But what they cannot avoid are gruelling climbs and steep, dizzying descents of some 900 feet.

Not surprisingly fell runners dominate, and as shown here in 2008 – demonstrated along one of the easier moorland stretches by the **Fat Boys Running Club** (based at the Scotsmans Pack pub in Hathersage) – ladders are the most common method of transportation.

From a record entry of eleven teams in 2008, the winning time was a staggering 48 minutes and four seconds, a time that would delight most walkers, even without the burden of bearing a barrel full of water weighing some 44kg.

▲ Writing on wheelbarrow racing in 1801, Joseph Strutt noted how 'the windings and wonderings of these droll knights-errant… produce much merriment.' Largely that was because in Strutt's day entrants wore blindfolds, whereas it is the donning of fancy dress, the extravagant decking of wheelbarrows and the consumption of half a pint at every pub passed *en route* that encumbers most modern day participants.

In Wiltshire the **Wheelbeero Race** (*above*) has formed part of the Pewsey Festival since 1980. But in Ponteland, Northumberland, where the New Year's wheelbarrow race is said to honour an early 14th century tradition of winter foraging, there is no stopping until the finishing line, where a silver salver, hot drinks and bacon sandwiches await at the Blackbird Inn.

Other pub-inspired races include the Wheelie Bin Grand Prix, held every July at the Three Horseshoes in Hernhill, Kent, Boxing Day pram racing at Windlesham, Surrey, and lawnmower racing at the Cricketers Arms, Wisborough Green in West Sussex. And yes, they do remove the blades before racing.

▶ Local produce and the humping thereof has inspired many a race.

For example, **Tetbury** in **Gloucestershire** was once the centre of a thriving wool and yarn market, before brewing took over in the 19th century. Hence in 1973 there was revived a race said to have been first run between sheep drovers in the 17th century.

Held on Bank Holiday Monday each May and starting by the **Royal Oak**, at the foot of Gumstool Hill, entrants carry a woolsack (weighing 60lb for men, 35lb for women) up a fierce one in four gradient, 240 yards long, to the **Crown Inn**.

The current individual record stands at just under 46 seconds, achieved in 2007.

In a similar vein is the **Oxenhope Straw Race**, held each July in **West Yorkshire** (*below right*). This started in the mid 1970s as a bet between two men as to who could carry a bale of straw the quickest between all five of the local pubs. Starting at the **Waggon & Horses**, and requiring pairs of runners to each down a pint (or a half pint for women) at all five pubs en route (now four since one closed), the race finishes at the **Dog & Gun**.

Top straw dogs have been known to complete the 2½ mile long course in 16 minutes, but others, preferring to take their time and show off their fancy dress, can take as long as two hours.

To date the event has raised over £300,000 for charity.

Another bet in a pub, this time at the **Beehive** in **Gawthorpe, West Yorkshire**, in 1963, led to the annual **Easter Monday World Coal Carrying Championships** (*far right*).

This requires entrants to hump a 1cwt bag of coal for just under a mile, uphill between the **Royal Oak** and the village maypole. The current record is just over 4 minutes.

▲ In June 1980 two drinkers in the **Neuadd Arms** in **Llanwrtyd Wells, Powys**, were arguing over whether men made better athletes than horses. Overhearing this, the landlord Gordon Green decided to settle the argument.

The result, the annual **Man v. Horse Marathon**, a three stage relay held each June along a 22 mile cross country course.

Although apparently some years it had been a close run thing, by 2003 the results read Horses 24, Men 0. Then in 2004 a south London marathon runner, Huw Webb, struck back for mankind, beating the fastest horse by just over two minutes, and scooping in the process £25,000 (being £1,000 for every year the prize money had accumulated).

For his part, Gordon Green has gone on to follow a long and proud line of publican-turned-promoter by launching a series of ever more innovative events in and around **Llanwrtyd Wells.**

These include mountain bike rides, chariot races, rambles, beer festivals and the now famous World Bog Snorkelling Championships, launched by Green in 1985 and, so far, not won by a single horse.

▲ **Ferret racing**, seen here at the **Famous Ale House** in **Swindon** in May 2007, is just one of many unpredictable forms of animal racing staged at pubs over the years. Some of the little critters took 15 minutes to scuttle along the 10m long runs of water jumps, bridges and see-saws, while others whipped through in seconds. But with bets being taken at 20p a time, no-one seemed too fussed.

Racing animals in pubs has not always been the highly regulated sport it is today. In 1938 a priest complained to *The Times* that pubs in Weymouth were staging tortoise races on their billiard tables, with toy jockeys strapped on their backs.

In the 1970s a Bishop Auckland pub planned to stage a mouse derby. Unfortunately all 18 runners were stabled together before the race, resulting in 15 pregnancies and three overtired males.

At the Barley Mow, Bonsall, in Derbyshire, hen races have been run every August since 1992, while further down the pecking order, as it were, woodlice racing has been a draw at the Mount in Stanton, Gloucestershire, for almost 20 years.

Some of the original contestants may even have finished by now.

Sightings elsewhere include maggot racing (at the Ashton Arms, Oldham, where owners are now barred from warming up their maggots under their tongues), and snail racing at Congham in Norfolk, where each race starts with the order, 'Ready, steady, slow!'

Chapter Seventeen

Dominoes

Originally the term for a long hood worn by medieval church canons, the word *domino* later came to denote the black cloak worn to conceal the wearer's identity at Venetian masquerades. Concealment being a vital part of dominoes, this explanation for the name's origin is often put forward. But it might equally derive from the Latin *dominus*, meaning master, or possessor.

One of the most reassuring sounds to be heard in a British pub is the soothing rattle and clatter of dominoes being shuffled on a table.

Along with darts and cribbage, dominoes seems as British as a pint of bitter and a packet of pork scratchings.

Yet the game is most definitely a foreign import.

The American ethnographer Stewart Culin, whose work in the late 19th century brought added respectability to the study of games, concluded that the earliest form of dominoes surfaced at least a thousand years ago in China.

Other sources go further back to China in the 12th century BC.

Apparently the earliest Chinese sets had 21 pieces and began with a double one, compared with the now familiar 28 piece sets starting with double zero that evolved, it is thought in Italy, in the 18th century.

Writing in the midst of the Napoleonic Wars in 1801, Joseph Strutt (*see* Links) was scathing in his description of the game.

Domino (note the singular), he wrote, 'is a very childish sport, imported from France a few years back, and could have nothing but the novelty to recommend it to the notice of grown persons in this country.'

Strutt went on to describe what is known as the 'block game' played with a set of 28 pieces, (which, he wrote, 'the players ridiculously call cards'), going up from double zero to double six.

This, almost certainly, was the most common form of dominoes played for money in pubs at the time. The aim was simply to get rid of all your dominoes as soon as possible, while trying to hinder your opponent by leaving him 'blocked' – that is, unable to fit a domino of his own on either end of the play.

If Strutt was correct in asserting in 1801 that dominoes had arrived from France 'a few years back', the French definitely had a hand in helping it to spread further.

Between 1793 and the Battle of Waterloo in 1815, some 200,000 soldiers serving with Napoleon's forces were transported to Britain as prisoners of war, including around 10,000 French and Dutch troops who ended up at a huge, 22 acre camp built at Norman Cross, Peterborough, in 1797.

To stifle their boredom, many of the inmates took to intricate craftwork, using wood, straw and bones left over from the camp kitchens to make miniature ships, dice boxes, ornaments and toys, as well as gaming chips, playing cards, cribbage boards and, as seen opposite, sets of dominoes.

Many of these objects were then sold from a stall outside the prison gates, partly to help supplement the inmates' meagre rations, but also to provide funds for gambling.

One of the conduits for this trade was a Mr William Powell. At the Old Bailey in December 1801 Powell claimed that while staying at the Green Dragon in Highgate, someone had stolen several boxes of dominoes from him, all recently purchased from French prisoners at Norman Cross.

He had been selling them on for three shillings a box, suggesting that this was a lucrative trade.

By the end of the 19th century dominoes had not only become »

Bones to pick – these dominoes form part of a collection of objects crafted by French prisoners at Norman Cross and held by Peterborough Museum. As well as 'bones', domino pieces have also been called 'stones', 'cards' and most commonly 'tiles'. Note that these 'bones' go up to double nine, and therefore a full set would total 55 pieces.

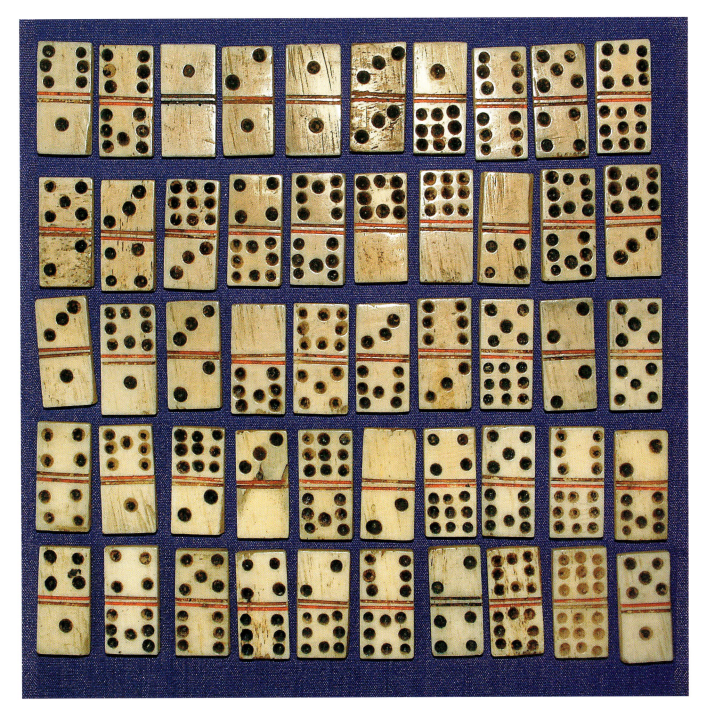

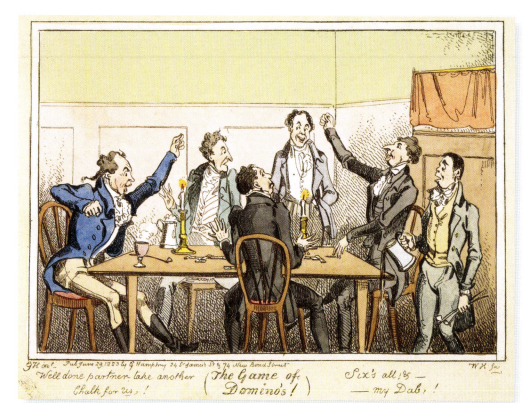

Well done partner- take another Chalk for us,! *(The Game of Domino's!)* *Six's all;& — my Dab,!*

▲ Dominoes is often thought of as a peaceful, reflective game for men of mature years. But in this scene at a London inn, published by **GH Humphreys** in **June 1823**, as in cafés and bars all over Europe, Latin America and the Caribbean today, it can also be a raucous gambling game.

The game of domino, domino's or dominoes crops up several times in court cases at the Old Bailey during the Georgian period.

In September 1799, James Syme was indicted for murder after a drunken row over a hand at the White Hart, Uxbridge.

The game was cited in two further trials on February 19 1800. The first concerned a murder at the Black Lion, Bayswater, while

a game was taking place. At the second, a fight broke out at the Kings Arms, Holborn Bridge, when one man accused another of hiding a domino up his sleeve.

Clearly dominoes was known to all those in court, since no explanation was deemed necessary.

Significantly, the defendants in these Old Bailey cases were all soldiers, who may well have picked up the game while fighting Napoleonic forces on the Continent.

Yet despite its potential for trouble, dominoes was one of the first pub games to come in from the legislative cold, as it were.

In 1852, Richard Ashton, a licensee in West Bromwich, was fined half a crown for allowing dominoes to be played in his pub.

But he took his case to appeal, successfully, and from thenceforth the game was deemed lawful, provided, of course, that it was not played for money, for drinks or played out of hours or on a Sunday.

In the USA in the late 19th century, ethnographer Stewart Culin described the Chinese workers whom he interviewed about their version of dominoes as men 'of the most ignorant class' who 'gambled ferociously at the game'.

But for Honoré de Balzac, writing in 1847, the game had rather more positive connotations.

'Many a man on the brink of suicide has been plucked back on the threshold of death by the thought of the café where he plays his nightly game of dominoes.'

» firmly ensconced in British life, but as many as thirteen different versions of the game were known, with such names as Tiddle-a-Wink and Domino Loo.

According to a revised edition of Strutt, drawn up by Jack Cox in 1903, one of the most popular variants was Matadore, imported from Spain, in the late 1870s.

Cox, incidentally, was much less sniffy than his predecessor, describing dominoes as 'by no means a mere game of chance' and one that had 'of late received much attention'.

This attention would continue throughout much of the 20th century, as dominoes leagues proliferated in all parts of the country (often doubled up with other pub games such as darts, skittles and cribbage).

In 1938 a Mass Observation observer noted that dominoes was played in two thirds of all the pubs in Bolton (or Worktown as the observers called it), and that one of two 'well known hang outs for domino fans' even had special tables for the playing of the game.

It was also noted that the domino sets used in Bolton went up not to double six, as was common, but to double nine, and therefore a set consisted of 55 rather than the usual 28 tiles.

Indeed there is still a large swathe of central Lancashire, encompassing Bolton, Oldham, Blackburn, Wigan, Preston and Salford, where the double nine set remains the favourite.

Why this is the case, when almost everyone else in the country plays with the double six set, no-one knows. But Lancashire players insist that theirs is the superior game. As one remarked caustically, the double six set is 'for children who can't add up'.

Another quirk in this part of Lancashire is that when playing the block game in pairs – in which each player draws nine tiles – the remaining 19 tiles (called 'sleepers') are left face down in the middle of the table. This pile is called the 'boneyard'.

To start, the first player places his tile on the middle of this boneyard. All subsequent tiles are then laid in the usual trail, but over the top of the sleepers.

There have been sightings of domino sets that go up to double twelves, while double 15s and double 18s are also on the market. These, however, are rarely, if ever seen in this country.

Dominoes variations

A wide range of dominoes games is played in Britain's pubs, some being found in only certain parts of the country, some having wonderfully enticing names that conceal their venomous intent, and almost all bearing pitfalls for the rookie challenger to fall into.

Among the illicit gambling games not recommended for the faint hearted are Ten Penny Knock, Blind (said to be popular in East Lancashire pubs) and Blind Hughie, once common amongst Fifeshire miners in the 1960s.

Then there are more regular games called Pick Up Three, or Doubles, Four-Ends or Double Cross, Honest John or Stormy Castle, and a derivative of the latter, delightfully called Slosh.

A further family of games has evolved in which, instead of blocking one's opponents, the aim is to score points with each move.

In order to keep the score in these games, at some point in the late 19th or early 20th centuries someone had the bright idea to use a cribbage board (*as seen on page 2*).

The most popular form of point scoring dominoes played in pubs today is called Fives and Threes (a synthesis of two older games known as All Fives, also known as Muggins, and All Threes).

In Fives and Threes, the player who puts a domino down is aiming to ensure that the outer pips, when added up, are either fives or threes, or multiples of five and three. For example, if the pips add up to 15, the player scores three points for three fives, plus a further five points for five threes, a total score of eight.

A third category of dominoes games may be loosely called Good Night Games.

These are usually quick rounds played at the end of the evening when the last round has been ordered, with the object being to get all the tiles back into the box.

One such game is called Boxer, in which each player turns up a tile at random. If a multiple of five or five or three, the player keeps it. If not, it goes back in the box. Whoever has the highest total at the end wins a small stake from the other players.

But there are countless other variations rarely seen in pubs.

To name but a few, other than Matadore they are Bingo Bergen, Sebastopol, Sniff, Colonel Cross, and Seven-Toed Pete.

Leave the British Isles and the possibilities expand even further, as can be seen on John McLeod's excellent website (*see Links*), which explains no fewer than 83 different forms of the game – an indication of just how great a variety of strategies and scoring systems can arise from a set of 28 tiles spread out on a table, with that satisfying clink and clatter that seems to belong so well in a British pub, but is in fact a global passion.

National Championships

Given all the subtle variations that exist in dominoes it would need a brave man to try to organise a national championships.

But there was once such a man.

In 1985, Keith Masters from Walsall, a regular player at the Bridge Inn in Wolverhampton, placed an advertisement in *The Sun*, and gained sufficient response to hold the first championships, with finals at Bloxwich.

From there the event grew and grew, with subsequent finals being staged at Ayr, Birmingham, Great Yarmouth and then Bridlington.

The chosen game was Fives and Threes, played with a double six pack. For singles matches, each player drew nine dominoes. For doubles, each player drew six.

Both games were one leg, and 121 points up.

But if that sounds simple, reaching a set of rules that everyone could agree upon required cutting through a dense thicket of local differences and house rules.

Nevertheless for over 20 years the competition thrived. By 1991 a total of 1,400 teams entered the pairs competition, starting with elimination rounds in local pubs.

But sad to say, the whole show eventually ran its course and the 2007 event was the last.

Some blame the smoking ban, though by far the more damaging factor was the decline in interest in dominoes at pub level.

That said, tens of thousands of individuals still play in pub leagues. But the regulars are all getting older, and if dominoes is to survive into its fourth century in British pubs, new ideas will be sorely needed.

Which brings us to the one sector of the game where there appears to be life aplenty...

▲ Bespoke dominoes tables such as this one at the **Atherton Arms** in **Atherton, Lancashire**, were once a common sight at British pubs.

To meet the requirement, the table must have raised edges around the top, to prevent tiles from falling off the edge during an over-enthusiastic shuffle.

There should also be a shelf underneath the table, since no self-respecting dominoes player would wish to get his tiles mixed up with beer slops.

In the absence of a tailor-made table some pubs provide lipped boards to place upon ordinary tables, while others also offer handheld racks for older players to line up their tiles, as in a game of Scrabble.

▲ Photographed by Vanley Burke, a foursome settles down at the **Bulls Head**, on **Villa Road, Handsworth, Birmingham** in the early 1980s.

Dominoes is hugely popular in the Caribbean, and so for many of the Windrush generation, in the often hostile atmosphere of British cities in the second half of the 20th century the game provided a social and cultural blanket no less warming than cricket or calypso.

What it did not do, at least not often, was to build a bridge linking these working men in pubs to their white counterparts apparently playing the same game.

Racism of course played a part, but just as crucial were the rules.

While the white teams favoured Fives and Threes, scored on a cribbage board, Anglo-Caribbean players stuck to a quick-fire Jamaican block, or partners game, in which two pairs face each other across a square table, and appear to spend as much effort on joking and riling their opponents as they do on the inherent mental gymnastics of the battle.

Ironically, this brand of dominoes is now the only one in Britain to be played at a national level.

▲ When a winning tile goes down in the **Anglo-Caribbean Domino League**, as here at the **West Indian Social Club** in **Rugby**, it goes down with a bang and a whoop. Elation plays a part, but such displays are equally designed to put opponents off their game.

Since the league was formed in 1989 and started attracting multi-national sponsors, Anglo-Caribbean dominoes has largely transferred from pubs to clubs, with its major finals taking place in hotels and drawing up to 2,000 spectators.

Teams bear such names as the Clapham Eagles, Luton Guns & Roses, Hampton Hawks (from Birmingham) and Walsall Lions.

Host teams are expected to lay on music and food. Team colours are obligatory and swearing is fined. Tellingly, a once male dominated game also now has a growing female presence and more young players than are generally seen in other British leagues.

Not everyone embraces this razzmatazz, least of all some of the older players. As one observer noted, the game is like bridge or poker, but with the Notting Hill Carnival passing through the room.

Chapter Eighteen

Board and dice games

A typical homemade merrills board or 'pound' from the Ryedale Folk Museum in Hutton-le-Hole, north Yorkshire, believed to date from the late 19th century. The identity of HP is unknown. This is one of several boards collected by the museum, which has also identified numerous examples of 'graffiti boards' around Britain – that is, boards carved or scratched out by players for impromptu games (including one in Westminster Abbey). Shown right from the museum is a merrills board carved onto the lid of a stable box.

Board and dice games are well suited to pubs. The sets can be kept behind the bar when not needed. They can be played on almost any table as and when required. They also have that ideal requisite, being playable in quick rounds for small stakes.

This chapter could have featured the likes of chess or draughts, both of which are commonly played in pubs. But because they are so familiar we will assume readers have prior knowledge.

Nine men's morris, or merrills
This, on the other hand, is a board game which has certainly been played in Britain for as long as chess or draughts, is still played in pubs across different regions, and yet which nowadays is little known to the general public.

Like many ancient games nine men's morris has gone under various names, the most common of which is merrills, or as Joseph Strutt called it (see Links) merelles, from the French *merelle* for counter or playing piece. Other names include meg merryleys in Lincolnshire, murrels in Cambridgeshire and morrice in Cornwall.

A Suffolk fisherman called Horry White (interviewed by Neil Lanham in the 1960s) referred to nine men's morris as either 'big morry' (for the game played with 24 holes, or 'stations') or 'little morry' (for the nine hole version). White recalled Suffolk horsemen playing these games on rainy days, using the top of a meal bin as the board and beans as counters.

Other names, no doubt based on variations of how it was played include 'ninepenny' (in Oxfordshire) and 'five penny morris', while in her mammoth 1890s study, *The Traditional Games*

of England Scotland and Ireland, Alice Gomme found nine men's morris being played with minor variations amongst children and agricultural workers in Dorset, Gloucestershire, Hampshire, Northamptonshire, Sussex, Warwickshire and Yorkshire.

But the game has long been played beyond these shores.

Archaeological evidence for it has been found in Egypt, Israel, Ireland and Norway, and even on the site of ancient Troy.

One theory is that the game came to northern Europe with Greek traders, or with the Romans. Another has it arriving in southern Europe from north

The fold stands empty in the drowned field
And crows fattened with the murrain flock;
The Nine Men's Morris is filled up with mud
And the quaint mazes in the wanton green
For lack of tread are indistinguishable

Act II Scene 2. *A Midsummer Night's Dream*
William Shakespeare c.1596–6

Africa, and that the word morris is a corruption of 'Moorish' (a link that has also been posited for the origins of Morris dancing).

As recorded by Shakespeare in the late 16th century (*see opposite*), and endorsed by Strutt two hundred years later, nine men's morris was commonly played outdoors, either by scratching the game's grid with its holes or 'stations' on the ground, or by digging shallow holes in turf. For counters players could use stones, seeds, whatever came to hand.

There is earlier, printed evidence of the game being played on a specially made board, the earliest being *The Book of Games*, commissioned by the Castilian king Alfonso X in the 13th century.

In Britain such boards were sometimes called a 'pound' or 'merels-pound'. Makeshift or 'graffiti' examples of these have been discovered all over Britain in cathedrals, abbeys, churches, castles and houses, carved onto furniture, or onto slabs of stone in the most inaccessible parts of buildings. (One assumes that in those instances the grids were scratched out by construction workers to provide a diversion, before the masonry was hauled into position.)

Examples at English Heritage properties alone include Scarborough Castle, Helmsley Castle and Whitby Abbey.

This concentration in north Yorkshire has led the Ryedale Folk Museum in Hutton-le-Hole, to conduct further research into the game, and for a few years to stage an annual 'world' merrills championships.

Although that died out in 1997, visitors to the museum can still try the game or buy modern sets.

Nine men's morris can also be played in a reconstructed Victorian pub that forms part of the Beck Isle Museum, in Pickering, and in a functioning historic pub nearby, the Station Tavern, Grosmont.

Other recent spottings of boards in use have included The Shoulder of Mutton, in Castleford, and The Bunbury Arms, at Stoak, Chester.

Because of the Shakespearean connection nine men's morris is also played in pubs in and around Stratford-upon-Avon, where an outdoor grid is laid out in gardens by the Royal Shakespeare Theatre.

The board one is most likely to encounter in a British pub (*see right*) is barely different from the 13th century Spanish board, in that it has three concentric squares with 24 holes.

Two players take turns to put all of their nine pegs into one of the vacant holes. If a player manages three in a line (called a 'mill') he can remove one of his opponent's pieces, as long as it is not in a mill of its own. Once removed, a peg stays out of the game.

After this first stage the players take turns to move one peg at a time, but only if there is a vacant hole next to it. As before, the object is to form a mill. A player can open up one of his own mills, by moving one of the pieces. If he then re-closes the mill with his next move, he is deemed to have formed another mill and can take off an opponent's peg.

A 'running mill' is where a skilled player repeatedly opens up one mill in order to close another, so that every move results in a loss for the opponent.

Play continues until one player is down to just three pegs, after which he may move those pegs to any hole left on the board. The game ends once a player has only two pieces remaining.

The author enjoys a game of nine men's morris by the fireside of the Red Lion at Whitworth, Rochdale, in Lancashire. Note that both players have one 'mill' each.

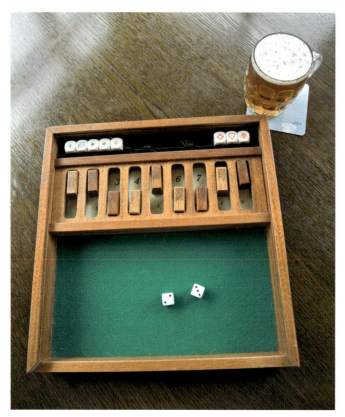

Shut the box boards from the Cock Inn, Luddesdowne, Kent (*above*) – supplied also with dice for crown and anchor (*see opposite*), and (*right*) from the author's collection. Both boards are numbered one to nine, but some modern sets go up to ten or twelve.

Shut the box

Shut the box is a dice game popular with gamblers and played in a baize-lined tray, with a sequential display of numbers.

Each number sits behind a hinged or sliding panel, so that the figure can be open or shut.

House rules vary, so it is always best to have these explained before playing. But the general pattern is as follows.

At the start all the numbers are open. The first player rolls two dice and must close any number, or combination of numbers, which add up to the total of the two dice. Thus a cast of six and three could be used to shut nine, or eight and one, seven and two, six and three, or five and four.

Once a number has been shut, it stays shut.

The same player then rolls again, and continues to shut boxes until – some say when the top three numbers (seven, eight and nine) have been covered, others that the numbers left uncovered add up to less than six – he can choose whether to proceed with one or two dice.

The aim of the game is, of course, to 'shut the box' by closing all the panels.

More often than not, however, before reaching that stage, a player finds himself stuck with a dice score that cannot be used because all possible combinations have been shut.

The numbers remaining open at this juncture therefore constitute that player's score.

There are different ways of calculating the damage. Some schools read the figures directly, so that an exposed one, five and nine would score as 159. Others add up, so that the same combination would total 15. If a player does manage to shut the box, their score is, of course, zero.

Each player has a round of throws, with the winner being the one with the lowest score.

Some people prefer a longer game, in which players drop out once they have accumulated 45 points by the adding-up method. In this case, the last player left gathers up the pool.

Another variation is that if any player succeeds in shutting the box, he wins outright and collects double the stakes from the rest of the players.

In a shut the box marathon, for two players only, the first rolls the dice and shuts the appropriate panels. The second player rolls and tries to open them again. If playing this version it helps to have a board with duplicate numbers below each panel so that both players can see what is going on.

The history of shut the box is itself an open case.

In Britain its first mention in print came in Timothy Finn's 1965 book, *The Watney Book of Pub Games*.

Finn had come across shut the box on the Channel Island of Alderney, and reported that it had been introduced from there to England by an enthusiast called 'Chalkie' Trowbridge, in 1958.

But in his 1975 update of the book (see Links), Finn reported that one of his correspondents had subsequently come across a 'very old and obviously hand-made board' in a pub in Hayling Island, in the 1950s.

In his *Games of the World* (1975) Frederick V Grunfeld suggested that fishermen in Normandy had played a similar game for two hundred years, although this claim has never been substantiated.

French games enthusiasts and historians, meanwhile, refer to the game as *fermer la boîte*, but are similarly unclear as to whether it is genuinely French or English.

To add to the mystery, shut the box is often confused with other games, such as tric trac, a form of backgammon (see overleaf), and snake eyes, a dice game which had nothing to do with boxes.

Commercial versions of shut the box have also appeared under the names Canoga and Batten down the Hatches.

None of which matters. Shut the box remains a fine game, and with solid sets still being manufactured, one that can readily be added to any pub's repertoire.

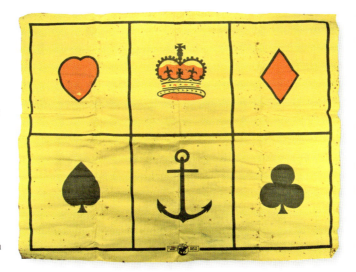

'Lay it down my lucky lads; the more you put down the more you pick up. You come here on bicycles, you go away in Rolls Royces. The old firm, all the way from 'Olloway. What about the lucky old mud hook? The old mud hook's badly backed. Any more for any more before we turn 'em up? Have you all finished, have you all done? Right, up she comes. Two jam tarts and the lucky old Sergeant Major.'

A First World War soldier acts as 'banker' for a game of Crown and Anchor, as recorded by John Brophy and Eric Partridge in *The Long Trail, What the British Soldier Sang and Said in 1914–18*. The 'mud hook' was, of course, the anchor, the 'sergeant major' the crown and the 'jam tarts' the hearts.

◄ As the name suggests, **crown and anchor** originated in the Royal Navy, and became popular amongst seamen and fishermen on both sides of the English Channel.

Because its 'board' is usually printed onto oilcloth, canvas or, nowadays, plastic, it is easily portable and so can be packed away at a moment's notice. Just as well since playing it for stakes in a pub is strictly illegal.

It can, however, be seen played legally at agricultural shows and at charitable events in the Channel Islands.

The St George's set seen here dates from the 1930s.

Each player places his stake on one or more squares. The banker then rolls three dice. A symbol which turns up on one dice pays evens, a pair pays 2–1 and three-of-a-kind 3–1. As the odds are with the banker, in the best run games the role of banker rotates among the players.

Crown and anchor has numerous international cousins. In the Flemish version *Anker en Zon*, a sun symbol replaces the crown. The French call it *Acre, Pique et Soleil*. The Chinese have *Hoo Hey How*, which is similar to the Vietnamese *Bau cua ca cop*, whose symbols are a fish, crab, prawn, rooster, gourd and a stag.

But whichever version you play, the banker always wins in the end.

▲ Strictly speaking, for **poker dice** to be played in a pub the licensee needs permission from the licensing committee for it to be played 'for small stakes only'. Hence it is more often spotted being played furtively in a quiet corner.

But in any case, since poker played with cards is now legal without a licence (see page 161), poker dice may well be seen less.

Each die is marked with ace, king, queen, jack, 10 and 9. The first player rolls all five and can then roll a second or third time, using all five dice again, or leaving some as they fell. The object is to build the strongest possible hand.

The scoring values of the various combinations (lowest hand first) are as follows: highest single die (ace high); a pair; three of a kind; a sequence; full house (pair plus three of a kind); four of a kind and best of all, five of a kind.

Once the first player has decided on his hand, all subsequent players are allowed only as many throws as the first one took.

Backgammon

Although rightly identified with Middle Eastern and Arabic cultures, backgammon has been played in Britain long enough for it to be considered as much part of the furniture as old familiars such as chess or nine men's morris.

How could it be otherwise with a name that, according to Strutt, derives from the Saxon words for *bac* and *gamen*, meaning 'back game'? (He also noted that in Welsh backgammon could be translated as 'little battle'.)

Modern scholars have argued over three main sources for its origins: a game called *Senet* in ancient Egypt; the Royal Game of Ur, discovered in Mesopotamia (essentially modern day Iraq), and the Persian game of *Nard*. This last variant appears to have the strongest claim since excavations at the so-called Burnt City in south eastern Iran in 2004 revealed a rectangular ebony board with 60 counters, thought to date back to around 3000 BC.

The Romans called a similar game *tabula*, hence until the 17th century in Britain it was called tables. The Anglo Saxon verses *Codex Exoniensis* tell of the delights of two brothers who 'shall at tables sit, while from them their sorrow glides away.' This 'pastime on board' allowed them to forget 'the miserable world'.

A 13th century engraving of tables, from the Harleian Collection at the British Library, as reproduced in Joseph Strutt's treatise of 1801. An ecclesiastical ban on all games of chance in the 10th century and a diatribe against this and all forms of 'the hellish art of dice' by John of Salisbury in the 12th century, failed to deter the clergy.

Over the centuries backgammon has fallen in and out of favour.

In the late 15th century it was eclipsed by chess, but was then revived across Europe in the 17th century and, according to Strutt, was 'a very favourite amusement' among 'persons of opulence, and especially the clergy'.

Jonathan Swift also mentioned it as a clergyman's foible, while Pepys enjoyed the odd game, with his wife or his friend Lord Bruncker (against whom he lost a crown after one game in 1665).

The French called it *Tric Trac*. In Germany it was *Puff*, in Spain *Tablas Reales*, in Italy *Tavole* and in Turkey *Shesh Besh*. The Scots called it simply *Gammon*.

In his 1844 book *Backgammon*, George F Pardon described it as 'a fireside, a domestic and conjugal game. It is not so obtuse as to banish conversation on general topics... the ever recurring rattle of the dice box keeps the ear alert and the attention alive; it has been found an anodyne to the gout and rheumatism, the azure devils and the yellow spleen.'

Despite these magical qualities, we read little of backgammon in pubs during the 19th or 20th centuries, until in 1975 Timothy Finn (see Links) noted excitedly, 'Few of the erratic bolts of fashion have matched the resurgence of backgammon.'

Indeed for a decade or so, as city slickers took up the game – playing a high stakes variant known as the 'doubling cube' – it seemed as if every trendy pub and wine bar was filled by the rattle of dice and the clinking of counters.

The moment passed. But the revival did lead to the formation of the British Isles Backgammon Association in 1989 (see Links), and at the last count there were some 30 clubs meeting at various bars, clubs and pubs from Scotland down to Kent and across to Wales and the West Country.

There may be fewer vicars and high rollers in evidence, and barely the whiff of a hookah. But those who play can rest assured that this is no imported fad, but a British tradition that has endured for a thousand years.

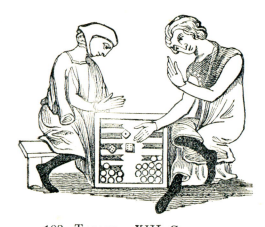

108. TABLES.—XIII. CENTURY.

For once the dartboard is ignored as the Coventry Backgammon Club get down to business at the Grade II listed Whitefriars Olde Ale House, parts of which date back to the 14th century, almost as old as the game itself.

◀ Tables on a table – the familiar pattern of a backgammon board is one of several games featured on the magnificent **Eglantine** or **Aeglentyne Table** at **Hardwick Hall,** in Derbyshire, evidence of how the game was a favourite amongst the elite of Tudor society.

Measuring 10' x 4' 3", the walnut table was crafted in 1567 to celebrate the marriage not only of Elizabeth 'Bess of Hardwick' and her fourth husband the Earl of Shrewsbury, but also those of both her son and daughter to the Earl's daughter and son.

Its delicate marquetry also depicts playing cards, musical instruments, heraldic devices and the Hardwick coat of arms, in which eglantine, a wild rose, appears as a symbol of chastity.

Chapter Nineteen

Card games

Described as 'the greatest gallant of his time', Sir John Suckling, depicted here at the height of his powers in 1635, may justly be considered Britain's first 'card sharp'. Heralded as much for his wit as for his poetry and plays, when not womanising Suckling was at the bowling green or the card table, winning and losing huge sums on a regular basis. Like so many gamesters he ended up in penury, in Paris, and according to John Aubrey's *Brief Lives*, 'tooke poyson, which killed him miserably with vomiting'. He was 33.

So familiar are most of us with the standard pack of playing cards that it is easy to forget their provenance and symbolism.

Why, for example, diamonds, clubs, hearts and spades?

Why is the king of clubs the only king to hold an orb, while the king of diamonds is usually depicted in profile, holding out an imploring, empty hand? And where did the joker spring from?

This is not the place to delve too deeply into these questions, fascinating though they are, largely because there are so many detailed sources in print and on the internet that the inquisitive reader can follow up.

But it as well to remind ourselves of just how embedded playing cards are in our gaming lives, and why certain types of card games seem inextricably linked with the pub while others are seen as more suited, as it were, for the parlour.

Britain's leading card historian, David Parlett (*see* Links), has written that although forms of playing cards were recorded in China as early as the 10th century, the 52

card pack we know today probably originated with the Mamelukes in 13th century Egypt, spreading to Europe, via Venice perhaps, rapidly thereafter.

For sure they had arrived by 1377 because in that year the cities of Florence and Siena banned a card game known as *naibbe*, to be joined *inter alia* by similar prohibitions of cards in Paris, also in 1377, Basle and Brussels in 1379, Barcelona in 1380 and Lille, in northern France, in 1382.

No doubt cards soon found their way across the Channel, although confirmation of this follows only in 1463–64, when a petition by tradesmen in London prompted Edward IV to issue a statute prohibiting the import of various foreign-made items, of which *cardes à jouer* were one, as were tennis balls, both manufactured in France.

A second reference to cards followed in 1496 when all apprentices were banned from playing card games other than at Christmas, and even then they could only indulge within their masters' houses.

It was around this time that the cards themselves started to assume the pictorial form we know today, based on French designs thought to date from around 1480.

Whereas in Spain and Italy the four suits evolved into coins, cups, swords and batons, and in Germany into hearts, acorns, bells and leaves, the French gave us *coeurs* (hearts), *piques* (pikes, later to become spades), *trefles* (trefoils, or clubs) and *carreaux* (diamonds).

We must also thank the French printing houses of Rouen for portraying our kings, queens and knaves – known as jacks from the 17th century – in the courtly fashions that their artists guessed were in vogue at that time.

For example the decorative lappets worn by the queens, and the flat caps sported by the knaves, have both been dated to the early Tudor period of 1500–40.

It is also interesting to note that while French cards of that period bore the names of actual kings and courtiers, those printed for the English were anonymous, and have remained so.

As stated in Chapter One, the first guides to card games in this country were penned by Charles Cotton, but published anonymously. His first book, *The Nicker Nicked, or, the cheats of Gaming discovered*, set the tone in 1669, and was then expanded into what was to become the standard work for a century, *The Compleat Gamester*, first published in 1674.

By then the image of the unscrupulous 'card sharp', ready to prey on innocents (particularly those from the countryside visiting the shady taverns of London), had entered the popular imagination in the person of Sir John Suckling.

Suckling may not have been the inventor of British pubgoers' favourite card game, 'cribbidge', as John Aubrey asserted – the Oxford English Dictionary states that the name is first recorded in 1630, when Suckling was just 21 – though he may well have improved it by adapting or adopting some of the rules from an existing game called noddy.

But he was certainly inventive. In his *Brief Lives* Aubrey describes how the devious Suckling had sent out to 'all Gameing places in the country' packs of cards each marked with 'private markes of his,' so that when he bowled up for a game he would know exactly which cards to play.

The result? 'He got twenty thousand pounds this way.'

If true (and Aubrey was not always the most reliable of chroniclers), that is at least £2.7m in today's money.

Small wonder, added Aubrey, that 'No shopkeeper would trust him for sixpence'.

Or that successive governments decided to clamp down on crooked gamesters, initially by imposing taxes on each pack (which also

put them beyond the means of the lower orders), and later, in the 18th century, by requiring card manufacturers to seal each pack before sale and also to print their name on the ace of clubs.

Take a look at that card in the next pack you come across and you may see that this convention is still sometimes observed.

As noted opposite, Suckling ended his days unhappily in Paris, ostensibly after being implicated in a plot to free the Earl of Stafford from the Tower in 1642.

But his beloved 'cribbidge' went from strength to strength, and after the Restoration was one of 20 card games described in *The Compleat Gamester*, as was all fours, another game still played in pubs and described below.

Otherwise, such 17th century favourites as Bone Ace, Lanterloo, French Ruff, Queen Nazareen and Beast are nowadays known only to card historians.

One other great survivor from that period, though not associated so much with pubs, is whist, a game that Edmond Hoyle wrote about so successfully in the 18th century, thereby laying the foundations for the Hoyle series on games that continues today.

Card games, one need hardly add, are perfect for the pub, beer slops notwithstanding.

But summarising all the many different varieties that are played would take a book of its own. What follows therefore is a brief description of the most common found in pubs today. »

Photographed for the *Daily Mirror* by Humphrey Spender in the 1930s, fishermen in the Cornish village of Mousehole enjoy a game of cards at the Ship Inn. The game appears to be cribbage but in this part of the country might equally have been euchre. Now listed Grade II, the pub remains a popular haunt for tourists.

Cribbage

In 2007 a reader of the *Daily Telegraph* wrote on its letters page, 'I wonder if we shall remember 2007 as the year we lost our pubs?'

The following day, journalist Michael Henderson added his own fears in a feature article.

'The English pub, one of our greatest gifts to civilisation, is in mortal danger.' He then added, 'Who, for instance, plays cribbage in a pub these days?'

The answer came the following day. Henderson, another reader advised, 'must be drinking in the wrong places'.

As indeed he was.

Cribbage is unquestionably the national card game of British pubs; its arcane rules as great a mystery to non-players as those of cricket to foreigners.

True, the game is in decline. There was a time when every other pub had its own cribbage school. Now poker is making a challenge (of which more later).

But cribbage is still the more common, and if you know where to look, you should still be able to find a game locally. There are also dozens of crib leagues in most areas of England and parts of Wales.

Indeed such has been its popularity that under the 1968 Gaming Act it, alone of all card games, was sanctioned in any British pub 'for small stakes only', whereas every other card game had to be dealt with according to its merit by the local licensing authority. (Since then the 2005 Gambling Act has granted poker equal status.)

As noted earlier, cribbage dates from at least 1630, and after being popularised in elite circles by Suckling and Cotton, trickled down to alehouses by the 18th century.

▲ Useful for scoring other pub games such as dominoes and table skittles, **cribbage boards**, as seen here at the **Greyhound** in **Claydon, Suffolk**, are a study in themselves, and almost certainly derive their form from ancient forms of peg boards that predate cribbage.

The standard board has double lines of 30 holes in groups of five for each player or pair of players, plus two game holes. As play progresses, players move their pegs (or matchsticks) up and down the line, so that the score can be easily seen by all parties at a glance.

Many a board seen in pubs will have been fettled up by a local from any old offcut of wood with perhaps a brass overlay. But much finer Victorian and Edwardian boards are also in circulation, made from such woods as mahogany, walnut and boxwood, with intricate inlays in rosewood, ebony, satinwood or ivory. Too good for the pub perhaps, but keenly sought by the growing community of cribbage board collectors on both sides of the Atlantic.

Seen below, part of a collection owned by Mike Millis, secretary of the Arun Crib League in West Sussex, is a more typical example, thought to date from the 1930s, of the sort of boards that breweries, distilleries and tobacco companies started producing for the trade from the late 19th century onwards.

Reflecting this, Old Bailey trials make frequent reference to the game, of which this one, in 1773, is typical. At the Kings Head near Cripplegate in London, 'John O'Connor and John Alsibrook were indicted, for that they by fraud, shift, cozenage, deceit, bad practice, in playing with one Richard Ryder, at a certain game of cards, called cribbage, did win, obtain and acquire to themselves, above the sum of £10' on four separate sittings.

Charles Dickens wove cribbage into at least eight of his novels. The game also featured in his last, unfinished work, *The Mystery of Edwin Drood*, in a fragment discovered by Dickens' biographer, John Forster.

In this snippet, the jackass auctioneer, Thomas Sapsea, explains the nature of a club to which he belonged.

'We were enrolled under the denomination of the Eight Club.

'We were eight in number; we met at eight o'clock during eight months of the year; we played eight games of four-handed cribbage, at eightpence the game; our frugal supper was composed of eight rolls, eight mutton chops, eight pork sausages, eight baked potatoes, eight marrow-bones, with eight toasts, and eight bottles of ale.'

The club was, added Sapsea with Pooterish pride, 'a little idea of mine.'

Four handed cribbage, in which two pairs of players go up and down the board twice (that is, to a total of 121 points), is still the commonest game played today.

Each player starts with five cards, and must discard one onto a pile placed face down on the table. This pile is the 'crib', also known as the 'box'. Each player in turn then puts down one card, face up and calls out its value. Scores are pegged up according to the accumulated total of cards thus displayed. If a player puts down a card that takes that total to 15 or 31 he scores 2 points.

Beyond this, there is no simple way of explaining the rules or the complex scoring patterns, and in truth no better way to learn than to play, preferably with tolerant, knowledgeable and patient friends. Otherwise, games proceed with such pace and fluidity that a novice is soon left behind.

But mastering cribbage is well worth the effort for the lifetime of pleasure and camaraderie that it engenders. Just as long as the spirit of Sir John Suckling is not hovering about in the ether.

Euchre

Whereas cribbage is played everywhere and anywhere, euchre, a bidding and trick-taking game with a restricted pack of cards and an unusual sequence of trumps, is the most important pub and club card game in Devon and Cornwall.

It is also billed as 'the national game' of Guernsey, and there are outposts in Hampshire and Kent.

The history of euchre is complex and sometimes contradictory.

Card historian David Parlett thinks that euchre began in Alsace, in the early 19th century. It next appeared in America, possibly carried in the luggage of German immigrants, although John Scarne, the US card expert, thought it was brought over by French immigrants to Louisiana.

But the real mystery is how euchre turned up in England, and in particular in the West Country.

Although there are no known references to the game in England before the 1860s, there is a »

▲ The Lancashire game of **crash**, a variant of brag, seen here at the **Middleton Archer**, is scored on a board with holes drilled in the form of a St Andrew's cross. Each player starts with his peg in a corner, the aim being to progress through six holes and reach the seventh, centre hole first. But if someone wins all four available tricks in one hand, (the 'crash') he wins there and then.

▲ For years it was thought that the mysteriously named **phat**, a variant of all fours (*see right*), was essentially a Norfolk game. Then recently it was discovered that there has been a phat league in Hereford for over 40 years, as seen here at the **Cotterell Arms.**

Because the game is a four handed game played to 181 points up, phat requires a peg board three times larger than a cribbage board.

Similar to phat is nine card don, also known as big don, long don, or Welsh don, played mainly in Lancashire and South Wales.

》 persistent story that euchre was brought to Devon by French prisoners of war, locked up in Dartmoor during the Napoleonic wars. There were Americans there too, sailors captured during the Anglo-American war of 1812. (They helped to build the parish church in Princetown.)

But equally there were French prisoners cooped up in hulks – decommissioned ships turned into makeshift prisons – near the Medway towns in Kent.

The Cornish theory is that sailors of the Royal Navy, having picked up euchre in Plymouth, spread it throughout Britain's coastal towns.

Equally, the game may well have been introduced by German miners, who came to Cornwall in the 19th century. There is a saying in Cornwall that 'wherever there is a mine in the world, you'll find a Cornishman at the bottom of it, and he'll be playing euchre'.

It is also said that even today you can get a game of euchre in Cornwall any night of the year, and most winter afternoons too.

Two of the most established euchre leagues in Cornwall, each with its own website, are in St Austell and St Ives.

All fours

A four-handed game played between two pairs, all fours is so-called because four points are contested: high, low, jack and game. These are won by taking the tricks containing the highest trump, the lowest trump, the jack of trumps and finally the 'game' point, in which the total value of cards captured in tricks are added up at the end of the game.

It is possible that all fours arrived on these shores either via France or the Netherlands at the time of Charles II's restoration in 1660. In *The Compleat Gamester*, published in 1674, Charles Cotton described it as 'a Game very much played in Kent', adding that 'although the Game may be lookt upon as trivial and inconsiderable, yet I have known Kentish Gentlemen and others of very considerable note, who have play'd great sums of money at it...'

Eighty years later the bursar of All Souls College, Oxford, felt it to be sufficiently corrupting to pen a critical, albeit often sardonic tract entitled, *Serious Reflections on the Dangerous Tendency of the Common Practice of Card-playing; Especially of the Game of All-Fours, as It Hath Been Publickly play'd at Oxford.*

By the early 19th century, and before poker caught on, all fours had become the main card game in America, where it was also known as old sledge or seven up.

But the mystery on this side of the Atlantic is how, in the 20th century, all fours appears to have thrived best of all in Blackburn.

One theory is that it may have been brought back from France in 1918, by men from the East Lancashire Regiment, many of whom had served as prison guards near Fécamp, in Normandy.

The abbey at Fécamp is where the liqueur Benedictine is made, which also explains why consumption of Benedictine is said to be higher in East Lancashire to this day than any other region in the world.

But of course it is equally possible that the East Lancs lads picked up the game from American soldiers in France.

Either way, the Blackburn and District All Fours and Dominoes League has a dozen pub teams playing on Sunday evenings in the summer.

▲ Full house at the **Watermans Arms** on the **Isle of Dogs, London**, a scene that would have been illegal before the 2005 Gambling Act came into force in September 2007. Before then, under the 1968 Gaming Act, the playing of **poker** for money in pubs would have required specific permission from local magistrates, permission that was rarely, if ever granted.

Now, in line with dominoes and cribbage, poker requires no permission, providing that it is played only 'on a low stakes basis'.

That means individual stakes limited to £5 and a daily limit on total stakes and winnings for the premises of £100.

But although the sums are low, for Britain's pub trade the change in legislation has been widely

hailed as a lifeline. Poker may be an American import, having evolved, according to the latest thinking, in French Louisiana in the early 19th century. But its recent popularity in Britain as an online game persuaded the government that reform of the gaming laws was the only sensible option.

Of course it is too early to judge just how much of a panacea poker

will prove to be in the long term. It could just be one fad among many in the always unpredictable tide of pub games history.

But based on evidence from those pubs that have embraced the game, some predict that poker could be no less of a catalyst than darts in the 1930s or pool in the 1970s.

Or as *The Publican* put it, 'Poker is the new Karaoke'.

Chapter Twenty

Pub quizzes

The Red Lion at Westhoughton in Lancashire – one of thousands of British pubs in recent years to have laid on quiz nights, or even 'nites', for its regular customers. But for tonight, or even tonite's snowball prize (*answer opposite*): what other game is the Red Lion in Westhoughton famous for?

Quiet please! All mobile phones switched off, and please write down your answers clearly.

Question 1: Who originated the police system?

Answer: Sir Robert Peel, in 1829.

Question 2: Why is this question relevant in the current context?

Answer: Because it was the opening question asked at the inaugural quiz night of the York Working Men's Club and Institute Union (CIU) in September 1946, home of what is now considered by the *Guinness Book of Records* to be the birthplace of Britain's, and possibly the world's first ever quiz league.

Question 3: That was in a club. So when, according to the London press, did quizzes catch on in pubs?

Answer: The listings magazine *Time Out* hazarded a guess in 2007 that pub quizzes took off after the launch of the popular television quiz, *Who Wants to be a Millionaire*, first broadcast in 1998. But in an account of his own pub quiz odyssey (*see below*), journalist Marcus Berkmann suggests that they were already established in the capital by the mid 1990s.

Question 4: Why does this offer conclusive evidence that London journalists should venture beyond the M25 once in a while?

Answer: Because if they did they would know that pub quizzes began in the provinces years earlier.

Question 5: And the first known quizzes in pubs?

Answer: Bootle, on Merseyside, formed a quiz league in 1959, with several teams representing pubs.

Question 6: If Bootle's pioneers, as has been said, were inspired by early television quiz shows, which shows might they have been?

Answer: Firstly, *Double Your Money*, first aired on the new ITV channel in September 1955...

Question 7: Hosted by?

Answer: Hughie Green.

Question 8: But did not ITV launch another quiz show that same month, presented by Michael Miles and called *Take Your Pick*?

Answer: Yes.

Gong! (Note, only older readers will understand this reference.)

Question 9: Which is Britain's largest quiz league today?

Answer: The Merseyside Quiz League (MQL). This grew from its roots in Bootle in 1959 to take in Waterloo and Crosby by 1963, followed over the next twelve years by leagues in Liverpool, Ormskirk, Southport, Formby, Warrington and the Wirral. By the mid 1980s the MQL had over 300 teams.

Today it consists of some 150 teams playing in six regions, each of which has two or three divisions, a system of promotion and relegation, and a series of knock-out competitions. The MQL also has a prize for individuals called the Mimir Trophy.

Question 10: Named after?

Answer: A mythological Norse sage who drank from a well of knowledge.

Question 11: Which of the following is the odd one out: Aberdeen, Aberystwyth, Lancaster, Sunderland, Rochdale, Stockport, Macclesfield, Leeds, Sheffield, Derby, Milton Keynes, Luton, Winchester, Bristol and London?

Answer: Luton. All the others have a recognised quiz league.

In fact there are over 200 quiz leagues in Britain today, many serviced by such companies as Redtooth, which sends out 4,000

I once took some American tourists to a pub quiz. They couldn't believe their eyes. They had expected Britain and the British to be eccentric, but never for a moment had they ever imagined that grown men and women would voluntarily sit in pubs once a week and write down answers to general knowledge questions on photocopied sheets. "And I thought Stonehenge was weird," said one man.

Marcus Berkmann in *Brain Men, A Passion to Compete* 1999

quiz sheets each week, Quizzing. co.uk (whose 2009 finals were at the Charlton Arms in Ludlow), 123quiz.net and Freequizzes.co.uk.

Question 12: What do the initials SWP stand for?

Answer: Apart from the Socialist Workers' Party, SWP stands for Skill With Prizes, the trade name for a coin-in-the-slot quiz machine, of which the first, The Quizmaster, appeared in 1985 and offered a jackpot of £10 (compared with the maximum £3 paid out by AWPs – Amusement with Prizes – such as fruit machines).

Question 13: In the context of quizzes, what was a 'deflowerer'?

Answer: Once regular players realised they could outwit the SWPs (for example by memorising answers or by playing only when the machines were pregnant with the coins of second-rate players), a class of hardened quiz pros emerged, some of whom, roving from pub to pub, won enough to earn a reasonable living.

Equally adept, if less serious, were sundry jazz musicians from London who enjoyed rich pickings from SWPs while on tour, idling away the hours between gigs. They called themselves the 'deflowerers' of quiz machines.

Landlords had other names for them, and their ilk, and either gave up their SWPs or installed a later generation of machines that had 'spoiler' questions to deter the serial gamers.

Question 14: Where would you find a group calling themselves 'The Thinkers and Drinkers?

Answer: This is the motto of the Lancaster City Quiz League, another of Britain's oldest leagues, formed in 1969 and immortalised in Ian Marchant's *The Longest Crawl*, an account of a month long pub crawl from Cornwall to

the Western Isles. Recalling his days playing for the Yorkshire House in Lancaster, Marchant considered the quiz league 'a monument to the glories of working class autodidacticism... You live and breathe trivia. You memorise everything, any list you can lay your hands on. You lay off the porn, and spend your free evenings surfing quiz websites. You never miss Fifteen to One.

'You are quiz...'

Questions 15–19: Name five pubs renowned for their quizzes.

Answer: The Gardeners' Arms, Hull (two themed quizzes a week); the Cock Inn, Luddesdown, Kent (20 teams of six each Tuesday); the Boogaloo, Highgate, London (said to run the best music and film quizzes in the capital); the Prince of Wales, also in Highgate, which

published its own quiz book, and Peter Kavanagh's in Liverpool, a cosmopolitan and bohemian delight, full of curios and with a famously tough but lively quiz every Thursday night.

Question 20: According to *The Publican* newspaper's 2008 *Market Report*, which activity is currently the most popular in British pubs?

Answer: Actually it is darts, but second comes pub quizzes, followed by pool in third place.

An estimated 44 per cent of all pubs now stage weekly quizzes, meaning that with leagues and other competitions, nearly a million questions are posed in British pubs every week.

Snowball answer from opposite: The other game at the Red Lion is crown green bowling (*see page 109*).

Now, how did you get on?

Whimsical names but a serious business – members of the Quiz Akabusi team dig deep at Ye Olde White Bear in Hampstead, London, where landlord Chris Ely, like so many of his counterparts, reckons that, Saturday nights excepted, quiz nights are his busiest nights of the week and, for a modest outlay, offer better value than a satellite TV contract.

Chapter Twenty One

Spoof and tippet

Having outwitted 140 competitors from nine nations, Dominic Graham of Canterbury celebrates victory in the 2004 World Spoofing Championships, staged at the Shepherd Neame brewery in Faversham, Kent. As this followed on from Sussex publican Mike Chappell's triumph in the previous year's contest, held in Sydney, there were immediate calls that as this was clearly a game that the English excel at, spoof should be included in the 2012 Olympics. Alas, the IOC have yet to respond.

Pub games do not come much simpler than spoof and tippet, gambling games whose origins are as much the subject of guesswork as are the games themselves.

There are claims, for example, that spoof, or 'spouf', was invented by actor Arthur Roberts, at London's Adelphi Club in the 1880s. But what were the rules of his spoof game? No one knows.

And how, for that matter, should we spell tippet? Is it tippet? Or tip it? Or even tippit?

Again, we can only guess.

All we can say for certain is that during the 1930s both games became popular in working class pubs on Sundays.

Why Sundays? Because whilst dartboards and cribbage boards were locked away as the law required, games that required only a few coins made for ideal substitutes, being easily concealed should a constable call by.

Spoof

The unusual feature of spoof is that the aim is to get eliminated, since the last man in pays for the next round of drinks.

Each player has three coins. How many of those coins a player elects to bring into play in any one go is up to him. It could be one, two or three, or it could be none.

Let us imagine that six players have agreed to join in.

On the given signal, all six place one clenched fist onto the table.

One by one, each player must hazard a guess as to the total number of coins clutched in those six sweaty palms. That total could of course be anything from 0–18.

No-one is allowed to call the same number, so some players may be forced to choose a number that does not correspond with their true estimation.

After everyone has guessed, the one who has called the correct number drops out of the game, secure in the knowledge that his next drink will be free.

In the final stage of spoof, when only two players are left, there are two possible endings.

In the West Country, they call this endgame 'kannoble'. In other areas it is called 'no bum shouts'.

Under this rule the first of the surviving pair must call out what he knows to be the possible total. Thus, if he himself holds two coins, because the maximum his opponent can hold is three, he must call two, three, four or five.

Where this convention is not adhered to, all sorts of chicanery and trickery, including 'bum shouts', are allowed.

In recent decades, almost certainly courtesy of ex-pat Brits in far off places, spoof has spread far beyond the tap room.

For example, two locations claim to have hosted the world's first spoof championships in 1983, Dubai and Tasmania, while The Gentlemen Spoofers of Seoul in South Korea (who graciously include ladies in their definition of gentlemen) took up the game in 1993.

A number of British breweries have also embraced spoof.

Guinness produced a set of coins and rules in the 1990s, as did Theakston in North Yorkshire.

Shepherd Neame's 2004 world championships are mentioned opposite, while the following year in Wales, Brain's Brewery got into the act with what they called the

Fifth European Championships at the Terra Nova bar in Cardiff Bay.

(Both these events, incidentally, were held on the eve of rugby internationals, thereby maintaining a longstanding link between the two games that may or may not be related to their thirst-inducing characteristics.)

Meanwhile, yet another event claiming world championship status started up in 2001 at the Nags Head, Edale, Derbyshire. Six players competed that year, using pseudonyms that are best left unprinted (although we can reveal without too much offence that one contestant in the 2006 event called himself Major Disaster).

Stranger still, or maybe not, comes news that for a while, at least before the banking crash of 2008, spoof caught on in the City of London, thanks to the chef Marco Pierre White. Apparently at stake in his games were the bills for both the food and wine that he laid on for contestants.

In other words, high stakes.

But strangest of all is the report – seemingly no spoof at all – that in 2007 the billionaire sports retailer and soon-to-be owner of Newcastle United, Mike Ashley, settled a dispute over £200,000 worth of legal fees with the firm Merrill Lynch, by playing a game of spoof. Which he lost, as did Newcastle, on all too many occasions under his ownership.

Finally, on a happier and saner note, mention must be made of the Spoofers Club at the aptly named Welcome Stranger pub in Liverton, Newton Abbot, Devon. There they play only for charity, with each spoofer paying one pound a go.

So far the club has raised over £4,000 for good causes, showing that spoofers need not be tight fisted all the time.

Tippet

The first known rules of tippet were recorded by the publisher and folklorist Alfred Nutt, in Alice Gomme's encyclopaedic work of 1894, *The Traditional Games of England, Scotland and Wales*.

He called it 'tip it', but it was otherwise pretty much the game we know today.

Rules do vary from region to region, however, so here follows the version favoured in Salford, Lancashire, in the 20th century.

Two teams of three sit facing each other across a pub table, captains in the middle. The captains toss for first go.

Team one then passes a single coin, or perhaps a ring, from hand to hand, under the table, amid a great deal of diversionary chat, banter, bluff and counter-bluff.

Finally, the opposing captain shouts 'hands up' and six closed fists crash down onto the table in front of him and his team.

He, or a nominated team-mate must then identify which of the six fists conceals the coin.

In doing this he can use a couple of early elimination ploys to help clear his mind. He can point to two of the opposing closed fists, which must be opened on demand. If the coin appears here, he loses a point.

He may also ask the opposing team to put their fists back under the table, 'tighten 'em', then bring them back onto the table top.

Even inexperienced players may, at this point, spot tell-tale white-tightened knuckles.

The final, forensic moment occurs when the questioner must make one last guess, tap the suspected fist and call out, what else but 'tip it!'

If correct, his team scores one point, takes over the coin and the game restarts. If wrong, the opposing team scores a point and keeps the coin for the next round.

Usually the game is played to eleven points up.

But in other parts of the country there are different versions.

In 'Up Jenkins!', the best known variant – possibly of Welsh origin, judging by the name – the guessing team are allowed a few more manoeuvres before making their final choice. They can, for example call for 'smash 'ems', when all opposing fists must be crashed on the table.

Or, if they call for 'crabs', the opposition must raise their hands so that only their fingertips touch the table. (The knack in this event is to tuck the coin out of sight between thumb and forefinger.)

The command 'church windows' means the hands must be held up, palms facing inwards.

If any of these commands results in the coin being dropped, then play passes to the other side.

Predictably there have been a string of world tippet championships, the first of which was held at the Red Lion, Llanafan Fawr, Powys, Wales, in 1995, followed in subsequent years by pubs in and around Caersws, in Powys, and Llandovery, in Carmarthenshire.

But the latest whereabouts of this tournament is a mystery, as is the fate of its organisers, The World Amateur Tippit Society, who will otherwise have to be fondly remembered for their acronym.

Somerset spoofers make a fist of it at the New Inn in Wedmore, venue since 2005 of the annual International Spoof Competition. From a field of 69 entrants, the 2009 winner was local vet Alice Swain. The New Inn is otherwise known for its alternative art show, the Turnip Prize.

Chapter Twenty Two

Dwile flonking

A 'flonker' wets his 'dwile' in ale on the end of his 'driveller' before preparing to hurl it at an opponent, outside the Lewes Arms in July 2007. Having originated in Suffolk, dwile flonking has spread to pubs and student unions all over England, and is now an annual fixture in Lewes. The strings tied around the flonker's knees are, of course, to prevent rats running up his trousers.

Historians of dwile flonking (or dwyle flunking) like to insist that its origins in Suffolk hark back to the Waveney Rules of 1585.

What they have been unable to tell us is whether those rules were as flexible in the 16th century as those which apply today (or at least apply at the start of a session... by the end, rules of any kind seem to matter very little).

The late Richard Boston, who in the late 1970s conducted a long-running investigation into dwile flonking via his *Guardian* column, unearthed no shortage of experts around the country.

In some dwile flonking areas, it transpired, the 'driveller,' as labelled in Suffolk, was called a 'swadger'. Swadgers, furthermore, were supplied by swadge-copers, and sold by the tardwainer's nard.

Decades on from these heady interchanges one hesitates to spoil the party.

But the truth is – subject to further research naturally – that all drivellers and swadgers in this story point back not to 16th century Waveney but to 1966 and a summer fête in Beccles, Suffolk.

There, apprentice printers Andrew Leverett and Bob Devereux and a group of their workmates successfully re-enacted an 'all but forgotten' Suffolk game whose rules had been found in an attic in nearby Bungay.

By the following year a Waveney Valley Dwile Flonking Association had been formed. We know this because The Three Tuns in Bungay applied for an extension in order to host the Association's dinner dance. Neither magistrate nor police inspector had a clue what dwile flonking was, but having been assured by someone in the public gallery that the activity was both harmless and ancient, the license was duly granted.

That same year, in May 1967, Pathé News filmed dwile flonking at the Wherry Inn in Beccles, a film that can still be viewed on their website (*see Links*).

Over the next decade dwile flonking gripped the nation's pubs and student unions.

What did it matter that Suffolk's county archivist could find no evidence at all of the game prior to 1966?

Besides, someone discovered that the word 'dwile' derived from the Dutch *dweil*, meaning both a floorcloth, or a drunkard.

Eamonn Andrews featured it on his television show.

So too did Michael Bentine on his ATV programme, *All Square* (a follow up to his BBC series *It's a Square World*). Indeed some revisionists have since claimed that Bentine himself invented the game as a television spoof.

But then Bentine never called it dwile flonking. He seemed to prefer the name 'nurdling', which in turn was taken up by the game's other great afficionado, the comic actor Kenneth Williams, who mentioned it on seemingly every chat show he appeared on.

This fascination endures today, culminating in web forums and even a virtual dwile flonking game on BBC Radio Suffolk's website.

It remains a media favourite too, still celebrated as if it were either quite the latest in English eccentricity, or in fact a game with centuries of tradition behind it.

Surely, a university-backed research study cannot be far off.

▲ Regulars at the **Lewes Arms** face the **Lewes Operatic Society** in their annual **dwile flonking** match at this celebrated East Sussex pub.

Each team has 12 players, many of whom don rustic garb. The first team forms a circle, or 'girter', and on the command 'Here y'is t'gether' from the referee (or 'jobanowl') they dance to traditional music in an anti-clockwise direction.

Taking it in turn to be 'flonker', one of the opposing team moves in the opposite direction and tries to swing the 'driveller' in such a way as to strike one of the circle with the beer-sodden 'dwile'.

A hit to the head, or 'wonton', scores three points; one to the torso (a 'morther') scores two, while a leg-strike (or 'ripper') counts for one.

Each flonker has two, or three attempts, but if he misses each time he must drink a pot of ale in the time it takes for the girterers to pass the dwile around the circle, chanting 'pot, pot, pot' as they do.

If the flonker is unable to empty the pot in time, he loses a point.

Theoretically someone keeps the score. But by the closing stages few care too much, and by the next day fewer still even remember.

Apart from Lewes dwile flonking can be enjoyed at several pubs, including the Farmers Boy at Kenworth, Bedfordshire and at the Racehorse Inn, Ipswich, where some players still sing the ancient dwile flonkers anthem, *Here we 'em be together*. This was penned by one Amos Thirkle, a former farmhand who is now considered the game's patron saint.

Chapter Twenty Three

Eating and drinking

The World Stinging Nettle Eating Championships at the Grade II listed Bottle Inn, Marshwood in Dorset, originated in 1986 when two farmers were discussing the length of stinging nettles in their fields. A regular then brought in his own 15' long nettle and in a moment of madness said that if anyone found a taller one he would eat it. Two American tourists duly obliged and the event has been open to all comers since 1997.

Competitions for eating, drinking and even smoking have featured at pubs and fairs since at least the 18th century.

In 1801 Joseph Strutt (*see Links*) reported that among 'Hot Hasty-pudding Eaters who contend for superiority by swallowing the greatest quantity... in the shortest time,' it was he 'whose throat is widest and most callous' who was 'sure to be the conqueror'.

Hasty pudding was an oatmeal porridge.

Two centuries later, from its inception as a limited edition in 1954 *The Guinness Book of Records* grew more bloated each year with ever more strange and stomach-churning eating and drinking records, until in 1991 the rules were tightened up, particularly in relation to those records involving the consumption of alcohol.

Over in the USA, where the hot dog makers Nathan's held their first weiner eating championships on Coney Island in 1916, there appear to be fewer inhibitions. As recorded by the International Federation of Competitive Eating in New York, records range from

Stinging in the rain at the Bottle Inn, June 2008. The winner is judged by the aggregate length of stalks whose leaves he or she has managed to eat in one hour. As of 2009 the record stands at 74 feet. Far from being dangerous, the young leaves of freshly picked stinging nettles (or *Urtica dioica*) are high in minerals and vitamins. They also make fine beer and tea.

asparagus (8.8 lbs consumed in ten minutes, at Stockton, California in April 2008) to watermelon (13.22 lbs in fifteen minutes at Brookville, Ohio in 2005).

British competitions are, by comparison, few and far between, and, no surprise here, in recent years those that have survived have become increasingly sanitised by health and safety watchdogs.

Or by the reluctance of the public to indulge.

In the latter category falls the 'biskeys and treacle' eating contest, until recently one of many pub-inspired and pub-fuelled events at the wonderful Egremont Crab Fair in Cumbria. In this, contestants had to down a teacake smothered in treacle, then whistle a recognisable tune.

A memoir of the Bull in t'Thorn, Winster, Derbyshire, recalls that in the inter-war years the pub staged individual contests for eating duck, tripe and potatoes, while for as long as anyone could remember in Frampton-on-Severn, the Three

Horseshoes ran an elver eating competition (elvers being baby eels, once netted in large numbers from the Severn). But this ceased in 1990 once the export of elvers to Japan, and a decline in their numbers, sent prices slithering up to over £500 a kilo in 2005.

In an attempt to maintain at least the spirit of this tradition, the pub tried substituting pasta for elvers, but too few people took the bait and so yet another eating contest died out.

Similarly in Oldham they used to have black pudding eating contests, now in Lancashire puddings are thrown (*see page 133*).

And so precious few eating events have survived, the two best known of which are featured here, involving nettles and pies.

But times, and tastes change, and it only takes one enterprising landlord or sponsor to tempt the nation's wide and callous throats.

Pork scratchings perhaps, or how about stuffed olives at your neighbourhood gastropub? »

▲ While Harry's Bar in Venice is famous for its Bellini cocktails, **Harry's Bar** at the Grade II listed **Clarence Hotel** in **Wigan** has been best known since 1992 as the venue for the **World Pie Eating Championships**.

Wigan being the self-proclaimed pie capital of England – locals have long been called 'pie-eaters' by their Lancashire neighbours – the contest is taken very seriously.

Every meat and potato pie for the event must measure 12cm in diameter and 3.5cm in depth, and contain 66 per cent meat.

As organiser Tony Callaghan told the BBC in 2003, the pastry cannot be too flaky nor the filling too absorbent, for fear contestants develop 'dry mouth', suffer from 'swallow-stall' or even worse, 'spongification of the belly'.

In its original form competitors had to eat as many pies as possible in three minutes, the record being seven pies scoffed by Anthony 'The Anaconda' Danson in December 2005. But then healthy-eating campaigners stepped in and the winner is now the person able to eat a single pie in the fastest time. So far, local pie-eater Adrian Frost holds the record, at 34 seconds.

(For a few years there was also an insistence, since dropped, that vegetarian pies be offered.)

Less frenetically, the Pork Pie Appreciation Society, formed 1984, meets weekly at the Old Bridge Inn, Ripponden, and every March organises a competition in which over fifty varieties from all over Britain are judged. Samples are also on sale to the public, making this a pie day not to be missed.

▲ Upholding a custom at least three hundred years old, a London docker successfully downs a **Yard of Ale** to toast the opening of the **New Gog** in **Canning Town** in 1958.

As anyone who has ever tried this feat knows only too well, it is not just a matter of downing the contents (typically three pints). One must also turn the tube to release air pressure, while tipping it very steadily. Otherwise, if air enters the bulb too suddenly the remaining contents will cascade into the holder's face with embarrassing results (as can be viewed in any number of clips on the internet).

The yard glass itself, known also as a Long Glass, a Cambridge glass or an Ell Glass ('ell' being an old measure of 45 inches), is first mentioned in February 1685, when, on the accession of James II, John Evelyn saw the Bromley militia drink to 'His Majesty's health... in a flint glass a yard long'.

Evelyn's contemporary, John Aubrey, further wrote that to drink 'by the yard' was to show that one was a man of fashion.

A century later, gentlemen in Hanley, Staffordshire, agitating for their town to be granted incorporation, inaugurated a mock initiation ceremony in which members had to drink a yard of ale.

And so to the present day, where we find yard glasses hanging over the bars of innumerable pubs, not least in two pubs called the Yard of Ale, in Birmingham and Stratford-upon-Avon.

Some gather dust. Others are brought down for stag nights.

But from time to time, formal Yard of Ale challenges also take place, for example at the Greyhound, Tinsley Green on Marbles Day, that is, Good Friday, (see page 112), at the Turf Tavern in Oxford on the university's Matriculation Day, and at the Ring o' Bells in Compton Martin, Devon, on Boxing Day.

Not all yard of ale glasses are one yard. Indeed the name 'yard' may have been adopted because the glass is the shape of a coaching horn, another name for which was a 'yard of tin', or simply 'yard'.

Hence there are different capacities, and therefore different record times. But two held by Peter Dowdeswell of Earls Barton in Northamptonshire would seem to be the ones to beat. In 1975 he sank a 2½ pint yard in 5 seconds and a 4 pint yard in 8.9 seconds.

▼ Depending on your tastes and capacity, the **pub crawl** – whereby a group sets out to visit a number of pubs, drinking halves or pints in each one – is either terrific fun and offers economic benefits to as many establishments as possible – or is a hateful excuse for braying inebriates to spill out onto the pavements.

But what cannot be denied is that the pub crawl has a long history and some unexpected practitioners.

In the late 1850s, for example, Karl Marx and two chums set off on a 'beer trip', calling in at every pub down London's Tottenham Court Road (of which there were then several). The trip culminated in the trio arguing with a group of Oddfellows, then throwing stones at streetlamps before being chased off by four policemen at two o'clock in the morning. Revolutionary stuff!

According to lexicographer Eric Partridge the term **'pub crawl'** first appeared in 1915.

It has not only been for pedestrians, however. After the First World War, sundry sons of cotton magnates in the Lancashire village of Shaw initiated a motorised crawl. Each put a guinea (21s) into the pot, then set off in their cars to drink a pint in each of ten local pubs. The first one back to the starting point won the pot.

Their capers ended in a crash. Not of motor cars but of the cotton industry itself in 1921.

Longer lasting has been the **King Street Run** in **Cambridge**.

This started in 1955, following a discussion among St John's College students about the body's capacity to retain liquid under controlled stress. To put their theories to the test the following evening the young scientists visited every pub along King Street, plus a couple round the corner, making ten pubs in all.

Thereafter 'The Run', staged on the first and last Wednesday of each term and limited to eight pubs, had to be completed in two hours, and anyone throwing up or urinating *en route* was disqualified.

Proctors banned the run in 1964, but it was reinstated in 1982 by the Cantabrigensis Hash House Harriers (based at the tiny St. Radegund pub on King Street), and run twice a year, with a tie awarded to anyone completing it. Past alumni include at least one High Court judge.

Today only three pubs remain, one of which (*below*) has been renamed after the run. But the tradition lives on, apparently with a newly devised 'River Run' which has ten pubs along its route.

▲ Apart from the irrepressible instinct of its entrants to don fancy dress and raise money for charity, there is no real competitive edge to the annual **Saddleworth Beerwalk** on the borders of Lancashire and Yorkshire. Staged every Whit Saturday since 1974, the eleven mile walk, which has ten beer stations along the way, is organised by the Round Table, and on a good day can draw up to 2,000 walkers and thousands more spectators.

Apart from sandwiches along the way and a warm glow of satisfaction, everyone who finishes the walk is given a glass tankard.

In Wakefield, West Yorkshire, opinion is divided on the Westgate Run. When it began on Friday and Saturday nights during the inter-war years, there were at least 30 pubs along the 500 yard Westgate. Since then several have closed or been turned into wine bars or discos. Many old hands also feel that binge drinking habits and coachloads of night-trippers from other northern towns have cost the run its appeal.

But for those who are curious, the most popular run takes place on the last Friday night before Christmas, starting at The Redoubt,

then continuing via another 7–12 pubs along a mile and a half walk to finish at the Black Rock in Cross Square. For those with the stamina, including bars and clubs there are over 20 ports of call in total.

In Glasgow, no-one knows when the Subcrawl started, but it certainly gained popularity after Iain Banks mentioned it in his 1987 novel, *Espedair Street*. The Subcrawl is so-called because entrants disembark at all fifteen stations on Glasgow's underground system and down a pint and a Scotch in the handiest pub.

In London a similar underground crawl along the Circle Line began in the 1960s and has since been turned by Kiwi ex-pats into a celebration of Waitangi Day, in February. With 26 stations along the line it can take six hours and cost at least £60 to complete.

Another London crawl, also with 26 stops but covering 18 miles above ground, is based on the Monopoly board.

Needless to add, details of all these and many other established crawls can be found on the internet. So could this be Karl Marx's greatest legacy of all?

Drinking contests

Whilst not every pub has its own yard of ale glass, there are, as most readers will no doubt be aware, plenty of other ways to stage drinking contests.

Not that many of them ever get into the record books.

In the 1920s, as legend has it in Leeds, the drinking champion of the Yorkshire Copper Works challenged his opposite number from Coghlan's Forge, at the Crooked Billet, Thwaite Gate in Hunslet. Such was the challenger's supremacy that he sank not only all eight quarts set out for him along the bar but also managed four of his opponent's.

From across the Pennines in the late 1940s comes the tale of Bert Foster of Oldham, who also happened to be a champion eater of black puddings. Foster was said to have been able to down twelve gills (or half pints) of beer during the time it took for Big Ben to be heard striking noon on the radio.

In other words, six pints in approximately 45 seconds.

Before *The Guinness Book of Records* (now *Guinness World Records*) stopped publishing drinking feats in 1991, we were informed that the official record for consuming a pint was 1.18 seconds, achieved by Bob Farrow, of Diss in Norfolk, in the 1970s.

But in the USA in June 1977,

Steve Petrosino outdid this at the Gingerbread Man bar and diner in Carlisle, Pennsylvania. First he sank a quarter of a litre (just over half a pint) in 0.137 seconds, half a litre in 0.4 seconds and one litre in 1.3 seconds.

There are, inevitably, other measures and combinations that have been subject to time trials.

Some of these may be found in the online *Catalogue of Ridiculous Records*, which seeks to boldy go where Guinness dare not tread.

Examples include the consumption of six pints and six shorts in eight minutes and 14 seconds at Slough in 2003; a pint of tomato juice (with Worcestershire sauce) in 21 seconds at Newcastle in 2002, and away from pubs, eight pints and a curry in one hour and 18 minutes, recorded in Birmingham in 2003 (to which the website adds this helpful warning, 'Non UK nationals may need to seek medical advice' before attempting this traditional British pastime.)

To which we must add our own rider. *Played in Britain* trusts that all its esteemed readers will drink sensibly, moderately and make no attempt to break any of the records so far mentioned.

But if they do, and do so in a pub, and turn their attempts into a regular competition, then by all means, keep us informed...

▲ Britain's smokers may have been forced to huddle outdoors since the smoking ban took effect on July 1 2007, but that has not stopped **The Bull** in **Harpole, Northamptonshire**, from staging its annual **pipe smoking** contest, an event once shared between three pubs in the village and said to go back to at least 1856.

That claim may well have a firm basis. Writing in 1801 Joseph Strutt (*see Links*) found two sorts of smoking matches at country fairs; those to see who could smoke a pipe full of tobacco in the shortest possible time, and those who could keep one burning the longest.

Only one example of the former seems to have survived, at the annual Egremont Crab Fair in Cumbria. Harpole's contest falls into the latter category, as seemingly do most of the world's other surviving pipe contests.

Another reason for not doubting the Harpole event's longevity is that it is held on Shrove Tuesday. Turning that final smoke before Lent into a competition therefore fits in with much else that we associate with the day (pancake races and traditional football games included).

Since 2007 of course the event has had to be staged outside, in a specially erected gazebo. Otherwise the essentials are unchanged.

Each contestant is given an eight inch long, clay churchwarden's pipe, as seen above, stuffed with a carefully measured plug of tobacco. They have two minutes to light up, after which the clock starts ticking. Anyone then unable to 'show smoke' to the referee's satisfaction drops out.

The 2009 contest attracted 17 entrants and was over relatively quickly, the winner having kept his pipe smoking for 41 minutes. But previous winners have managed well over an hour, while the record at the British Pipe Smoking Championships – last staged at the Old Silhillians Club, Knowle, near Solihull in June 2007– was one hour and 38 minutes.

Elsewhere, a dozen or so pipe clubs keep the home fires burning, in private premises or at pubs.

For example the South West Pipe Club meets at the Kings Arms, Buckfastleigh, in Devon, while the Pipe Club of Norwich meets at The Nelson.

Or rather, in its back garden.

Chapter Twenty Four

Lost games

Just as karaoke machines have taken the place of the 'old joanna' in pubs, so too, from the 1930s onwards, did the flashing, buzzing pinball machine put paid to the staid old bagatelle pin board. Most surviving examples now hang on pub walls, as quaint decorations, although one or two such as this board at the Cock Inn, Luddesdown in Kent, still get the odd airing. In some pubs Space Invader games from the 1970s enjoy a similar, retro-style appeal.

In the history of games, as in the game of life itself, there have always been winners and losers.

Fashions change. Technology moves on, as do public tastes.

Of course just because a game is no longer played in a pub does not mean that it disappears altogether.

Billiards and snooker may have been eclipsed by pool, but there are plenty of outlets where they can still be played.

Not so cock fighting or bull baiting, for obvious reasons, but also the likes of loggats, popular amongst one generation, discarded by the next.

Some games disappear simply because a landlord moves on, or because they were the brainwave of a regular, who then sobered up.

Conger cuddling, a form of skittles with humans on plant pots as pins, and a large dead conger eel as the wrecking ball, ended in Lyme Regis after a 30 year run in 2006, when animal rights activists threatened a campaign against it.

Other games, of much greater repute and longevity, fade away almost unnoticed. One of the organisers stands down or dies.

Or, more often, the community most identified with that particular game breaks up as local industries go to the wall.

On the other hand, few games are lost entirely, in the sense that as long as one set of rules and equipment is preserved (or is at least documented), it only needs someone to knock up a new set and bring it back to life.

All the games featured in this chapter fit into this category. For now they appear to be lost. But who knows, one day they might be found.

Knur and spell

Last seen in 1995 being played outside the Hargreaves Arms at Laneshaw Bridge near Colne, Lancashire, knur and spell, often dubbed as 'poor man's golf', was once one of the most popular games in the industrial north (although a number of similar games have been recorded in other parts of Britain, as listed below.)

Unlike golf, the aim of knur and spell and its variants was not to land the ball in a hole, but to hit it further than the opposition.

Knur and spell was also much older than golf, possibly of Viking origin. According to the *Oxford Companion to Sports and Games* (*see Links*), in old Norse the word *knurspel* meant simply 'ball game', *spel* meaning game, and *knur* being a knot of wood, from which the earliest balls were probably made.

Yet by 1801, according to Joseph Strutt, the game was known as 'northen spell' (*sic*).

Confusingly, this was not *spel* in the sense of a game, but 'spell' as in a northern dialect word meaning a piece of wood.

This 'spell' was laid on the ground, balanced on a small peg, with the knur placed on one end.

The player would strike the other end of the spell with a long-handled club, thereby launching the knur into the air, so that he could then thwack it, on the rise, as far as possible. The spell thus performed the same role as the trap does in the surviving game of bat and trap (*see page 114*).

As described on the right, other methods of launching the knur also evolved, as did the composition of the knur itself.

Knur and spell, nur and spel, kibel and nerspel, buckstick spell and ore, dab and stick, nipsy, peggy, piggy, billets, bungs and barrels, buck and stick, stick-in-the-mud, bad i'th'wood, tipcat, cat, catty, cat and dog, dag and trigger, trip it and miss it, tribet, trippet, trippit and coit, dab, peg, trip, kit kat, cat and kitten, whacks, waggles, peg and stick, munchers, katstick and bullett, and hornie holes

Just some of the names by which games similar to knur and spell have been known as in various parts of the country, several of them children's games subsequently adapted by adults.

In early centuries knurs – hardly larger than a marble in size – were either carved by hand from wood or horn (so that they had a dimpled surface, like a golf ball), and then weighted with lead, or, they were made from much heavier lignum vitae and turned on a lathe.

But in the late 19th century an ideal, mass-produced substitute presented itself, in the form of 'potties', glazed china balls at a penny a piece, designed to stop kettles from furring up.

Glass knurs were also used, these being balls left over from the grinding process used to produce sandpaper.

As to the matches, each player was given a fixed number of hits, or 'rises', struck in blocks of five at a time. Each hit was then measured in units of 20 yards, or 'scores'.

In the form of match known as long knock, involving several individuals, the player to have achieved the longest rise overall was the winner. So, for example, Joe Machin's record breaking rise at Barnsley in 1899 was expressed as 15 score and 14 feet (that is, 914 feet in total).

When only two players were in action, aggregate distances over a set number of rises were the determining factor. Only complete scores counted however. So, if the pottie landed even an inch short of the line marking the number nine score (that is, the 180 yard marker), the shot would count only as eight score.

If a player missed the knur, he could not take the rise again, and if the knur could not be found within five minutes of it being struck, that rise counted as nil.

As can be imagined, this last rule led to all kinds of chicanery, with supporters treading a rival's pottie into the mud »

▲ Knur and spell players Bert Warren and Bill Shutt square up outside what is thought to be the **Alma Inn, Laneshaw Bridge,** just outside Colne, c.1900.

In Colne and Lancashire generally players were called 'tippers'. In Yorkshire they were known as 'laikers' (from Old Norse meaning to play or perform).

Over the centuries there were five methods of setting up the knur for a 'rise', or strike.

The earliest, as described opposite, used a spell, or piece of wood, balanced on a peg.

Even simpler was to throw the knur up into the air by hand, or to cradle it in a small hollow at the end of the bat, before lofting it upwards and striking it on the rise.

Then, as seen above and right, in the 19th century spring loaded spells appeared. A sharp tap on the release mechanism sent the knur up into the air, its height and trajectory having been carefully calibrated by tensioning the spring.

Often using their own home-made spells, top players were said to have been so adept at this that they could hit a knur blindfold.

Clever though this method was, in the 20th century a much simpler method was adopted. Called the 'pin', the knur was suspended in a wire noose from a gallows-like frame, as demonstrated by Ned Helliwell (*right*), at the **Spring Rock Inn, Greetland, Halifax,** in 1964.

Those who stayed loyal to their spring-loaded spells disdained this method, saying that anyone could hit a stationary knur.

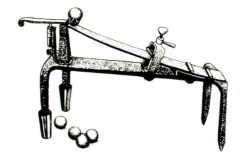

» surreptitiously. Or, children would be sent out with spare potties to drop one in a more advanced position when no-one was looking.

Other examples of foul play were to dab Brylcreem on an opponent's pottie so that it could not be hit cleanly, or to meddle with a player's striking position – the setting up of which was a finely tuned operation requiring the ground to be levelled and coated in ash.

Because knur and spell needed plenty of clear space – top players could hit the knur 200–300 yards – it was mostly played on moors, racecourses or showgrounds.

But from the 19th century onwards the game was largely organised from pubs.

For example the All England Knur and Spell Handicap of 1870, at Belle Vue, Wakefield (later home to Wakefield Trinity rugby club), had five promoters, four of whom were publicans.

Huge crowds and heavy betting characterised many of these encounters. In 1859 a match between Jackie Jagger and 'Bill at the Mount' – players often used nicknames – was said to have attracted a 10,000 crowd to Wibsey, near Bradford, with some wagers being staked of £50–100, the equivalent of two years' wages for working men at that time.

Hence the chicanery.

Legend also has it that in 1937 more people attended a world championship match at the Alma grounds at Laneshaw Bridge (Lancashire's Billy Baxter v. Yorkshire's Jim Crawshaw), than attended a high level derby cricket match between Colne and Nelson barely a mile away, a match that itself drew a huge crowd paying 6d a head to see Colne's Indian professional, Amar Singh, up against Nelson's legendary West Indian, Learie Constantine.

But if the 1920s and '30s represented a high point for the game, after the Second World War steady decline set in.

Firstly, fewer young players showed an interest, so that when the Spring Rock Inn at Greetland staged three challenge matches in 1964, the winner was 78 year old Ned Helliwell (*seen on page 173*).

Meanwhile open spaces became harder to rent out. The supply of potties dried up. Then in the 1970s the collapse of local industries devastated communities that had supported the game for so long.

And yet, in 1969 when the world championship was revived, an estimated 5,000 gathered at the Spring Rock. Yorkshire Television was there too, with cricketer Fred Trueman presenting.

For a brief while all boded well until, at the 1973 championships,

The knack with nipsy was to strike the egg-shaped projectile on its snout (the black patch) so that it flipped up and could be struck a second time for distance. Seen here is one from the author's collection, placed on an ordinary brick. But serious players always carried their own bricks, including a stonemason whose own favourite was made from white marble.

at Dodworth Colliery sports ground in Barnsley, to the ire of Yorkshire spectators, a Lancashire electrician, Stuart Greenfield, retained his title, and to the even greater dismay of the broadcasters and the sponsors, Webster's Brewery, the event ended in clashes between miners and the police.

There would be two further world championships, at the Red Lion, Stainland in 1979, and the Bradshaw Tavern, Halifax, in 1991.

But since that aforementioned match at the Hargreaves Arms in 1995, knur and spell appears to have gone into hibernation.

Centuries of tradition ended, seemingly within one generation.

Or might readers in Lancashire and Yorkshire have other ideas?

We can only hope.

Nipsy

A simpler, 20th century version of knur and spell, nipsy was another miners' game once popular in the Barnsley area, where as recently as the 1960s there were 50 pub and club teams in two leagues.

The nipsy was an egg-shaped piece of lignum vitae, usually painted white, which was set up for striking by being placed on the top edge of a brick (*see below*).

The stick used was either a pared down mattock or pickaxe handle, or a railway brake stick.

Originally nipsy was a game for individuals. But when the first league formed after the Second World War it became a seven-a-side team game. Each player had seven rises, or hits, the team's total yardage then being totted up.

Distances were measured by means of a long rope marked off with metal tallies, but were always more modest than those for knur and spell. The typical range was 90–130 yards, although in 1962 at the Pheasant Inn, Monk Bretton, near Barnsley, a school caretaker called Joe Cook reputedly managed 208 yards. If true, this was a truly prodigious hit, and one that has never been beaten since.

Nor will it, so it would seem. By the 1990s only six nipsy teams were left, from pubs and clubs in Brough Green, Athersley, Worsborough and Silkstone.

And now there are none.

Peggy

Similar to nipsy, before it was appropriated by adults in the 20th century, peggy was a children's game, known by a whole host of names (as we saw on page 172).

In the 17th century John Bunyan called it 'cat', while in Cumbria, the Kendal *Boke of Record* for April 1657 warned that if anyone over the age of twelve was caught playing 'Katstick and Bullet' he would be fined 12d, or jailed for two hours.

The katstick, or peggy, was a piece of wood about two inches long, tapered at both ends, which was struck with a short club.

Thereafter the game differed considerably from nipsy.

Once the peggy had landed, the captain of the striker's team had to estimate how many strides it would take a member of the opposite team to reach it on foot.

If his challenge was accepted and the opponent managed it, the yardage would not count.

This was therefore a game fraught with guesswork and laughter, and one in which lanky kids were particularly welcomed.

Peggy was most popular in Lancashire and Yorkshire. Stan Laurel (Laurel and Hardy) played it as a child in Ulverston, then part of Lancashire. But for adults it did not catch on until the 1960s.

There was a peggy league in Castleford, formed at the George and Dragon in 1969, and in 1975 32 peggy teams from both sides of the Pennines staged their own War of the Roses at Brighouse.

But no sooner had it caught on, peggy then faded away. No reason.

That is how it goes in the world of pub games.

Billets

The final game in this seemingly lost family tree of knur and spell-related games, billets was played with a four foot long club, with a groove cut into its head.

Onto this groove was balanced a curved piece of hard wood, the billet – about five inches long and resembling a drooping sausage – which was then flipped up and struck, again for distance.

Some players, it is said, stored their precious billets in manure. Others pickled them in old ale or rum. It must have been an aromatic old game.

As in knur and spell, distances were measured in scores, the longest hit recorded being eleven score in 1882. Betting was rife too, although the nominal prize, as in quoits and other 19th century contests, was a copper kettle.

Billets seems to have been most popular in the vicinity of Heptonstall and Mytholmroyd in West Yorkshire, but seems to have petered out in the 1970s.

For a while after that a set of clubs and billets was kept at the Robin Hood Inn, at Cragg Vale, high up above Mytholmroyd.

But then the landlord moved on, and now no-one knows where the billets might be, though perhaps the nearest manure heap would be the first place to search.

▲ When in 1889 *The West London Sketcher* & *Theleme* reproduced this drawing of a **bumble puppy** board at **The Doves**, on the banks of the Thames, it was described as 'a Hammersmith curiosity'.

Writing in 1801, Joseph Strutt believed that the game, originally called **nine holes**, had become popular after London magistrates banned skittles in 1780, hence it became known as 'bubble the justice' as a deliberate jibe at the authorities. The vulgarity of its other name, bumble puppy, wrote Strutt, was 'well adapted to the company' who played it.

There were actually two versions.

When played on the ground, metal balls, stones or marbles were aimed from a distance of five or six feet at a board with nine, numbered holes. When played on a raised board, as above, balls were rolled down the sloping top towards nine numbered arches.

But this was no English game. Another report from the 1880s described a similar board being found in a former smugglers' pub in Wallasey, Cheshire. Its finder was told by a retired seaman that it was a French game, probably crafted by visiting or imprisoned sailors.

The old sea dog was right. Nine holes or bumble puppy were in fact versions of the centuries old game of Trou Madame, which is still played in France and Belgium.

In 1959 the landlord of The Doves, now The Dove, George Izzard (*see Links*), called his board the last in England. But if it was, his successors cannot have been impressed and the board has not been seen since the 1960s.

Spot the peggy – not easy, being only a couple of inches long. But it is there, to the right of the brick, having been flipped up by the mayor of Oldham on the village green at Bardsley, in 1960. The Daisyfield Inn at Bardsley was later the venue for the peggy world championships, an event which, like the mayor's attempt, seems not to have been a hit.

Lawn billiards

We conclude our survey of lost games, and our round of British pub games overall, at the Freemasons Arms, on the fringes of Hampstead Heath in London.

As noted in Chapter Three, the pub is, as of mid 2009, the last bastion of Old English skittles.

But the official title of the skittle club, it may also be recalled, is the Hampstead Lawn Billiard and Skittle Club, and lawn billiards is most definitely defunct, and has been for over 30 years.

Before explaining how lawn billiards was played, however, one issue must be clarified.

Although we do not know when the game was first played at the Freemasons – it may have been in the 19th century, but equally not until after the pub was rebuilt in the early 1930s – we do know that from the late 1940s onwards the notion circulated that lawn billiards was in fact another name for 'the ancient game of pall mall'.

This may have been a deliberate distortion by the Freemasons' players in order to glean greater credibility. It could equally have been the landlord's way of jumping onto the 'Olde England' bandwagon that was so much in vogue in the post war period.

Certainly a steady stream of photographers turned up eager to capture this 'ancient game.'

Now pall mall, also known as paille maille, pell mell and, to Samuel Pepys as pele-mele, was indeed a fairly ancient game. As its name suggests, its origins may have been Italian (*palla* meaning ball, *maglio* meaning a mallet). But most accounts call it French, and say that it was introduced to England by Charles II.

The game was played on a huge outdoor alley some 1,000 yards long, on a strip of land which would later become the London street, Pall Mall. The object was to hit a small ball with a mallet up the length of the alley in as few strikes as possible, and then loft it up through an iron hoop on a pole.

But fascinating though this is (and *Played in Britain* will return to pall mall in our forthcoming study, *Played in London*), it has very little in common with lawn billiards.

Instead, the rather more mundane roots of lawn billiards lie in a game Joseph Strutt called 'ring ball', but which was known in the Low Countries as *closh* or *beugelen*.

A clear depiction of it from the mid 17th century can be seen in Liverpool's Walker Art Gallery, by the Dutch artist Jan Steen.

Indeed *beugelen* is still played in the Flemish province of Limberg.

By the 19th century a game very similar to this was being played in the gardens of country houses in both England and the USA, under the name of either lawn billiards or 'troco'. ('Trucco' or 'trucks' were themselves earlier variants of table billiards.) Lawn billiards was also on offer at Lord's cricket ground in the 1830s.

But according to one writer, by the 1930s only one venue was left, the Freemasons.

The aim of lawn billiards was to propel one's ball through a hoop placed in the centre of the court, or rink. If it passed through without touching another ball, it scored one point. If it canoned through off an opponent's ball, it scored two. A normal game was 21 up.

But if that seems easy, it was not. For a start, at the Freemasons the hoop measured 7¾ inches in diameter, while the lignum vitae balls, each of which weighed 8lb, were 7½ inches in diameter. Not a lot of room for error then.

Harder still, the hoop swivelled on a pivot, so that whenever it was struck from the slightest angle it

would turn (whereas in *beugelen* the hoop is fixed, a small but crucial difference in terms of tactics and playing techniques).

A further complication was the method of propelling the balls.

Instead of maces, as used in early billiards, or cues as in later billiards, in lawn billiards each player wielded a four foot long rod with a small iron hoop on the end. These hoops could be used to propel the ball along the ground, or to scoop it into the air.

To make sense of this, readers may wish to access the British Pathé website, where there is a short but evocative newsreel filmed at the Freemasons in 1933.

As a young student in London during the early 1960s, your author well remembers watching action at the Freemasons, similar to that shown on the newsreel.

To witness a game at first hand was both a pleasure and a privilege. The players could exert screw and spin on the ball, or fling it in the air to perform devastating drop canons. Or they would clip the hoop so that it would turn just a few inches and thereby stymie their opponent's next shot.

By then most of the players were ageing, however, and as their numbers fell, in the 1970s the pub took the fateful decision to evict them and extend the beer garden.

And now, three decades later, the Freemasons' diminishing number of skittlers must fear that this story could easily repeat itself.

To borrow that well worn phrase from Oscar Wilde, for a pub to have lost one traditional game may be regarded as a misfortune.

But to lose two would look like carelessness.

And to us gamesters who cherish our heritage, it would also be unthinkable.

Still stored in the skittle alley at the Freemasons Arms, these two hooped rods and this lignum vitae ball are all that remain of lawn billiards. By rights they should be in a museum. Yet there is always the hope that someone, somewhere, may seek to revive the game, in which case these artefacts will form a vital resource.

▲ Posing on a damp day in 1951, the **lawn billiards** players at the **Freemasons**, **Hampstead,** were used to photographers in search of quirky material. Fred Pyle on the right featured regularly, and in true pub game tradition was always described as the 'world champion'.

Despite its name, lawn billiards was never played on turf at the Freemasons (or at least not after the 1930s). Instead, it was played on wooden blocks laid in a keyhole shape, the square bit being where opening shots were played from.

Mostly the court was covered with sand, so seeing it exposed like this would have been unusual.

Yet should anyone be minded, in this image, in the artefacts seen opposite, and in the numerous rules that survive from the 19th century, there exists more than enough information for this truly artful game to be revived.

And should that happen, future players please note. This is not 'the ancient game of pall mall' (nor 'pell mell', as commemorated on this spot in the Freemasons' garden).

It is a game in its own right. We hope, not lost. Merely temporarily indisposed.

Links

Where no publisher listed assume self-published by organisation or author

Where no publication date listed assume published on final date within title, ie. 1860–1960 means published 1960

Abbreviations:
UP University Press

Sports and games

Arlott J *The Oxford Companion to Sports and Games* Paladin (1977)

Beauchampé S & Inglis S *Played in Birmingham* English Heritage (2006)

Bentine M & Ennis J *Michael Bentine's Book of Square Games* Wolfe Publishing (1966)

Boston R *Beer and Skittles* Collins (1976)

Brailsford D *A Taste for Diversions: Sport in Georgian England* Lutterworth Press (1999)

Cotton C *The Compleat Gamester* Cornmarket Reprints (1972)

Finn T *Pub Games of England* Queen Anne Press (1975)

Finn T *Watney Book of Pub Games* Queen Anne Press (1966)

Gomme A *The Traditional Games of England, Scotland and Ireland*, orig pub 1894-8 Thames & Hudson (1984)

Griffin E *England's Revelry: A History of Popular Sports and Pastimes 1660-1830* Oxford UP (2005)

Grunfeld F *Games of the World* Plenary Publications (1975)

Hornby H *Uppies and Downies* English Heritage (2008)

Inglis S *Played in Manchester* English Heritage (2004)

Physick R *Played in Liverpool* English Heritage (2007)

Strutt J *The Sports and Pastimes of the People of England* (editions of 1801, 1855 and 1903)

Taylor A *The Guinness Book of Traditional Pub Games* (1992)

Willughby F *Book of Games* (c1660s) Ashgate (2003)

Pubs and pub history

Beed E *70 Years Behind Bars* (1984)

Brandwood G, Davison A, Slaughter M *Licensed to Sell* English Heritage (2004)

Browner JA *Wrong Side of the River: London's disreputable South Bank in the 16th and 17th century* Essays in History Vol 36 University of Virginia (1994)

Clark P *The English Alehouse - A Social History 1200-1830* Longman (1983)

English Inns Illustrated Odhams Press (1960)

Girouard M *Victorian Pubs* Yale (1984)

Haydon P *The English Pub* Hale (1994)

Hissey JJ *The Road and the Inn* Macmillan (1917)

Izzard G *One for the Road, the Autobiography of a London Publican* Max Parrish (1959)

Long G *English Inns and Road Houses* Werner Laurie (1937)

Magee R *Stalybridge Pubs and their Licensees 1750-1990* Neil Richardson (1991)

Mass-Observation *The Pub and the People A Worktown Study* Century Hutchinson (1987)

Protz R & Sykes H *The Village Pub* Phoenix Illustrated (1998)

Roadhouses and Clubs of the Home Counties Sylvan (1934)

Temple Thurston E *The Flower of Gloster* Alan Sutton (1984)

Wentworth Day J *Inns of Sport* Whitbread Library, Naldrett Press (1949)

White TH *England Have My Bones* Collins (1936)

General history

Graves R & Hodge A *The Long Weekend: A Social History of Great Britain 1918-1939* Faber & Faber (1940)

Vale M *The Gentleman's Recreations: Accomplishments and Pastimes of the English Gentleman 1580-1630* DS Brewer (1977)

Williams WB *The Amusements of Old London* Muller (1971 facsimile of 1901 edition)

Bat and trap

www.batandtrap.co.uk
www.batandtrap.org
www.batandtrap.org.uk

Board and dice games

Bell RC *Board and Table Games From Many Civilizations* Vols 1 & 2 Oxford UP (1969)

Brophy J & Partridge E *The Long Trail: What the British Soldier Sang and Said in 1914–18* Andre Deutsch (1965)

Pardon GF *Backgammon: Its History and Practice* Bogue (1844)

Parlett D *The Oxford History of Board Games* Oxford UP (1999)

www.backgammon-biba.co.uk
http://covbackgammon.co.uk
www.dicecollector.com
www.gammoned.com
www.traditionsofsuffolk.com

Bowling games

Pilley P (ed) *The Story of Bowls* Stanley Paul (1987)

www.britishpetanque.org

Card games

Parlett D *A Dictionary of Card Games* Oxford UP (1992)

Parlett D *The Oxford Guide to Card Games* Oxford UP (1999)

www.davidparlett.co.uk
www.pagat.com
www.cbcs.us
www.staustelleuchre.com
www.stiveseuchre.com
http://aruncrib.co.uk

Cue games
Clare N *Billiards and Snooker Bygones* Shire (1996)
Mitchell JR *Billiards & Snooker, a trade history* BSAIF (1981)
Shamos M *The Complete Book of Billiards* Gramercy (1993)
www.aebba.org.uk
www.chesterbagatelle.co.uk
www.lewesbarbilliards.org.uk

Darts
Chaplin P *Darts in England 1900–1939 A Social History* Manchester UP (2009)
Croft-Cooke R *Darts* Wyman & Sons (1936)
Peek DW *To the Point: The Story of Darts in America* Pebble Publishing (2001)
Waddell S *Bellies and Bullseyes* Ebury Press (2007)
Wellington A *The Various Dart Games and How to Play Them* Universal Publications (1939)
Young J *How to Play Darts and New Games for the Dart Board* Foulsham (1938)
www.patrickchaplin.com
www.justinirwin.com
http://pagesperso-orange.fr/philippe.plouviez/javelot.htm

Dominoes
Berndt F *The Domino Book* Bantam (1975)
Leeflang KWH *Domino Games and Domino Puzzles* Hamlyn (1976)
www.dominorules.com
www.gamesmuseum.uwaterloo.ca/Archives/Culin/Dice1893/invention.html
www.pagat.com/tile/wdom
www.peterborough.gov.uk/page-488
www.xs4all.nl/~spaanszt/Domino_Plaza.html

Knur and spell
Breeze P and Greenfield S *Colne Giants - tales from the forgotten world of knur and spell* Posh up North (2002)

Pitching and tossing
Charman A *History of Southwater: Part Two* (1977)
Smith HJ *History of Southwater: Part One* (1907);
www.benward.tv
http://lewes.lions105se.org.uk/index.html

Pub quizzes
Berkmann M *Brain Men* Little, Brown (1999)
Marchant I *The Longest Crawl* Bloomsbury (2006)

Pushing and shoving
Walton I *The Compleat Angler* Harrap (1931)

Quoits
Davidson P *Memoirs of Childwall Quoiting Club and its Members* PH Young & Son (1934)
Metcalfe A *Organised Sport in the Mining Communities of South Northumberland 1880-89* Victorian Studies 25 (1982)
Tranter N *Organised Sport and the Working Classes of Scotland 1820-1900: The Neglected Sport of Quoiting* in Holt R (ed) *Sport and the Working Class in Modern Britain* Manchester UP (1990)
Tranter N *Quoits* in Jarvie G & Burnett J (eds) *Sport, Scotland and the Scots* Tuckwell (1999)
Welford G *Darlington Quoit Club - A History of the Game of Quoits* Mawers (undated)
www.amber-online.com/exhibitions/quoits
www.lindahome.co.uk
www.quoits.info
www.quoits.ndo.co.uk
www.suffolkcamra.co.uk/quoits

Rifle shooting
Spittle F *Ring My Bell* (1995)

Ring games
Tressell R *The Ragged Trousered Philanthropists* Penguin Classics new edition (2004)
http://worldringboard.piczo.com

Skittles
Gosson S *The School of Abuse* (1579)
Herbert AP *The Water Gipsies* Methuen (1930)
Jones J *The benefit of the Ancient Bathes of Buckstones* (1572)
Kessler L *La Quille Vivante* Joël Cuénot (1983)
Smedley N *Life and Traditions in Suffolk and North East Essex* Dent (1976)
Walker D *Games and Sports* Thomas Hurst (1837)
www.bamptonauntsally.org
www.oxfordauntsally.co.uk
www.irishskittles.com
www.londonskittles.co.uk

Table football
Lott J & Brainard K *The Complete Book of Foosball* Table Soccer Publications (2000)
Lott J & Brainard K *World Table Soccer Almanac* Table Soccer Publications (2007)
www.britfoos.com

Table skittles
Bates A *The Drama: Its History, Literature and Influence on Civilization* Historical Publishing Co (1906)

Twisting and spinning
www.putandtake.co.uk

Wesbites – games
www.tradgames.org.uk

Websites – archives
www.bbc.co.uk/nationonfilm/topics/entertainment
www.britishpathe.com
www.oldbaileyonline.org
www.pepysdiary.com
www.thepublican.com

Websites – heritage
www.english-heritage.org.uk
www.historic-scotland.gov.uk
www.cadw.wales.gov.uk
www.heritagepubs.org.uk

Websites – general
www.british-history.ac.uk
www.oxforddnb.com

Newspapers & magazines
Country Life; The Countryman; The Daily Telegraph; Darts World; The Field; The Independent; Licensed Victualler's Gazette; Literary Gazette; Morning Advertiser; Newcastle Weekly Chronicle; News of the World; Norfolk Mercury; The Publican; South Wales Echo; The Sunday Chronicle; The Sunday Telegraph; The Times Online Digital Archive 1785-1985

Credits

Photographs and images

Please note that where more than one photograph appears on a page, each photograph is identified by a letter, starting with 'a' in the top left hand corner of the page, or at the top, and continuing thereafter in a *clockwise* direction.

All English Heritage and National Monument Record photographs listed are either © English Heritage or © Crown Copyright. NMR. Application for the reproduction of these images should be made to the National Monuments Record, at Kemble Drive, Swindon SN2 2GZ. Tel. 01793 414600.

English Heritage / National Monuments Record photographs

Keith Buck: back cover d, back flap, 34abcd, 35bc, 89c, 91c, 99a, 136b, 151, 152b, 154a; Alun Bull: 33a, 144, 158a; Steve Cole: 1, 65, 88ab, 89b, 91ab, 124c, 135b; Nigel Corrie: inside back cover, 37b, 38abc, 39abc, 55, 59ad, 78abc, 79, 92, 103, 137a, 161, 176; James O Davies: 47b, 49, 97, 138a, 139abc; Derek Kendall: front flap, 4, 15bc, 33b, 89a, 124a, 125, 152a, 172; Bob Skingle: 60a, 82ab, 83abc, 150ab

Photographers

Tony Bartholomew: 76a, 77abcdfg; David Brett: 142c; Vanley Burke: 148; Bruce Cairns: 142a, 184; John Cocks: 80a, 81ab; Eddie Garvey: 110, 111ab; Peter Holme: 16, 107ab, 109abc; Sue Hudson: 17; Simon Inglis: back cover ac, 22, 30, 32, 44, 46cd, 51, 52ab, 54a, 56, 61, 90ab, 93, 94, 95, 99bc, 100abc, 101, 104, 105ab, 114a, 119abc, 123, 127, 128, 129bcd, 130abcd, 135a, 136a, 160, 163, 174; © Alistair Laming / Alamy: 170b; Bob Lamoon: 116ab, 117a; Paul Lapsley: 66, 67abc; Ian Macdonald: 75; Ben May: 117bc; David Norman: 84, 86; Martin Phelps: 141ab; Chris Prichard: 143a; Jean Segers: 120; Michael Slaughter: 96ab, 124b, 126, 130e, 134b; Roz South: 132a, 166, 167; Jaqui Strevens: 46b, 47a, 48a, 50ad, 165; Arthur Taylor: 7, 35a, 147, 162; © Phil Taylor: 132b, 133; Matthew Whatley: 64a; Michael Williams: 149abc; Kev Woodward: 141a

Archives and agencies

Courtesy of The Advertising Archives: 19; Reproduced with the permission of Birmingham Libraries & Archives / Benjamin Stone Collection: 45; Bodleian Library, University of Oxford (268 c.82 p54, Boy's Own Book 1870): 24a; The Brighton Argus / Simon Dack: 129a; Britain on View / John Miller: 15a; © City of London / Heritage-Images: 13; © Corbis: 12, 57; Dorset Media Service: 168ab; Getty Images: inside front cover, 2, 6, 31ab, 64b, 112, 156, 169b, 177; Graham Robinson Photography: 68b, 69, 121ab; Harold Samuel Collection, City of London / The Bridgeman Art Library: 11; Huddersfield Examiner / Trinity Mirror: 142b; Hull & East Riding Museum, Hull Museums & Art Gallery: 42a; IWCP News Service / Laura Holme: 85, 87abc; Reproduced by permission of Lancashire County Library and Information Service, South East Division: 173a; Mary Evans Picture Library / Arthur Rackham: 118; Mary Evans Picture Library: 146; © Mirrorpix: front cover, 157; © Museum of London: 115; © Museum of London /

Heritage-Images: 43; © National Portrait Gallery, London: 10a; © The Trustees of the National Museums of Scotland: 40a; © NTPL / Nick Guttridge: 155ab; © Newsquest (Herald & Times). Licensor www.scran.ac.uk: 73; Northampton Chronicle & Echo: 171; Reproduced courtesy of Oldham Evening Chronicle: 175b; Peterborough Museum & Art Gallery: 145; Press Association Images: 113ab; Ric Mellis Productions: 62, 63; Ross Parry Syndication / Halifax Courier: 173b; Reproduced with the kind permission of the Royal Pavilion & Museums (Brighton & Hove) HA107083: 131; © South Lanarkshire Libraries. Licensor www.scran.ac.uk: 70; © 2002 Topfoto: 68a; Tredegar House, Newport City Council: 119d; Western Daily Press: 50c ; Wigan Evening Post: 169a

Donated photographs

English Heritage wish to thank the following individuals and organisations: Blackthorn / Gaymer Cider Company: 21, 50b; Daniel Brévière: 23bc; Brewery History Society Archives, Birmingham Central Library: 60b; Childwall Quoiting Club: 80b; Kevin Cook: 153ab; The Countryman: 24b; Michael Davies: 46a; Toni Dolan: 27; Gerald Eaton: 71; Graeme Eddie: 77e; Linda Evans: 76b; Ruth Gillan: 74b; Hammersmith & Fulham Archives & Local History Centre: 175a; Hampstead Lawn Billiard and Skittle Club: 54b; Hexham Courant: 140; JW Lees / Moy Williams: 159; Stanley Lowy: 20, 36ab, 37a; Mike Millis: 158b; © Norfolk Museums & Archaeology Service: 41, 134a; Gordon Padmore: 98; Pennine Heritage Network: 173c; Philippe Plouviez 23a; Steve Pyatt: 53abc; Margaret Rushmer: back cover b ; Saddleworth Round Table: 170a; Scunthorpe Telegraph: 143c; Shepherd Neame: 164; Claire Shuttleworth: 143b; Tablesport / Stuart Timbs: 102; John Tutchings: 155c; Jim Winters: 72, 74; Worcester News: 138b; www.suffolkcamra.co.uk/quoits: 76c; www.ville-hasnon.fr: 25; Dave Ziemann: 137b

Books

English Inns Illustrated Odhams Press (1960): 108; Strutt J *The Sports and Pastimes of the People of England* William Tegg (1855): 10b, 40b, 114b, 154b

Acknowledgements

Over some 30 years of visiting goodness knows how many pubs, I must have spoken to hundreds, if not thousands of games players and publicans, without ever getting beyond first name terms. It was always useful chat, though, and I offer my sincere thanks to all of them for their patience and good humour.

For more specialised information and advice on the whole spectrum of pub games I must thank the following individuals: Dr Patrick Chaplin; Erik De Vroede, curator of the Sports Museum, Flanders; Barrie Pepper; the late Robert Buchanan Morton; the late Rob Magee; James Masters, John McLeod, and the staff at the British Library, Boston Spa, Wetherby, West Yorkshire.

On behalf of myself and *Played in Britain*, thanks also go to those who assisted in relation to specific games, as follows:

Bagatelle: John Allen; **Bar billiards:** Nigel Ryall, Nick Barnett, Ken Hussey, Graeme Le Monnier, Ric Bethell; **Card games:** David Parlett; **Crown green bowls:** Iain Foster; **Darts:** Nigel Thompson, John Gwynne, Paul Robson, David Mealey, Tom Dempsey, Tony Cryer, David Bailey, Phil Kempton, Xavier Deltombe, Corine Deliot, Terry Holden, Stan Lowy, Marijke de Hollander; **Dominoes:** Keith Masters, Trevor Hoyle, and the staff at Peterborough Museum; **Marbles:** Sam and Julia McCarthy Fox; **Pétanque:** Andy Clegg, Simon Crompton, Gary Wild; **Pool:** Bob Blakeborough; **Pub quizzes:** Ken Needham (York CIU), Philip Cornwall; **Pushpenny:** Dave Burrows; **Put and take:** Ron Mills; **Quoits:** Peter Brown, Linda Evans, Richard Macdonald, Jim Winters, Colin Gray, Charles Wheeler, Stan Smith, Geoff Hare, Henry Pattinson, Charles Cody, Dave Watson, Peter Bowerbank, Una Oakes, Aaron Gubb, Rae Gardiner, Joe Wooldridge, Graeme Eddie; **Rifle shooting:** Barry Smith, Adrian Bull; **Ring games:** Joe Norman, Adam Pratt, Luke Turner. Sophie Blakes, Will Clarkson; **Shove ha'penny:** Nigel Jones; **Skittles:** Guy Tunnicliffe, Paul Robinson, Peter Greene, Barrie Martin, Charles Finch, James Clarke, Tom Brady, Michael Thomson, Tim Lethaby, Tony Hockerday, George 'Nev' Taylor, Trevor Tunstall, Steve Pyatt, Peter Stevens, Alan Birch, Graham Brown, George Lambert, Dave Jones, Mike Davies; **Table football:** Tim Baber, Dave Ziemann; **Toad in the hole:** Ben Ward.

Played in Britain would also like to thank Michael Slaughter and Geoff Brandwood, John Travers (Gambling Commission), Peter Clare (EA Clare & Son Ltd), Suj Summer (The Watch-Men Agency Ltd), Sue Hamer (Pennine Heritage Network), Paul Jackson (The Countryman), Helen Mason (Ryedale Folk Museum), Rachel Bourke and Brian Pengelly (Shoot Out Club), Sarah Belizaire-Butler (Clarion Communications), Mark Duffy (Ilkeston Advertiser) and John Herbert.

I am also grateful to my fellow *Played in Britain* authors, Steve Beauchampé and Hugh Hornby, for additional research, and to series editor Simon Inglis, who was at all times a pertinacious, patient and peerless editor, and Jackie Spreckley, who orchestrated the whole production and performed wonders with picture research.

Finally, I hope this book will eventually make sense to my three very young grandsons, the 'Special Ks' – Kazunori, Kento and Kai.

Played in Manchester
Simon Inglis (2004)

Played in Birmingham
Steve Beauchampé and
Simon Inglis (2006)

Played in Liverpool
Ray Physick (2007)

Engineering Archie
Simon Inglis (2005)

Liquid Assets
Janet Smith (2005)

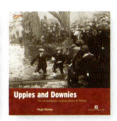

Uppies and Downies
Hugh Hornby (2008)

Great Lengths
Dr Ian Gordon and
Simon Inglis (2009)

Played in Glasgow
Ged O'Brien (2010)

Played on Tyne and Wear
Lynn Pearson (2010)

Future titles

The British Olympics – Britain's Olympic heritage 1612–2012 Martin Polley (2010)
Played in London – charting the heritage of the capital at play Simon Inglis (2011)
Bowled Over - the bowling greens of Britain Hugh Hornby (2012)

For more information **www.playedinbritain.co.uk**

Index

▲ Time to reflect after the rigours of the **Woolsack Race** in **Tetbury, Gloucestershire**, in May 2006.

Joseph Strutt was in reflective mood too, after completing his mammoth study, *The Sports and Pastimes of the People of England*, over 200 years ago.

'The task, in truth, is extremely difficult,' he admitted, 'and many omissions, as well as many errors, must of necessity occur in the prosecution of it... especially when it is recollected that in a variety of instances I have been constrained to proceed without any guide, and explore, as it were, the recesses of a trackless wilderness.'

Amen to that. In these tough times for Britain's pubs, *Played at the Pub* has ventured often into the wilderness. But it has also found itself in many a garden of paradise. For there never is one single trend, and certainly no finishing line.

And so, though time is called on our present labours, we raise our glasses to those who will take up this enduring tale, secure in the knowledge that as long as there are pubs, there will always be games.

Beer and skittles – a winning combination, if ever there was.